TIED TO THE WIND

Afric McGlinchey

Tied to the Wind is a book of intense sensations, and kaleidoscopic atmosphere. I could almost feel its heat, smell its exotic fragrances. Beautiful and transporting.
— Sara Baume, *A Line Made by Walking*

I loved Afric McGlinchey's lyrical and haunting memoir. Simultaneously intimate and epic, McGlinchey's search for belonging voyages the reader through a sequence of unforgettable landscapes, braiding beauty and challenge into a book that lingers long in the reader's heart.
— Grace Wells, *When God Has Been Called Away to Greater Things*

The hugely attractive and magical power of Afric McGlinchey's writing is found in the beautiful clarity of her storytelling, highlighting the intensity of formative years. Served up like postcards, this narrative cuts to the marrow of a family torn in all directions by culture, career and geographical location. Tied to the Wind is a mighty piece of work: powerful, insightful and fascinating – absolutely wonderful.
— Cónal Creedon, *Second City*

Exquisite – a beautifully-written, lyrical charm.
— Paul McMahon, *The Pups in the Bog*

Afric McGlinchey's long-form debut steals beguilingly across the spiderweb between poetry, memoir and novel, offering an exquisitely rendered narrative of a young, hurting, growing life. Lush, sensitive, harrowing, gloriously written.
— Mia Gallagher, *Beautiful Pictures of the Lost Homeland*

I loved the book. Searingly beautiful prose.
—William Wall, *Alice Falling*

Waves of memorable images, where love is challenged, and home is ever in question. Where to be, how to be and how to love are the kinds of questions Tied to the Wind asks; it's a courageous and moving piece of work.
—Paul Perry, *The Garden*

ISBN: 978-1-913642-58-7   SECOND EDITION

The author has asserted their right to be identified as the author of this Work in accordance with the Copyright, Designs and Patents Act 1988.

Cover design by Aaron Kent

Edited & typeset by Aaron Kent

Broken Sleep Books (2021)

Broken Sleep Books Ltd
Rhydwen,
Talgarreg,
SA44 4HB
Wales

Tied to the Wind was awarded a Literature Bursary by the Arts Council of Ireland.

Contents

4.

9.

Author's note

I have deliberately glossed over certain elements and changed names to protect the privacy of individuals. The timing of certain events has also been changed to facilitate flow. As memory is fallible and slippery, the narrative is cast as auto-fiction.

Because part of the book relates to my experience of living in countries where citizens were classified according to definitions of race, I have used the terms 'black' and 'white', as broad descriptions of skin colour.

For my brother and sister
and in memory of my parents

Tied to the Wind

Afric McGlinchey

We don't see things as they are;
we see them as we are.
— Anaïs Nin

1.

The first migration (or running away, after the first slap)

Salthill, Galway. Gates ticking by like dark shirts on a line, black as the blobs of rage in my chest, which fade as I begin counting *one two five eleven* because I am four and know numbers, just like I know that we're nearly at the blue sea because the wind is blowing us a salt kiss; and daffodils bounce yellowly on their stems like a brass band marching to a silent tune *three seven* and birds follow us, air-surfing from telegraph pole to tree, and I look through the bars of each gate, to strangeness, to a different front door and *this is my foot* I say staring down *and my other foot, one two,* I tell Ivor, who doesn't know how to count yet, because he's only three – and then I look up and the sky is sending messages I can't hear, something to do with the clouds coming in, eating up the sun, all the high flying blue vanishing, until everything is as grey as the sandpaper road under our bare feet, and I know that green is softer than tar so I cross over, calling Ivor to follow, *see the grass* I say, turning around, but my little brother is whimpering and, trotting towards us, long-haired and horned, is a billygoat monster – *trip-trap* – from our fairytale book, and then I'm running back, dragging my little brother's hand, past gate after gate, blundering into a question: *how will I know my own home?*

2.

A death in the playground

Lusaka, Zambia. I have three friends at my new school. Anna and Gabi, both Italian, are only five-and-a-half. Anna has specs with big frames and a chocolate beauty spot to the right of her mouth, which God added like a full stop. Gabi is short-haired, a tomboy with a loud Nepalese accent. Maggie is a tumble of dark curls and *giddy*, her mum says. She has to be my number one friend because she's Irish and nearly-six, like me.

Maggie and Anna do the clapping in slow-motion to show me the pattern: *A sailor went to sea sea sea*...and the blue sea arrives in my head with a horizontal swoosh. A big feeling of emptiness follows. I miss Galway, the ocean practically at our front door. As I watch their flickering hands, I stumble back against a potting table, and the scent of its cedar wood pricks my nostrils and I fly

high up to the galley in the cathedral in Letterkenny, my aunt playing the organ, the choir singing, white incense trembling up like a nervous genie, and I'm leaning over the galley railing to look at all the lit candles far below and...

crash! An upturned red clay pot at the edge of the potting table tumbles to the floor, uncovering a coiled garden hose. Only it isn't a hose.

Near the open door, Maggie screams and flees, the other two scrambling after her. But I stand still as a tree, the snake only a few inches from my chest. It is acid green with black markings, rearing up like the letter Z we've just been practising in class, forked tongue flickering from its open jaw. The caretaker rushes in. He lifts a spade, twists it edgewise, then hammers down. As the spade finally slices through the muscular rope of the snake's body, the head falls to the dusty wooden floor. *A boomslang. One bite and you can be dead in twenty minutes*...the caretaker's growly voice, one hand at the back of my head as he ushers me out.

It might have slept for months and then just slipped away without hurting anybody. But I toppled the pot. And now it's dead, and Maggie says her *amai* says that means I'll have bad luck for seven years.

Lightning

Lusaka, Zambia. Still in my baby dolls, I tiptoe across our scrappy patch of garden. Pull two long fat carrots from the vegetable plot. Wriggle through the tiny mesh door of a rabbit run, to say hello to our new pets which have come with the house. I've named them Lightning and Thumbelina, on account of one being white and the other tiny.

Next thing, Lightning shivers under my arm, scoots out and lollops down the driveway and I'm screaming *No no no no!* reversing, hooking the latch so I don't lose Thumbelina too, and then sprinting after him to the gate. But the car I've heard shrieking has already sped off along the empty tar strip track, whirring into the magenta and yellow sunrise. I drop to my knees. Blood trickles into snowy fur, his neck dangling back, eyes dull as down-there well water.

Sorry, sorry, Lightning, I whisper, sobbing. Just like the snake, it's my fault he's dead.

In which my father is a sun and I star too

Lusaka, Zambia. Men in uniform smile and make room for my mother who swishes her emerald green dress as she lifts me on to the first tier of the stand and steps up after me, until we are at the very top, and the men on the tiers below are still gazing up at her, but I look beyond them, to the parade ground, to my dad standing to attention in front of his men. My usual perspective of my father is from the waist down: khaki trousers and lace-up black boots. Now I am high above him, like a bird, and can count six gold buttons like glinting mini suns on his dress uniform. If I had a watch, I bet it would say noon, because all the soldier-shadows are practically invisible, like time. And time is like bathwater, and the present is a small lull between swish and swash.

Chucking their boots together, neat as pleats in an accordion, the shiny soldiers with water-pellet-foreheads hold their rifles tight to straight-as-matchstick bodies, and President Kaunda pulls his portly self up with the help of his arm rests and nods to my father's salute, and then it's the anthem, all the rollicking drums and the marching make my chest ching-ching like the cymbals. *Victors in the struggle for the right, we've won freedom's fight, all one, strong and free.*

After crackly loudspeaker speeches and wheeling birds and floppy clouds lazily swimming in the pool-blue sky, trumpets swagger up and call out a tune that I recognise: *I'll be here, in sunshine or in shadow…*and that's the cue, and we descend again, one-two, one-two feet per step, and Mum gestures where I should go, and I'm faltering towards the president's seat, in the centre of a line of dignitaries. *Don't trip, don't drop, don't fall…*and then I'm right in front of him, offering the posy of shamrocks, which my mother revived with a hiss of water from her spray bottle before we left, and I risk a teetery glance up to his brilliant teeth. And close up, how round and dewy his face is, as though he's a sprayed posy too, and my eyes dart back down until they land on his giant panda paws clasped over mine, black over white, and he says *Tell your father that he is very important for our army.*

Blurred walls and nights

Lusaka, Zambia. Through my open window, a swampy, boggy, tendrilly, green-things-growing, wet-earth aroma, the summer storm aai-yaai-yaaiing from its far edge now, and brief on my cheek, the soft pelt of my mum's mink, and I touch her silver dress, which blinks rapidly, as though many-eyed, the fringe at the hem swishing left-right-left, and her *goodnight!* tinkles across the ting-ting of water dripping from the eaves, and then she's gone, leaving the air of her scent, like the last notes of a song, and I'm lifting my head to the sill to watch as she swims with my bow-tied father, into the glittering street.

Shutting the door of another house

Fly away Anna. Fly away Gabi. Fly away Maggie. There they go, three specks vanishing like the silent popping of bubbles.

Only, it's not them leaving; it's *us*. Again.

Just a bit further north, says Dad, to a place called Broken Hill, where the president wants him to train more of his soldiers.

For my sixth birthday, Mum and Dad give me a doll with long brown locks, just like Maggie. I'll call my doll Maggie, I tell them. So I don't forget my first best friend.

Water baby

Country club, Broken Hill, Zambia. Straggle of damp hair across my face. I wipe it away. The water is up to my chest. Tipping onto my back, I kick it into rain. Spin. Spew fountains from my mouth. Underwater, I hear my mother's voice warble, just like the first time I went deeper and deeper, my feet becoming webbed as I paddled beyond ships and sunken cities, yellow-green seaweed curling around me, pale jellyfish floating like bathing caps, until I glimpsed the sunken treasure, a shining gold coin, and dived, holding my breath until I had it in my hand, and only then did I push off the tiles, back to the surface, to my mother's delight: you're *swimming*! Just like a water-baby.

Mum says water is my element because I lived in my own little pool inside her tummy, before I was even born.

White sun-beds, umbrellas, diving board. Light sparkles across the club pool. Two white-painted swans dip their necks towards us. I squeeze the sting from my eyes. Mum is standing in the water in her green bikini, sun-browned, with Molly in her arms. Let's teach her to swim, she says and pushes my baby sister towards me. Molly floats, her body a pale, shelled bean. I reach for her, turn her around, push her back. Her head hits Mum's bare belly and we laugh. If I pushed hard enough she might go back inside and I'd have my mum all to myself. She could be a water-baby inside and I'd be the one outside.

A place snaps its vowels against the wind

Broken Hill / Kabwe, Zambia. Broken Hill is a good name for a place where they do mining. It rushes a picture into my head, of rocks tumbling and cracking at the bottom of the quarry, making a copper fracture. But one of the officers says this town's new name is Kabwe. Why did Mum and Dad tell me its old name? Now I have to change the taste of the place in my mouth, the sound of it, the energy, and it makes me feel twisty, like pitching head over tail, or rolling into a surprise cartwheel. To say *Kabwe* jostles me out of copper, into brown-muddiness. I have to invent the place all over again, and myself in it.

Red memory, collapsible as a swing

Kabwe, Zambia. Most days, when officers and their wives visit, we are ordered to go outside and *count the grass.* But grass is non-existent and the air is a burny-yellow pulse. Unkind scrub and thorn and beyond the fence, bush.

The house is a ship, and around it flows a sea of red dirt. The high red steps of our verandah unroll down from the roughly-built house like a giant's tongue. I sit next to Dad's freshly polished army boots, laces woven in and out of dozens of eyelets. A beetle scurries by, shiny and dark as their leather. Rustles and hisses, occasional screeches. I slide onto my belly on the cool red-polished concrete floor. Open my copy. The high dial tone of the cicadas, and dizziness from the heat, disappear as I become engrossed in writing a series of cursive a's and e's and o's between narrow red lines flanked by wide blue ones.

Ivor's raggedy fringe is so long it covers his eyes. Molly's curls are as pale as the sun. They are sitting in the new swing set, the kind with sides to hold you in, so you feel as though you are flying in a green crate. Come in the swing Tosha, calls Ivor, but I'm busy right now. Ivor rocks the swing higher and higher, and Molly squeals with excitement. She is two and a half and already a thrill-seeker. The whooshing air sharpens to a blade. I look up in time to see the swing tilt and freeze – a silhouette against the sun – as though considering options. Then, it creakingly topples, slow as a tree, and crashes to the dirt. Ivor, vaulted over Molly's body, thuds to the ground.

Molly:
You were on the swing too, Itosha. Which is why it was top-heavy.

You may find yourself

among white
butterflies
of vertigo.
You may try on
recklessness
to see if it fits.
You may recognise
yourself
in a doorway
to the sky.
You may feel
alive,
electric,
or flinch
darkly
in fear,
asking yourself
how did I
get here?

It's raining hands

Kabwe, Zambia. Outside the window, hot sticks of rain. Beatrice is scrubbing my feet with a nailbrush. It is screamingly ticklish. I dissolve in hysterics, jabbing my foot against her belly. Her blue-and-white check dress, musky, wood fire scent. Soft shuffle of her flip-flops across the terracotta tiles. Her hands on my head. Hands cupping a heel. Hands wrapping a towel around my skinny body, which vibrates in response to her touch.

Dad:
We never employed women, only men.
But we had Beatrice.
There was no Beatrice.
But I remember her bathing us.
Don't argue with me. You're wrong. We had a policy of not employing women, because your mother thought they would be tempted to steal her things.
So who took care of us? When you and Mum weren't around?
Black Halawa. The cook.

Accidental Tinkerbells

This farm, where I have to stay until my parents get back from Ireland, is completely unlike our place. The heat, unrelenting. Marie's parents, so different from mine. Her father is tall, thin, unassuming, drives a *bakkie* and wears a bedraggled straw hat, Fedora style. Always stares at the sky. Marie's mother is frowsy, stern, wears an apron, the kind you hang from your neck. Always carrying something – a wooden spoon, a bucket, an axe.

Is your brain a dead leg? she roars at the tractor driver, who has driven over a tree stump in the yard. The tractor trails a tiny shadow, so I know it must be nearly noon. Bloody numbskull! She stands in front of him, legs spread, hands on hips, glaring. He stares at the ground, feet shuffling. The women harvesting the sugar cane in the field opposite the yard, lift their heads. As one, they straighten up, feet invisible, heads held erect, silhouettes against the sun. They walk away. It's probably time for their break, but it feels like a protest.

*

Off you go, you two, says Marie's mum. To the store for me. Here's a list. Put it on my account. Marie and I hop on our bikes and pedal fast along the dirt road towards a vastness of hazy sky. A boy sprawls in the dirt near the *khayas,* playing with a wooden tractor. About our age. I can feel his eyes entering our backs, jealous of our bikes.

The last light dissolves into spider legs. Finally a cooling relief. Some hours later, the generator goes silent. A moonless, starless blackness. Occasional woo-wooing of an owl. Sudden volley of barking from startled dogs. Whisper of hundreds of fruit bats spiralling into the night. Or was that sound a snake under the bed? My neck prickles.

Across the room, Marie is sound asleep. The bedside tilly lantern attracts flying ants and moths, wings whirring like shuffled cards. Sometimes they get through the net and brush my face. I turn off the lantern, pull the net down tight and tuck it under the mattress. Flick on my torch, dance into the pictures, faint over the words. Each click plants a magic in my mind. Tinkerbell, darting from open-necked flowers like a bright dragonfly in a feathery sky, becomes more real than the big empty feeling of homesickness inside, more real than the insects circling, scooting, gliding, swivelling; than all the yowling night noises. Gradually, I fall asleep.

In the morning, all over the concrete floor, dozens of pale fairy wings.

Dissolving

Moth wings and dead flies line the windowsill. It's been weeks and weeks of soggy Weetabix and the kitchen is always stiff with the smell of onions and boiling milk and I'm forgetting my mum's face, even though I still hear her voice in my dreams, and I'm wondering if my little sister will remember me, and Marie and I hide under blankets from twirling, trembling thunderstorms, and sometimes I wander from room to foreign room, looking for something familiar, and I wish I could talk to my brother. Are they all ok? Without my family, I'm a sentence with most of the words missing. And my memory of our house is slipping and sliding like an egg off a plate. And every night, even when I pull the darkness over my head, my hidey-crying sounds pool around my bed, leaking towards Marie's bed on the other side of the room, and my heart is an ache on a loop and I'm scared of even thinking the thought, *will I ever see my family again*?

Escape

When I hear about what happened, I feel as if my heart has been driven over. The man who was supposed to be taking care of my little brother and my baby sister, has been beating Ivor, just for being homesick and scared and asking for me. So Ivor took Molly from her cot that night and ran away. Just as the sky was whitening, the Buckleys found them gone, and called the police, who found them spooned on the verandah of our locked-up house, blanketless, after a long walk in the clattering dark. So clever of Ivor, when he's only five, to look for the big mahogany tree that told him he'd found our house. When the police arrived and tried to lift Molly, he screamed and clutched her and called for me. Only after they promised to ring the Walkins, did he let her go.

Marie's parents said Ivor could come here. But Molly has to stay with the Buckleys.

So now I have Ivor with me. But what about Molly, he says. And keeps saying her name as he paces in the yard near the tractor, his voice shrill. She'll miss me. She'll think we've left her. Why did Mum and Dad go away? When are they coming back?
Soon, I say, though really I don't have a clue, and sometimes panic that we'll never see them again. But I'm the big sister, and I have to make Ivor feel better.
When they come home, they'll bring us all presents, I say. Meanwhile, let's go explore the barns. They have hens here. We can collect eggs for Mrs Walkin.

I can't tell him that Mum's sister Judy is dying, and dying sometimes takes a long time, so we don't know when they'll be back. And Auntie Judy has a baby too, and someone has to mind it, along with my auntie's other child. And sad husband.

Meanest, most selfish self

Long past the tucked-up hour, the whole place in heavy silence. Gradually, night growing a dark shape into the room. A spike of fear, until I realise that the tottering arrival is Ivor. *Tosha, Tosha…I need to go to the toilet.* I am fake sleep-breathing, willing him to go away, my chest rising and falling. *Toshaaaaaa,* he whispers in a whimpering lament, and I shirk under my sheet to muffle the pleading, because the long drop is outside, in the pitchest of blacks, where snakes and bats and *tokoloshes* poke and scrape and slither. *Go ask Marie,* I say, and he stumbles and trips across the room and prods her, and Marie groans, *No.* Itosha is your sister. She must take you. And he yearns back to me, all leaky-mouth from tears that have dripped, and I coil up away from him. It's too scary outside, Ivor. Pee into your water glass. It's not a pee. No Ivor, I can't take you. Try to hold on until morning. And making little sniffling gasps, he fades from the room.

Crime and punishment

I'm being yanked out of bed by Marie's furious mum and she's dragging me down the corridor to the bathroom-with-no-toilet-in-it. What a selfish sister you are, not taking your little brother to the loo! she shouts at me, her voice the bellow of a hundred thunders. Well, you can wash his dirtied sheets. Right now! And she dumps a Tilley lamp beside the bath, which burns a circle around me. She hands me a bar of soap. Get to it.

The flickering oil lamp creates giant shadows that waver all over the walls and ceiling. A scuttle. Is it a rat? A snake? Enough of your snivelling. Come Ivor, Mrs Walkin says more gently. You're going to sleep in your sister's bed.

The bathroom smells of musty towels and Pears soap. I stoop over the bath, rubbing and sniffling. In the battered mirror, I look like a scratchy ghost. The water's cold. Rust coils its yellow-brown fingers around the plughole and in a streak below the taps. And it's hard to see, and the double sheet is massive, and my hands are hyper-tense as they make invisible contact with the slimy, skinny muck.

After settling Ivor, Marie's mother comes back to check on me, still kneeling on the knee-biting concrete floor. She makes me twist the sheet by myself, haul the sodden sheet to the scullery and straggle it over the clothes horse. Watches with folded arms while I fumble to get it spread out properly. There's nearly no night left when she she says I can go back to bed. My nightie is drenched and I don't have another one. Marie is asleep, and I don't want to wake her to ask for a spare. Climb up onto the high feather mattress, as damp as though I've peed all over myself. Ivor and I are top and tail, a faint pooey whiff from him. A guilty swoosh. She'd wiped his bum with the dirtied sheet but not washed him properly. He's fallen to sleep, at least.

Thoughts churn until dawn.

Feeling bodiless as the light seeping in through the curtain, I float over to Marie, touch her shoulder. When she stirs and sees me, I tip my head in the direction of the door. Quietly, so Ivor doesn't hear, we soft-pad down to the pantry.

Black hound, swallowed sun

I follow Marie past the sugar cane fields, our tyres hissing in the dirt. I'm watching the bunched hem of Marie's dress flutter with yellow and white stripes, like trapped butterflies, when Ivor's high-pitched voice rings out. Wait for *me!* Sugar cane stalks stand east and west of us. I glance back over my shoulder. And see a huge black shape flinging itself out from the sugar cane...a massive black shape leaping...a *monumental* black creature, leaping...from a row of crops, leaping out...and knocking...Ivor...to the ground...leaping out of the row of cane and... knocking him to the ground, sinking its teeth into Ivor's buttocks and holding on...and holding on...its mouth foaming, teeth holding on, holding on...foam spewing from its mouth, and it's shaking its head from side to side, foam flying, as though...as though trying...as though trying to tear my brother, my little brother...into shreds...his one, long, piercing scream...and then, a deafening crack. Marie's father, with a rifle.

*

Ivor stares at me through a sealed, barred window, his face dirt-streaked. He's in quarantine. That means he has to stay all alone in that room for two whole weeks. I am not allowed in to say *sorry* for leaving him. *Sorry* for last night. *Sorry* for not looking after him, when I promised. People usually die, Marie whispers, when they've been bitten by a rabid dog. *Rabid*. The word has a fright and a madness in it. I want Ivor to see me through the window at least, but Mrs Walkin takes me to Marie's room so I don't see them injecting him. Rocking, arms crossing my belly. It'll be my fault if he dies. When Mrs Walkin comes in to kiss Marie goodnight, I cry for my own mother. Cry when I smell Ivor-smell in my bed.

The next day, through the barred window, I catch sight of the doctor flicking the huge syringe while a nurse tries to hold Ivor still. The doctor has to come and puncture deep into Ivor's small belly-button every day, every day, every day, every day, every day, every day, every day, every day, every day, every day, every day, every day, every day, every day, every day...

He is one gutsy little boy, I hear Mr Walkin murmur to his wife. Hasn't cried once since the first day. Brutal injection. I've heard that even grown men scream they'd rather die.

The heart is a lonely bear

Mrs Walkin says Dad is coming home, but Mum is staying. What if Dad's plane falls out of the sky? What if Mum's sister dies and she is sad for the rest of her life? What if Ivor dies and I'm sad for the rest of mine? Or he lives, but he's all wrong in the head? What if bad things are happening to Molly right now? What if she doesn't know us when we all go back to being a family? What if these bad things are happening because of the snake? What if it's my turn next, and I get bitten by a scorpion? What if Mr Walkin had killed Ivor when he shot the rabid dog? But he didn't he didn't he didn't and Ivor's going to be ok, and Dad's going to be here soon, and Molly is fine fine fine, and Mum's sister is going to get better and Mum will be happy and come home *lalalalalalalalala...*

I hate Ivor being all alone in that room I'm banned from. Black clouds are milling about on the horizon, ready to charge in with a storm. I'm sitting on the verandah step, staring at the bush, imagining I can see the eyes of a wild dog staring back at me.

Happy birthday, says Beatrice. I start. That means I'm seven now. Look, a present from your *amai* and *deddee*, she tells me. One hand holds a huge green bin bag. The other is on my shoulder. She moves her hand to stroke my thin hair. I glance up at her uncertainly. Could it be a puppy? She nods to me and I unknot it. Inside is a big blond teddy bear, with a friendly, sewn-on black nose, and amber glass eyes. Under his left foot, a label. *Made in Zambia.* My bear is a Zambian, like Beatrice.

I ask her to help me carry him on my back, the way she does with her own baby. Instead, she zips up my rain jacket and slides my bear down the front, so it's just like the kangaroo pup's pouch in my animal book. This way is better. Now you can see him all the time, she says. When you see him, you can know he is there.

The present

She is a collie, five years old, abandoned by her owners who have left the country. Even though I have been asking for a dog forever, Dad says Cara is for Ivor, so he can learn not to be afraid of dogs.

And I know the underneath reason is to say sorry. Because he wasn't there.

Pushing down fear

Kabwe, Zambia. My father seizes me from behind and flips me onto his shoulders. It's so high up here, so far from the ground, but it's the first time I can ever remember my dad playing with me, so I try to hold back my shriek. I *try*, but it peals out of me. Ah now, don't be a baby.

My slippery palms are sliding all over my dad's sweaty head, fingers getting caught in the damp black curls stuck to his forehead. Pulling my hands away, he holds them stretched out in his own. Now he's stumbling forward again. Daddy, watch out, I scream, as he trips over a tuft of scrub. The powdery dust of the parched grass kicks my nostrils, along with a whiff of the brown drinks he likes. He curses and drops my hands to steady himself. I latch back on to his forehead. Cara is leaping up against his long rifle legs, barking. Another jolt, as one of his boots shoots out. The shell-shaped clouds on the horizon are bouncing as though on a trampoline. Next thing I'm on the hard, dusty ground and Cara is anxiously licking my face.

Dad whirls around to check Mum's reaction. She's standing on the vernadah, tapping the toe of a heeled sandal against the step, one fist clutching the hem of her sundress patterned with poppies, the other hand holding a cigarette, staring far away to where her sister is buried.

Memory, wrung out

Mum, by the line, squeezing Ben's body after spinning him in the washing machine.
My teddy, I wail. You're torturing him!
Don't be ridiculous, Tosha. He's just a toy.

I stare at her wringing hands and a familiar sensation charges into my body.

At the back of our first Zambian house, by the *khayas*, a wood fire, sending up laces of smoke.
A doorway into a sandy yard, where I saw a skinny woman's hands swiping after a squawking
feather-frenzy, whirling, like a shaken yellow duster, head thrusting forward. Slow motion
puffs of air as I stood riveted, watching its silhouette skitter among the huts. After seizing
its scrawny throat, she twisted its neck and plopped the shuddering body – thwack! – into a
galvanised bucket.

Mum is hanging Ben up by his ears. Itosha, stop being silly. He'll be fine once he's dry. He was
so dusty and you were sneezing in bed.

Dad says that the neck vertebrae are the most breakable parts of a body. I couldn't have heard
it, but in my head, the crunch of the creature's bones was like my mum breaking a handful of
skinny raw spaghetti before plunging it into boiling water.

Did we eat crispy roast chicken that night?

White sky, black afternoon

Kabwe, Zambia. Charcoal-scented smoke through the open window from the *braai*. Low drone of adults, occasional crack of laughter, like a twig breaking. Girls first, says Luke, the biggest boy, who is twelve, and Irish, like us. His sister Caz and I pull down our knickers. Pull up our summer frocks. Bend over the bed, he says. Why? It's your turn now. Because, he says, we need to get a better look. The other boys are jostling and clambering behind him. He sighs at our stares. Ok, I'll give you this bar of chocolate.

The eiderdown is forest green. We take the chocolate, kneel over the bed. I can feel the lump of a scab on my kneecap, as though I'm kneeling on a beetle. Luke, is behind me. He pushes me on to the mattress. All of a sudden, trepidation, followed by something sharp and cutting, like a sword or an arrow, or a stick, stabbing right inside me. I pull in air on a long string. What are you doing? Stop moving, he complains. Hand pressed into the centre of my back, holding me down. Stop, stop!

He giggles and shoves harder. When I scream, he withdraws it swiftly, and he and the watchers run out of the room. Feel a trickle down my leg, pull up my knickers, sit on the bed, squeeze my legs together, desperate to press my hand over the pain. Gulp back sobs and wipe furiously at my sniffling nose. Push the chocolate off the bed. It lands on the floor with a thud. Open-mouthed, Caz stares at the threads of blood sliding down my leg. I stumble to the loo to examine my hurt. Drop the lid, lean against the cistern, pull up my knees to my chest, wrap them with my arms.

Time swishes like water, becoming deep and strange. Maybe three hours go past, or twenty minutes.

Caz knocks and calls my name. Eventually, I open the door.

The adults are getting darker with each drink. Rowdy tang of char-grilled steak, pork chops, chicken, skewered peppers, onions and mushrooms, jacket potatoes wrapped in foil. Caz and I shrink past their dangerous faces. Beyond the fence, a thicket of dense bush full of trees: *mufuti* and mountain acacia, large-leafed *mahobohobo* and *mazhanje* trees. Beatrice taught me their names, but I still can't distinguish them all. The trees whisper. In the African stories, Beatrice said, trees always know when there's trouble.

You stare
into a puddle
so intently,
you almost fall
into the clouds.
Fynn's long coat
beside you.
Let's do a skydive,
you say.
You? he says,
jump from a plane?
You shrug.
All it takes is
twenty seconds
of insane
courage.
Above you,
the trees
whisper.

Eye is a spike

I start screaming.

Maggie, my doll, named for my first friend, has been tied to a tree and shorn. Her lovely, long wavy hair, flung in scissored clumps to the ground. Dress and knickers, lying in the dirt. Limbs wrenched off. The smooth plastic of her body, stabbed with a skewer, rude as a defeathered chicken. I spend the rest of the afternoon tenderly pressing her limbs back into the hollows of the joinings, covering her little pink torso with plasters that I find in the bathroom cabinet, sobbing violently over the sticky black remnants of her head.

The culprit, we find out, is Caz and Luke's four-year-old brother.

I imagine he was just being curious, pleads their mother apologetically. Looking for a belly button and whatnot. Playing cowboys and Indians.

Ah, pet, consoles my mother. Don't worry. We'll get you another doll.
But there can never be another Maggie, can't she see?

I squat against a tree, watching a snail's trail up the red brick boundary wall, waiting, waiting to go home. Wish *they* were all dead, lying on the ground, skewered.

Gifts and other lures

Kabwe, Zambia. A small girl strokes my sister's blond hair. In response, she reaches for the girl's plaits, little black spikes all over her head, like cloves in an orange. The other kids laugh.

Is it true, says Samuel, affecting a taller posture so he's up to my height, that where you come from, weddings are inside, and very small?
Weddings have to be inside, because we get a lot of rain, I say.
Samuel glances up at the flamboyant tree, alight with coral petals. The tree is our umbrella if it rains. Don't you have trees?
Yes, but it's also cold, I say. Not like here.
I start to feel disloyal to Ireland. Cast about for something positive to say.
The best man announces something in Bemba. The women ululate. What are they saying? I ask Samuel. They are saying that Kinglsey gave many, many cows for his bride's *lobola*.
In Ireland, the man doesn't have to buy his wife, I pounce, superior at last. She's not for sale. She marries him for free because she loves him.
Samuel's smile is tilted.

Drums rattle to announce the meal. Wafting up from the tables standing in front of the flamboyant tree, aromas of spinach with peanut butter, tomato and onion. Huge tureen lids are lifted from dishes of meat or chicken. The sun is belting down, and I'm glad we're in the shade of the tree. Saliva surges. People line up to heap their plates. I scoop some rice and chicken on to a plate.

After the feast, Samuel slips off his school lace ups. I go shoeless too, tucking my socks into my new black patents. Step gingerly, braced for the appearance of a snake or paper thorns. Samuel flies freely across the hard hot ground. The other boys race after him as though he's the pied piper.

I like Samuel, on his own. But I'm not going anywhere near a bunch of boys. Sit glumly against the trunk of the flamboyant. Watch bees landing on petals. A dog with its long strains of *find me*. A spider scurrying down a thread to the crook of a lower branch. Light glints across the beautiful, quivering web. But it's a trap. Like chocolate.

Questions fizzle and go out

White with black spots. Just like Spot, the dog in my blue-and-white diamond book from school, as though he's come alive. I watch him scrabble a hole under the next door fence, and slither through from the bush-side, towards the huge trees. The sky is heavy with threatening rain. Grabbing my leftover crust from my lunchbox, I squat down, arm outstretched. And, simple as that, I have a new friend.

The next-door house is empty. Red dust whirls into a pile against the concrete steps of the verandah. Spot shakes vigorously and then settles on the bed I've made with an old sheet. I kneel and empty my bulging pockets. Out topple the biscuits I stole from Cara's basin. Spot nuzzles my lap, light as the breeze nuzzling the leaves. I spell out his name in the dust.

The hours, days, weeks merge, with their banging screen doors, sudden rains, mud that coats my calves. Spot and I play in the concrete boat in the no-neighbour's back yard. It has two sun-faded wooden planks for seats. I am Long John Silver voyaging across the red sea, and Spot is my trusty look-out.

Ivor and Molly splash in the plastic paddling pool, occasionally calling my name. They probably think I'm somewhere, reading. I don't respond, because Spot is my secret.

Everything ends with a warning nod from our next-door-but-one neighbour to my parents. A white van; two men. Spot's pleading eyes. I scream and grip tight, but they yank him from me. Because of the two long drag marks his frantic claws left, springing two beads of blood, they jab me with a tetanus injection. But that's nothing, compared to what happens to him.

My father comes to the empty house and sits on the step beside me, where Spot used to sit. The only way to confirm that a dog has rabies is to put him down he says quietly, after a short silence. But he didn't have a foaming mouth, I wail. He didn't act crazy, and he never bit me! I loved him, and you killed him! And I bet he didn't even have rabies! Did he? My father shakes his head once. But he might have had, he says, his green eyes drilling into mine. We couldn't risk…

My mouth opens. Then closes again. Broken glass thoughts.

Stinging insects and words

Kabwe, Zambia. I go round the side of the house and squat to pee, my knickers pulled down between my knees, feet apart, so I don't wet them. Force my pee fast, feeling sure someone's behind me, staring at my bum.

The someone is a mosquito. Smack!

As the sun droops redly into bed, insect sounds intensify. I swat at squads of mosquitoes trying to stand on my skin to gorge on my blood. Two victories, splats of brown-red, on the concrete.

Bedtime. Shrouded by the bliss of my cool, water-sprayed net, I'm misted into the universe of Neverland. Pause to take a few sips of water and hear the world again. A lift of breeze bangs the screen door. Birds chip the air, or maybe into wood. Another bang. Mum and Dad are having a drink on the verandah, outside my window. Just a little longer, my father says in a low voice. I hear him shove something up against the screen door. One of his boots, maybe. We'll be moving soon, he says.

And I'm the door, feeling the boot shoved into my mouth. The tree, feeling the stab of a bird's beak.

Thoughts walking out

Our visitor rubs his face against my legs. Mum has been reading to me from a book of animal facts, and she says cats have sweat glands on their cheeks. They rub against you to mark their territory. So I belong to *him*. Can he stay? I ask.

Mum looks at Dad.

I'm not going to give him a name. If he decides to leave, it will be easier if he's nameless.

He circles my pillow repeatedly before settling into it. That's what they do, Mum says, as though preparing the room, the bed, the pillow, to accept his vibrations. He's embedding his scent.

His eyes gleam in the moonlight flowing through my un-curtained window. Cats have iridescent membranes in their eyes for gathering the palest traces of light, Mum says. Only all that scattery light prevents them from detecting fine details. I wonder if he can see *me* clearly, if he has fixed me inside the animal kingdom of his mind.

How many places can you be at once? I'm already inside all my own memories, and inside my mum's head and my brother's and father's and sister's. And outside too – my hands, and arms and legs, and in the mirror, my eyes. Does the mirror know a bit of me that the cat can't see?

I leave the windows open so NoName knows he's free to come and go. Sometimes, when the moon is skating across the treetops, and the warm air is humming *come out*, he wriggles between the burglar bars, and I wish my body could follow. But my thoughts can, at least. Out they go, over the security fence, into the bush, where I prowl like a cat – a *big* cat – hunting for prey.

Half my heart is jumping out the window

In the car, drenched with the heat, crushed between boxes and Molly, who is sitting on Ivor's lap, I think of the inferno it must be for the cat, who's inside the box on my lap. I open the flaps a little, to let in some air. We slow-pass roadworks, men sprawled on the verge, eating roasted *mealies*. My mouth floods with saliva for one of those charred cobs to chew on. The warm air is thick with diesel oil and the labourers' acid sweat. NoName presses his head out of the box and lurches for the pop-out back slit of the window, his belly resting on the latch. Wriggles further through the open slot. My slippery hands try to keep a grasp of his hind legs. The combined stench of Mum and Dad's cigarettes, gravel snapping against the underbelly of the car, speed of the roadside treeline rushing back as we rush forward and the feeling of losing my grip on the cat, trigger nausea. I swallow.
Daddy, the cat is nearly out the window. I say.
Well, hold on to him, he says, glancing at his rear view mirror. But I'm guessing he can't see because of the ceiling-high boxes.
Dad I can't, he's, he's…oh he's jumped out!
I scream and scream and my mother puts her hands to her head and goes Seán, Seán, until my father slams the brakes in a fury. I thud to the ground before the car's even stopped. The heat belts me across the face. Through the dry crackle of the bush, swiping at tribes of mosquitoes, alert for snakes, Ivor and I hunt for the cat. Here, kitty kitty! I call frantically. Psss, goes Ivor, just once, like the puff of a tight jar of jam when you get it open. Enough now, says my father. He's gone. And then, just like that, we find him, curled like a leopard on a nearby tree stump. Like Houdini. Like the Cheshire cat.

As Dad approaches, NoName's tail becomes a swaying flagpole, the growl in his throat starting up like a motorbike. Let me, Dad. Crooning, I gather him up, and settle him into the box. Dad tapes the flaps and pierces some holes. NoName scrabbles furiously. Relief and sorrow conflict in my chest.

Mum hears me sniffling, and turns right around to catch my eye. Think of it as an adventure, darling. You'll make new friends. And our new house has its own pool. It'll be fun living in a city. But I've swum underwater, can't hear her words clearly. Bet we won't have a low-bellied tree that carries colour and sound like the one in the empty-house yard. Or bush so close we can smell lion, elephant, hyena. And there'll be no one like Kingsley, Dad's friend, who invited us to his wedding and let us sit in his shiny bronze Cadillac and pretend we were James Bond. Or Samuel, my nearly-nearly new friend. Wish I could leap through the window too.

Diamond words

Evelyn Road, Ndola, Zambia. In bed, I listen to Mum and Dad's muted voices through the thin wall, talking about our boxes arriving from Kabwe. She says 'crushed' or 'damaged'; he says 'pulverised', 'mutilated'. More syllables seem to mean more drama. I collect new words, taste the sound of them in my mouth.

Our new house is at the corner of a crossroads with Broadway and Evelyn Road. Our new school is just across the wide Broadway Avenue. The cathedral is opposite the school. And the president's house is further down Broadway. All the important places in a box with four quarters.

My new teacher, Sister Mark, is tall, a slice of raven hair peeping from her veil, and a confounding accent that Dad says is German. Each day, she hands out a familiar blue and white diamond-patterned book to each pupil. Some of the spines are splitting, and I sellotape them before returning them. After a couple of weeks, Sr Mark allows me to take home six books at a time to repair and as a reward, I can also move on from the baby books (Janet and John) to The Famous Five, who say 'ravenous', meaning really hungry. I already know 'famished' and 'starving'. Mum would say 'peckish'. My brain begins building colonies of new words.

The girls' uniform comes in sky-blue, or russet, or lemon yellow. *Stimulating, appealing, energising,* Mum says. Assembly is a rainbow every Friday. Ivor's bones jut like tent poles from his blue shirt and grey shorts. *Dull, bland, insipid.* It doesn't seem fair that the girls get to choose colours and the boys don't, but he doesn't care.

Dad says all you have to do is use a new word six times and it becomes yours. *I am ravenous for toast and marmalade. The birds are ravenous for worms. The cat is ravenous for freedom, or someone to snuggle. The ravenous, ravenous earth opens up its mouth for the rain. Ravenously, I swallow the word ravenous.*

The pack

Evelyn Road, Ndola, Zambia. Shuffling sounds from the living room. Someone is pushing a pyramid of chips into the centre of the table. While the adults are in poker moods, we can be in midnight feast moods.

I like Mum and Dad's new friends. They're fun. Robert Rawson is a Major in the Zambian army, like Dad. He's *rather* British. He used to live in India, and speaks like the queen. So does his wife Eleanor, even though she's from South Africa. I've never seen such a tall woman. Amazonian, Dad calls her. The Rawsons have three daughters, blue-skinned and bone-thin, each with a waterfall of white-blond hair. Marlie's seven, nearly my age, Jessa is six (same as Ivor) and Antoinette's the baby. The Jane Blonds, Dad nicknames them.

While the adults are busy, we creep into the pantry, hunting for biscuits. Ivor climbs up to find the biscuit tin on the top shelf.

Callie, that's a big bet, we hear Robert Rawson say to my mum. In for a penny, she replies. I'm out, says Eleanor, his wife. A slapping of cards on the table.

Ivor uses a penny as a lever. The lid twists open. I slide a pile into the scoop of Marlie's held-out nightie. With the heel of my hand, I erase evidence of crumbs from the shelf. Chips! hisses Jessa. Don't move! I mouth, finger on lips. We draw our breaths, silent as spies.

A crease in the kitchen light, tall, statuesque silhouette in the doorway. Without pressing the pantry switch, Eleanor lifts a cigarette carton, deadpan, as though oblivious of all of us in the small dark space with her, our bodies pressed together, rib to rib, tight as cards in a pack. Priceless, I hear her murmur as she wanders back out.

We hear groaning. Bloody hell, Callie! A sliding of chips, commotion of curses and laughter.

We wait for three beats before creeping back to our room for the feast.

Looking until there's no distance left

Black's skin is very dark, smooth as a plum, with an *achromatic* sheen. Achromatic is my new word. Eyes black as watermelon seeds, and white, white teeth. He often chews on a stick. His hair is short and tufty, and once I asked him if I could touch it. He obliged by bending down so I could reach. Soft and a little oily. His hands have pale palms, nearly the same colour as mine, very clean, deep line markings and sometimes I stand and watch him washing dishes, how the soapsuds spill between his fingers, and the gestures he uses as he flips a plate, rinses it, settles it on the draining board. I go outside to the pool, sit at the edge cooling my feet, and stare at my own unsatisfying hands, with strings of vague, broken and splintered lines.

Black squats down in the dirt, beckons us over, and shows us the coiled dark metallic brooch of a centipede. Teaches us the word for it: *chongololo*. I say it over and over. Is he dead? I ask, as the creature remains unmoving in his hand. Eh. He's playing dead. That is what he does to keep safe.

This moment of an almost-elsewhere

My arms, floating up and down like wind-swayed branches as I tightrope walk the driveway kerb. My little sister Molly and her new friend Jessa – Jane Blond number 2 – are pretend-pushing Mum's sky-blue Peugeot, the ragtop roof rolled down, and Jessa trips on a red bucket and comes to show me her sore knee. From the house, music and laughter. *I'll nip down and get a few more,* calls Mum, swinging open the screen door, tripping down the steps, into the car – *chunk* – and she reverses, and I scream but nothing comes out of my mouth…white noise, clouds swishing together, the car halting, Mum flying out to find

Molly lying between the wheels. A high narrow whirling in my body, as though I'm a silver fish just hooked and lifted from the blue sea, and *Please*…did my prayer fly fast enough? Heaven seems so far away…it was only a split-second, but I was supposed to be in charge, and now my Mum slides out my sister and clutches her body, soft and limp as a pillow, and…*Thank God,* says Mum in a cracked voice, as Molly utters a pale whimper, her thin body trembling like a dragonfly.

A little wind runs

Doug
the sky-diving
instructor,
glances up at you.
Found the loo okay?
Waits for your breezy nod,
before commencing
the drill.
Behind him, a girl,
staring at you,
as though working out
how to salvage a chandelier
on the verge of falling.
Instructions
rush past.
You glance up
at the cumulonimbus
sky,
slide out
of how to do
the landing.

Between one heartbeat and another

Christmas Eve. The moon is riding a massive black horse across the window. I twist and turn and thump my pillow, nerves like knives squealing across dinner plates. Will he find us here, in hot Zambia, far from the snow?

Creak of the door. Instantly, I'm a *chongololo,* playing dead. Through almost closed lashes, I can see Santa, shadowy as a moving tree, wheeling in – a doll's pram. He stops at the end of my bed. I can smell the brandy that my father left out for him. Strangely, a reek of cigarettes too. Santa, smoking?

From his own centipede-circle shape on the pillow, NoName lifts his head and makes a low growling noise. He doesn't like men, not my dad, and imagine, not even Santa! His fur has gone electric, his eyes are glaring. I risk a peep.

Tiptoeing out of the room, Santa is wearing nothing but a short maroon smoking jacket, hanging open, just like

my father.

All night, questions rumble like bees circling above my head.

Unravelling in the dark

A voice mutters on the other side of the dusty confessional screen. On cue, I begin, Bless me, Father, for I have sinned... A pause, which balloons into a silence. I have no idea what to say next. Well, child, go on then. No need to feel shy. Do you ever disobey your parents?
Um...well, I do read in bed when it's a school night, even though I'm not allowed.
Anything else?
Um...and my brain is a blank.
So you're a good girl then?

This confined dark. Like the outhouse on the Walkins' farm.

No! I'm *not*, Father. My little brother nearly died and it was all *my* fault, because I wouldn't take him to the outhouse, even though I was supposed to be minding him, because my parents had gone away, and he ended up doing a poo in his bed, and when I got in trouble with Mrs Walkin, I was angry at my brother for telling on, and the next morning I left him behind and went off with my friend, and then...

I tell the whole story to this shadow on the other side of the screen. Reveal my own guilt, which I hadn't mentioned to anyone, even to myself.

... and now I have a black blot on my soul...

How could *anyone* forgive my inexcusable acts, even someone kind, like God?

Mournful in a short white dress

Evelyn Road, Ndola, Zambia. I am already eight, way past communion-age, because I switched schools at the wrong time. And now my once fairy-tale dress is too short, flaring out from the waist and stopping way above my scabby knees. I gaze in dismay at all the other girls. Every one of them is wearing a long dress to the ankles. Long!

In the cathedral, I kneel beside a line of flowing white satins and laces, occasional flash of white sock tucked into white pumps. Like Samantha in *Bewitched,* I brood into vanishing. Run my tongue over my upper teeth, which jut out, like cliffs. Drop my head for the prayers along with the others, as though we are birds dipping our thirsty heads to drink.

There's no Santa. Maybe no tooth fairy. What if God is made up too?

I quickly apologise to Him for such a wicked thought, in case He's listening, in case He really exists. After all, didn't He save Ivor from dying of rabies? Didn't He save Molly from being run over?

The priest lifts a gigantic host towards the light – sharp cut-out of an ironed sun on a wan day – and I ready myself for the walk up to the altar, squirming about the fact that my legs will be the only ones visible. Even though they are bare every day, somehow, on this occasion, the exposure feels like *sacrilege* (Mum's word).

Even worse, when the priest finally lays the host on my stuck-out tongue, it won't come un-clung. I strain to scrape the dissolving God away, without the sin of chewing. All of a sudden, I shudder violently, as though a lizard has just run up my leg, at the thought of my body being occupied by the Body of Christ.

At the breakfast celebration in the school hall, I sit at the long table. Fields of open mouths. Red tongues, yellow candles, red serviettes, yellow eggs.

Trying not to think about His body being mashed up by my digestive process, His blood, swallowed by the priest, I console myself with another thought: at least no one can see my legs now.

In the wake of a crop

A scorching day, flawless blue sky. Mum's newly blond hair lilts behind her in the wind. I love being alone with her, just the two of us, in her blue sports car. But I'm mournful about the drastic cut I've just had. Float my hand over my shorn head. At least you have a lovely cool neck now, says Mum. When I don't respond, she changes tack. How was school?
Someone asked if Ivor and me were twins, I say. People will think we're both boys now. Twin *boys*.

My mother smiles, glances over, ignoring the bitterness in my tone. Ivor and *I*, she says breezily. Actually, twins run in our family.
Despite myself, I become interested. Really? Who are the twins?
Well, your Auntie Iris and Uncle Will are twins. And your Auntie Judy, the one who died, had twins. A boy and a girl.
I didn't know she had a boy too, I say. Another cousin!
Mum pauses. He died soon after she did. He was only a year old.

The lights change to red. Mum slams on the brakes and extends an arm to keep me from hitting my head on the windshield. She gasps and I think it's the jolt. She releases a long breath and then says, I had twins too, before you. Like Judy, a boy and a girl. But they were stillborn.
Stillborn? I say, although I sense the answer already.
She looks down at her hands. They were born too early, at seven months. They didn't get to live at all. Not even to draw one breath.

I stare at her, feeling an undulation I can't name. It ripples across my shorn head. Twins, floating in some limbo, like water babies. Twins, in Mum's tummy before me.

Did she name them? Did she see them? Did she hold them? Is there a grave? No. No. No. No. Dad made her pregnant straight away, she says, to help take the sadness away. And then she had me.

So I'm the eldest by default.
So I have to make up for two.

So my presence is due to their absence.

Souls are fluid and alchemical

In class, I am seated between Kevin and his sister Jeannie. They both have fuzzy hair and linseed skin. They are twins, alike as a pair of polka-dot socks, except Kevin smiles more whitely, readily, and Jeannie has five freckles across the bridge of her nose. At rest-time, we cross our arms, lay them on our desks, lean cheeks on our arms, first this-way, then that. Smile at each other, first me-and-Jeannie, then me-and-Kevvie. I like your new haircut, says Kevvie. Cool. I smile back. At least my hair can't static-float into snarls anymore when it's hot. And my neck *is* cool.

Maybe the souls of my ghost siblings came from heaven and landed in these two bodies, in the very class I'm in. It's a kind of miracle. Here they are; my lost twin brother and sister, like ink soaking through from the other side of a page.

Parlay by moonshine

Evelyn Road, Ndola, Zambia. So hot, as though the sun was still up. And the night has forgotten it's supposed to be dark – it's *ridiculously* light, Mum would say – so I have to run outside too, and sit on the top step of the pool. The moon is a gigantic melon, the hugest I've ever seen it, as though it's crept close to our planet. An avenue of light crosses the water, which magnifies my long toes (like my mother's) and my hands (like my dad's).

In the distance, I can hear yowling. NoName has gone hunting. Or tom-catting, as Mum says. An *ahem* at the side gate. It's Black.

Look Black, I say (keeping my nightie on; I was about to slip it off and jump in). It's like daytime. Black stays where he is, but opens the gate. Yes, but it's not daytime. And remember, after midnight, the *tokoloshes* come out. I grin at him, reaching out my arm to cup the buttery moon in my palm. If the *tokoloshes* come, you can protect me. He smiles. Black, why are you called Black? He laughs softly. I can ask the same thing. Why are you called Itosha? Maybe because you are an African girl? I giggle.

Black, do you believe in God? Of course. Do you talk to him? Yes I do. But most times, for guidance, I pray to my ancestral spirits. His words come slowly, like fat raindrops that plop one-by-one on the pool at the very end of a storm.

Mum says I have a guardian angel. So it's kind of the same thing, isn't it? Have you come out to talk to your ancestral spirits? I ask, trying out the new word in my mouth, somehow understanding the meaning without being told.

I like to come out these warm nights, for some peace, and space. I like the quiet. I can think my thoughts. And you? Am I disturbing a conversation with your guardian angel? I twirl my hand in the warm water, thinking about Santa wearing my father's smoking jacket. No, I say, just with the moon. You can *see* the moon. It's definitely real. I'm not so sure about angels.

Ah, many things are real, even if they are invisible. He squats down beside the gate, and gazes up at the moon. If you listen, you can feel them.

Back in my room, I lean on the sill. Maybe my name is a sign. Maybe I *am* meant to be an African girl.

Low body-whirling

Evelyn Road, Ndola, Zambia. Every time my dad passes, NoName growls deep in his throat, the tip of his white-tipped tail curling slowly in a circle, like the second hand on a clock. Three times a day, Dad goes, *I'll kill that cat*. One Sunday afternoon in October, he discovers a mess of cat poo in the bath, like roadkill smashed flat on the hot tar. He drop-kicks NoName right out the front door.

Dad makes me clean up the stinky, diarrhoea-like slather. NoName probably had a bad tummy and couldn't make it outside in time. I ask Black for his rubber gloves and a dust pan. He follows me to the bathroom, gives me a nod to scoot, and finishes the job.

I sprint up and down Evelyn Road, asking everyone I pass if they've seen a grey cat with white markings. No one has. The next day, I come home from school to find that he still hasn't returned.

Mum sits on the bed. Darling sometimes it's important to consider that there might be a reason for a person's actions. When your father was a small boy, a cat clawed wildly at him, and one of its claws locked straight through his lip. He was taken to the hospital with the cat still attached to him. He's hated cats ever since.

NoName has left us for good, I gasp sobbingly in the kitchen. Come, says Black, and takes me to his *khaya*. He goes in through the tatty door to the dim interior, emerging a moment later with a catapult. This is for you. You can knock the sweetest pomegranates from the top of the tree, he says.

The sturdy forked twig, like a tiny divining stick, is wrapped in thick rubber. A smooth, sand-coloured leather pouch, drilled with holes on each side, is attached to the rubber, which folds back and is bound tightly to the stick with strong string. You made this? He nods. At the top of the tree, the largest, reddest pomegranate I've ever seen juts mockingly, like a baboons's bum. I scoop up some stones, aim, and fire. After several goes, the coveted pomegranate is mine. Sitting on his step, we split it and share the seeds. You mean it's mine for keeps? He nods, and I hug him.

I keep the catapult under my pillow. Every now and then my hand creeps to it.

Christmas beetles in the crackling bush

Luanshya, Zambia. Dart's ears waggle the horseflies away, her mane the gleam of a snowfield from a Christmas card, swishing tail a dark tip. She snorts, and the sound is like wind flapping a flag. One of her eyes is blue. She's blind in that eye, Mrs Vant tells me. I choose her.

Ivor and I, along with fifteen other kids, spend the morning learning how sit in a saddle, how to trot, hold our reins. Ivor has chosen the biggest, wildest horse, though he is the smallest boy. During lunch-break, we watch a long line of thumb-sized soldier ants bearing our crumbs towards their anthill home. Then, a long trek. Ivor is the first to try jumping over a log.

The afternoon light, rocking motion, this new, springy odour settling on my skin. Sunlight glints through the acacias. *I am a girl on a horse.* Then Dart is spooked, jumping from the alarm bell of a snake or a cricket. She flares and ramps up on her back legs. I scream. Rein her in! Mrs Vant shouts. But I've lost the reins. Hand clutching a fistful of mane, I call, whoah, whoah girl... as we fly across the mole-rutted *vlei.* She only skids to a halt when we reach the dam.

The others catch up. After the horses have had a drink, Jenny's horse paces up the grassy slope of the dam wall and the other horses follow. Jenny is fifteen, and Mrs Vant's daughter. Dart snorts and heaves. *So high.* And only about six feet wide. *Don't look down.* Next moment, Dart shies... loses her footing...and we are somersaulting over the side of the high wall.

Twigs in my hair and a lip bitten bloody. Dart scrabbles to standing. Come on, up you get, back on the horse, calls Mrs Vant from the top of the dam wall. But I can't. I refuse Ivor's offer to come down and give me a leg up. Dart and I plod back to the stable yard, shamed and alone.

The 21-mile trip back to Ndola in the van is slow and it's quick. Dusty pick-ups and clean white cars, black-and-white painted kerbs, a lorry carrying logs. The sun drops swiftly, red as the flaming lilies in the roadside flowerbeds. Rosy clouds turn into galloping horses. Soon, we're beyond the tree-lined streets of the town, the white buildings with Dutch gables, and on the Ndola Road, bush either side of us. Ivor is sparkling, singing along with the other kids, while Jenny plays her guitar. I feel too miserable to join in, until Jenny pauses and gifts me her 100-watt smile. That was some gallop to the dam, Tosha. And you stayed on.

The source

Evelyn Road, Ndola. Mum, why am I afraid of things and Ivor isn't? The rhythmic shick-shick-shick of the chopping knife. Soft suck of the fridge as I open it, take out a natural yoghurt. The fridge resumes its usual droning. I lick the lid before folding the silver circular foil into quarters and popping it in the bin. Select a granadilla from the fruit bowl, bite into its wrinkled skin, squirt the seeds into my yoghurt, use a finger to stir.

Itosha! Mum clucks. Maybe it's because you had a fright when you were small. Onion slices in a waterfall of half rings. You toddled into the garage in Galway and somehow the door slammed shut. You were in the dark for a while, I think, before I heard you.

As soon as she says it, I'm back there in that high wire pitch of terror. Dark, loud as boots, looming over me. A butting of heavy furry snuffling things against my knees. Something wet sliding over my foot. Beating and screaming at the great shut barrier until, at last, rescue. *You silly goose; it's just Laika's puppies.*

And then I get it. Ivor doesn't fear anything, because

he has blocked everything out.

Swallow the white flicker

At the club poolside, we share a Sparletta Creme Soda, passing the bottle from mouth to mouth. The green fizz prickles my nose. My brother dares me to try a swallow-dive. Thinking myself into the shape of a bird, I hop onto the highest diving board. As I inch closer to the edge, a great swirl spins in my belly. *Don't jump.*

The shimmering surface, silver apparitions turning into the shapes of birds. Go on, Ivor calls. I lift my arms the way I saw the other divers do, skyward like an arrow, then bounce up, ready to curl for my downward flight.

My chest clips the board – whap! – and I barrel into the pool. A red gash. Gulp chlorine, erasing the taste of green soda.

Half-past dread

Cups of wind
in her torrent
of dark hair.
On the sill
of her left ear,
a mother
of pearl
seagull, twin
to the one
in your right.
Behind Doug,
the instructor,
(who is shouting
to be heard
above the wind)
the girl stands
skinny as a flagpole
against a rock,
hair long as
Botticelli's Venus.
It's at you
she stares.
And then
she walks over
and speaks.
Don't
jump.

Crossing a ditch

Dominican Convent, Ndola. Sr Mark tells us it's a French word, showing us the little hat on the 'ê'. *Fête* I say to myself.

The sports field is wrapped in *kikois* and shorts and t-shirts and floppy hats. Aroma of coffee, toffee apples, candyfloss, cakes. Queues for archery and fortune telling.

Around teatime a silver spot in the hazy sky becomes visible, growing larger, until we can hear the *cutacutacutacutacuta*. Leaves and insects and people flurry away as the rotor blades fray to a *sheeasheeasheeasha*, and the khaki machine with its monster dragonfly-bulbous eye lands and finally falls silent. A moment later, the 'Flying Nun' (a friend of my parents) swings down the steps.

*

1, *Evelyn Road, Ndola.* Black tells us that he needs to go and look for his wife, who vanished last night, after a big fight. Your lunch is ready on the table, he says. Don't swim until I come back.

We're playing favourite ads. *And all because the lady loves Milk Tray,* intones Molly. *Happiness is a cigar called Hamlet* says Ivor. *Shhh…you know who,* I quip. *Put a tiger in your tank* goes Ivor. *It's finger lickin' good,* I announce. I'm bored says Ivor. I know, I say. Let's have a *fête.*

An oil drum in the dry ditch between our house and the road. We twist it lengthways so it becomes a bridge. Trestle table between two guava trees. I dress the bare board with a cloth, assemble some shirts and dresses, the ones that were packed in a suitcase for charity. Molly checks reachable branches and searches for fallen guavas, lemons and oranges. I knock down two pomegranates with the catapult Black gave me – I use it nearly every day, and my hit rate's getting better. Ivor climbs up shelves for Mum and Dad's cartons of Peter Stuyvesant in the pantry. Brilliant, I say. Will you run down the road and tell people we're selling stuff? I'll look for more things. Molly can arrange the table.

What's our line? I press palms together, waggle my fingers and blow. What about: *Sunday Sale at Number 1 – cigarettes, cheap cheap!*

Legs or tails

People cross the drum. A few oranges spill from my fruit pyramid. I drop down to gather them up. Between the upside down V of the trestle table, I see a jamboree of legs: blue-black, pale, dusty, skinny, one lifted as the owner reaches for something on the table; legs in raggedy shorts, bouncing up and down, his flexing toes.

A garment of clothing has fallen too. Look. I hold up the black see-through *negligée* of my mother's. What am I bid? The women bend over, cackling, slapping their knees, shaking their heads. No one wants it, even though it's so pretty.

A couple of them select fruit. One man buys a raw-sienna belt of my father's for 50*ngwee*. I rub my finger over the embossed coin. Etched in a circle around a mealie cob in the centre: *Grow more food for mankind.*

The rest swoop on the cigarettes like herons over a shoal of fish. We sell them singly, for 5*ngwee* each.

By 3pm we have sold all five cartons: 150 cigarettes. We sprint to the shops and buy a dozen packets of sweets with our earnings. Ivor stuffs his face with a whole family-sized pack of liquorice allsorts. Twenty minutes later, he's vomiting.

Black appears by the time the sky stops being blue. Judging by his face, I'm guessing he found his wife and they had another fight. Look, I say. Liquorice and also the mealies Ivor had for supper last night. Can you see? He gets the dust-pan and sweeps up the claggy mess, then stares down at the wet empty circle as if it's a crystal ball. I can see trouble.

Blood brothers

Glimpse of empty road and streetlights wafting in the front door with Mum and Dad when they get home. Their voices are honey. *Phew.*

Cigarette smoke and alcohol on Mum's breath. We were just about to go to bed, I say, glancing at the last seconds of *Bewitched* and hoping for magic. What's the matter, darling, she says. You not feeling well? Ivor is balled up and clutching his tummy, groaning. My tummy hurts. I glower at him, sending a telepathic message not to tell. Dad, from the doorway of the pantry. Callie – did you move the cartons? No. Why? I can't see them anywhere. Mum swivels after him. My heart is beating so hard, I can see the edges of my vision throbbing. They're not here. Good grief. Have we been robbed again? Over she goes to her bag, pulls out a crumpled, empty packet and peers inside it. She looks at her watch. Itosha, do you know anything about our missing cigarettes? I weigh up options. Then imagine what they'll say next: *We need to wake Black and ask him where he's put them.*

And then they'll find out he wasn't here, minding us, and he'll lose his job. Nothing for it but to distract them with the truth. You know, my teacher says smoking is really, really, bad for you. And I don't want you to die. Itosha. Where. Are. The. Cigarettes. A tiny whisper. We sold them. You did WHAT??

*

Whatever you do, don't cry, Ivor murmurs. We are kneeling beside each other, next to the bed, bracing ourselves for the first lash. Curling snakes in my stomach.

His shadow looming on the wall, whistle of the thin, flexible riding crop. Ivor makes not a sound. So I hold it in too, but gasp with each successive whip-whip-whip, squeezing Ivor's hand tight. One, two, three, four, five, six, seven, eight, nine, ten, eleven, twelve...

That's enough Seán. Mum's grey voice in the doorway.

After Dad follows her out of the room, we stay knelt over the bed as we catch our breath and check out the welts on our bums. They begin to trickle red. Ivor turns to me. We won, he says. How do you mean? I ask him. Because, we didn't cry.

Give or take a mission

The long wait for the moon landing is so boring, when the moment actually happens, I'm following a gecko up a wall.

Just as well they replay it, over and over.

Ivor and I waddle around, each in three pairs of tracksuits, jumping from one bed to the other. Ivor wants to be Neil Armstrong. I let him, because I like the name Buzz.

Two minutes, twenty seconds, I say. Tranquillity here: we're going for landing, over. Do you copy that?

Roger, says Ivor, we copy. Looking good.

He makes his voice go deep. Tranquillity Base here; the Eagle has landed. That's one small step for man; one giant step – Ivor takes a mighty step – for mankind.

He thumps hard against the wall, and the flimsy single bed jerks.

Magnificent...desolation, I say, turning a 360 at the wondrous sight of the moon. I'd staged the room with a pair of knickers thrown on top of Molly's dollhouse, along with grey socks. The huddle looks like a fascinating rock formation.

The heat, which is coming up from the floor, down from the ceiling and in from the door, is starting to make my skin itch. I strip off in a sudden frenzy and wipe my face with a sweaty upper arm. Phew! Shall we go for a swim?

Instantly, Ivor strips his layers off too, down to his underpants, aeroplanes his way to the pool. I'm going to become a pilot, he shouts, before dive-bombing in. You mean astronaut, I shout back, following suit.

Subliminal bat-squeak

Black has invited the three of us to his house for lunch. We skirt the swimming pool, carefully avoiding the ten-foot-long pole topped by a leaf net and go through the little gate at the back of our courtyard. I'm curious to see inside his *khaya* and to meet his wife.

Pungent with wood smoke, it's dark in his thatched *rondavel*. One tiny window, with a green cloth hanging over it and the same kind of fabric hanging from the open door too. Four milky-green enamel plates, a gas canister, a few limp clothes by the wall. There are only three worn-smooth *batonka* stools. Black sits on one. Ivor takes the second. I glance up at *Amai* Halawa. Black nods to me. It's ok. She will sit later.

Molly sits cross-legged on the smooth, polished mud floor and pushes her sticky hair from her forehead. There is no table. I fan myself with my library book: *The Castle of Adventure*. *Amai* Halawa thrusts an enamel plate with a chipped rim at me. Not covered in a *doek,* her hair flops like wilted pea pods from the top of her head. I've never seen her close up before. Her skin is black as treacle and she has a way of looking at me that makes me feel as though little snakes are climbing up and down my spine. She is wearing a dirty housecoat, with a sarong wrapped around it. The same patterned green as the curtain hanging in the doorway, which casts an underwater gloom into the room. She is silent, but a storm cloud whirls around her like the smoke from the *poiki* pot.

Black tells us about growing up in Malawi, a country north of Zambia. The turquoise lake with multi-coloured fish, the beaches, fishing with his father in his boat. Why did you leave and come here? I ask. His wife clicks her tongue against the roof of her mouth. He shouts at her in Bemba, then immediately apologises to us.

The fried fish is burnt. The *nshima* is lumpy and grey, like badly-cooked porridge. I can't eat it, even though I know it's rude not to. The spinach with peanut butter I can manage. Mmm...I look up and smile at her. It's delicious. *Tsikomo, Amai.* I have learned people-pleasing skills from Enid Blyton, which sometimes means knowing when to lie. *Amai* speaks to Black in Bemba, scrapes her food back into the pot and, swaying her bottom and slapping her flip-flops across the floor, walks out of the room.

An hour made of words, a meal and questions

What did she say, Black? He closes his eyes for a moment. She was reminding me of *The Story of the Poor Man*, he says. A story? Can you tell us? He sighs. *The poor man does not know how to eat with the rich. While the rich eat only the body of a fish, the poor man eats the head too, rushing, licking his lips, upsetting the plates. But even though his manners are as loose as an empty hessian sack; even though he comes to the table with dirt under his nails; even though the face of the poor man has many, many lines from the hunger and thirst in his belly; even though to be poor makes a man feel like an animal who would even eat grass; even though the poor man has no proper conversation to share with the rich, how rich this pleasure is, for a poor man.*

Is that the end? The three of us look at each other. That's not a story, says Ivor. Black laughs softly. It is a parable.

What is the parable saying? Are we rich? Is he poor? But he is the one offering *us* food!

It's stultifyingly hot. I want to get up, stand in the doorway, but I'm scared of *Amai*. Black commences eating again, rolling the *nshima* into a ball with the tips of his fingers, scooping up some gravy and spinach with it and popping it into his mouth. I swallow a mouthful, grimace. Black nods in the direction of the pot and I quickly tip my *nshima* back into it. He throws his eyes in the direction of the doorway. Surreptitiously, I peek at him to see if he opens his mouth as he chews. He doesn't. I glance down at his pale, clean nails, then at my own grubby ones.

It's siesta time. He makes us promise not to swim until he gets up to make tea for us, in an hour. And if we're quiet, he might make us some buns.

Remember, the creator is watching, even though he stays in a far place. His eyes are on Ndola, on this very house. His eyes are on you. Read your book, he says to me. Play with your doll, he says to my little sister. And you, he turns to Ivor, eh. Play with your marbles.

When we exit the *khaya, Amai* is nowhere in sight.

*

A few days later, I hear the low voices of my parents. *Amai* Halawa went missing again, and was finally found by Black, hanging from a tree.

Here-now-gone

Did we do anything to make his wife mad? Maybe it was because I didn't finish her *nshima*? *I am the one with no manners.*

Black is not at work.

I've already experienced death. Some deaths I've even caused. The grasshopper whose legs I snapped off, so easily. Flies I'd stood on after I found them flailing in a glass of water and lifted them out by a wing. The snails whose shells I painted with toxic lead colours.

Everything, everyone dies. My aunt, her little boy, my grandfather. Lightning. Spot. One day, I will die too. All alone, at the drop of a hat, on a lonely day. It hurts, this stone in my throat, when I think about dying.

There was a storm in her brain, Black told us.

One of the girls at school is saying she will have to go to hell and get burnt.

Not wanting to think of *Amai*'s face and hair and legs and arms on fire, I get my yellow rope with the wooden handles and start skipping furiously. *Lalalalalalala. One, two, three-four-five, once I caught a fish alive...*

All night, as my sister sleeps like a starfish through a crackling rainstorm, my heart accompanies the galloping heaves of darkness awakened by lightning, like a filmstrip of the storm in *Amai*'s brain.

Blackest furies whirling around trees

All morning, the sky has been threatening a downpour. We need to leave now or we'll get caught, says Dad. Molly and I aren't allowed to go with them, because Dad doesn't want a 'scene'. Not even Mum is going to the airport.

Ivor's jaw is clenched. He's been expelled for having had another of his black furies and throwing mud at a nun. But it was because he saw her kick a dog! And still, they are sending him to boarding school in Ireland, where he'll be all alone. And he's only seven!

Come on now, says Dad gruffly. You'll make loads of friends. You'll love it. And you'll come back for the holidays. The air hostess will take good care of you, and hand you straight over to your aunt when you reach Dublin.

Dad is lifting Ivor's black trunk into the boot of his green Peugeot, his name in large white painted letters on the lid. Mum comes out of the house and strokes Ivor's head. I've prepared you a special picnic for the plane, and packed your comics and your soldiers, she says. Auntie Iris will meet you on the other side. You wait and see, you'll love it in Killashee. It's one of the best schools in Ireland. But Mum – and his voice is so small, in the melancholies – I won't know anyone. What if I wet the bed? You're a big boy now, she says. You won't wet the bed.

And then it's the last minute. Cara presses her long snout into his hand and whines. He squats down and strokes her. I can't stop the tears, looking at him in his blue short safari suit. He hugs Molly first, and then Mum. Take care of Cara, he says, his skinny arms going around me tight.

Behind us, Black is standing at the front door. Ivor walks over to him and, just like a man, shakes his hand.

Last touch I say, and our hands brush as he climbs into the passenger seat next to Dad. They drive off, just as the first heavy drops hit the ground.

A whistling sky

Up the gangway,
into the Cessna.
Door clamps shut.
Four novice jumpers,
all huddled,
helmeted.
Fynn,
in some preparatory space,
fingers tapping absently,
ta-ta-ta.
Wheels juddering
the length
of a short
weathered runway;
a sudden
buffeting lift.
The high-wire
pitch builds.

Bricks and wishes

Molly and I wake up a week after Ivor's left, to find a red brick on the floor, glass all around it. Someone has smashed a window pane, the only one not burglar-barred. How did we sleep through that? The wardrobe in our room is open and our clothes are gone, and in Mum and Dad's room, theirs have vanished too. In the kitchen, the radio is absent. In the lounge, no TV. Money and watches that were sitting on Mum's and Dad's bedside tables have been taken. We heard nothing.

What do you think, Black, Dad asks him at breakfast. How did they do it so quietly? They spray a gas, so you cannot wake up, Black says, as he lays a tray of boiled eggs and toast on the sideboard. Unbelievable, says Mum. They filled our suitcases, unlocked the front door and just sauntered out.

We get the window fixed. When Dad goes back to the bush for another six weeks of training, Mum becomes jittery, her voice brittle and her movements spiky. Especially after she wakes one morning to find that her handbag, which sleeps on her bed with her at night, is missing. They went fishing, says Black as he's setting a teapot on the table. That is what they do. They push a rod through the burglar bars and hook it by the straps.

And Mum goes sharp as a hook and I am one fish away from drowning in air when she accuses Black of stealing eggs. He looks at her in silence. Takes off his apron and places it on the counter. For you to say that, Madam, means I must go now. The trembles start in my legs and voice. Mum! He probably used all the eggs in that cake he made for us! How could you think he would rob us? He's our friend! But Black has already walked out and when we run to his *khaya*, we find he's taken his things and has gone.

Mum goes all rigid, as though she has a tension in her chest. She consults her neighbours to ask their domestic staff if they know where he is. Please, she says, we need him back.

A wishbone dangles from the kitchen window latch. What is it saying? Is it *juju*? Reach up for it. Molly and I insert our little fingers on each side of the bone knuckle. Snap. I screw my eyes tight. What did you wish? asks Molly. You know what I wished. Don't say it or it won't happen. But now we've broken it, she says. A wishbone gives luck only when it's broken, I remind her.

A fortnight later, after my dad gets back from the bush, Black returns. We cling to him.

A storm

The wind cries and pushes trees into diagonals. Lightning blitzes through my thin curtains.

Dad arrives back from the vet without Ivor's dog.

A particularly loud crack, like a snapped plank, has me sitting bolt upright in the bed. As the thunder rolls away, I think I hear scratching and whining at the front door. A thought swishing wetly in some deep-down place. I pad down the corridor. Almost don't recognise the drenched mangy wreck flopped on the doorstep. Cara! I say, and drop to my haunches to stroke her.

Something is very wrong. The corners of the hallway seem to tilt on an axis, like a catamaran, as I run for my dad. Warm some milk for her, he says, swinging his feet to the floor and pulling on his maroon smoking jacket.

He gathers her up and carries her into the living room. I sit cross-legged beside her and lift the saucer to her mouth. Amazing, Dad says, as he sits on a pulled-up armchair beside us. She made it through 16kms of torrential rain. Cara takes a couple of sips. I fetch a blanket. Eventually her spasmodic shudders slow down. Me in my baby dolls, hair like a hammerkop's nest, Dad on the pulled-up armchair, in his maroon and gold smoking jacket. Her rattled breathing. What's wrong with her, Dad? It's cancer, darling, he says softly. I think of my auntie Judy, Mum's sister, the one they went to Ireland for. The one who died. Isn't cancer something only people get? I pull the blanket around Cara's shuddering body. She gives me her soft eye. All that love, melting. No, he says, dogs can get it too. Dad leans to stroke her matted fur too. Incredible. She must have escaped from the vet's. It's been raining needles of steel for hours. Steel that could penetrate the walls of even a strong body. *How did she not get killed on the highway? How did she know the way home?*

My stroking hand senses something. Daddy? Daddy…? He nods. She's gone. Interior feeling of a balcony collapsing. I let out a wail. *Ivor asked me to mind her.* It was going to happen anyway, pet, says Dad, his hand on my shoulder. They were going to put her down because of her pain. Her heart and mind must have kept her alive long enough to get here. I sniffle, continuing to stroke her. My bent sorrow, and another feeling. She made it home to me and my dad.

Insomnia

A mozzie whines and tries to push through my mosquito net. An owl whoo whoos. I peep out the window. There he is in a tree, eyes lit up like a pair of miner's lamps. Is it a sign?

Someone turns a radio volume alarmingly loud, and then off. I flop down into bed again, billow the sheet off my sticky body, flap it a few times to cool down. Want to cry, but all I can manage are a few grunts that hurt my chest. My eyes are sticky too, and it feels as though my left eyeball has shifted in its socket from being rubbed so furiously. I squeeze them hard. Blink for a hundred counts. My palms itch. Scratch for a hundred scratches. My mouth is dry. Flash to the route to the loo. Then to Ivor at the Walkin farm. Then to his faraway boarding school. Then to Cara. He'll feel her death, surely? He'll ask about her in his letters. And what should I say?

That percussion of Christmas beetles, laying over everything. My bed, floating on a gold sea of land, below hundreds of silvery stars. Black says that stars are souls flown up. Maybe Cara's a soul now. Gulp down water from my night glass. Tiptoe to the bathroom. Splash water on my face. Brush my teeth. Lie back in bed and hold my breath for twenty counts. Stare into the night that won't let my body give in to sleep. Feels as though a bumbo marble has rolled into my throat. Can't swallow it down.

A face that shows the present

1, *Evelyn Road, Ndola, 1ˢᵗ April.* Mum's voice is curt. Itosha, use your napkin. Where are your manners? Molly pulls a face at me. Feel like a squashed ant. I lift the napkin. Underneath it, a tantalizing box. My dad lowers his paper. What's that then? he asks.

Gold markings, a circular black face. Narrow black leather strap. On the face, I can read a name: Orbis. I fly up and round the table to hug my mother. Oh Mum, I love it. She smiles. Happy birthday, darling. What about me? Dad says. I rush around to hug him too, my nose wrinkling at his cigarette smoke. Double digits, says Molly. Ooh, you're old.

Hurry Tosh, we have to leave in two minutes. I have a meeting at the barracks and your mother needs to be early for her new job at Barclays.

In the car their cigarette smoke flares behind them and I choke spasmodically and ask for a window to be opened. Oh Itosha, don't be so dramatic, says Mum. It's still chilly.
Please? It's my birthday, I say.
Oh, alright.

I keep looking at my new watch. The second hand beetles forward past the digit marks, faster and faster, dizzying me older and older and older. I don't want to grow up into the world of smoking adults. I'd rather be like the lost boys in Peter Pan and stay a kid forever.

Little sister

Molly, with a perfect copycat accent, flinging her tea set out of the window, like Eva Gardner in Green Gables. *I'm just biting my time until Oliver gets home.*

*

Molly, a blind worm in her hands, silvery grey, waxy, wildly wriggling. She creates a home for it in a Peter Stuyvesant box, with leaves and grass. A few minutes later, she tells me it has emigrated.

*

Molly's scrunched-up face when she smells Brussels sprouts, her nose turning into a mushroom, tiny toddler teeth wide in a grimace. Or her mouth open wide to wail, lips making a rectangle of her mouth, blaring louder as we crack up.

*

Molly and I sit on the floor, facing each other, listening to *Seasons in the Sun*, seeing who can cry first. I stare into her Cadbury's milk chocolate eyes, which remind me of Cara, dripping and collapsing on the step, and beat her to it.

*

A yellow-headed, green-bodied lizard appears from a gap between two rocks to watch Molly playing with her invisible friends.

*

Batman Molly, flying around the club swimming pool. A black and red hand-towel knotted at her throat as she sings, 'Dana danadanadanadanadanadanadana Batman!' then skids on the wet tiles and topples in, cracking her skull, clouding the water pink in seconds. Floating, face down, until a woman swoops in and lifts Molly out, leaving her cloak sagging heavily in the bloodied scurry of shallow water. Later, a trophy: six stitches, scored across her forehead.

Puppet mouths

1, Evelyn Road, Ndola. The Jane Blonds, Molly and I decide to put on a puppet show, as my dad is home from the bush.

The adults all troop down the long parquet corridor, past Mum and Dad's room, Molly's and my room, the box room, Ivor's room, and finally to the den, a rectangle of fort boxes and our yellow-red-blue looping art on the wall. They pay for their tickets. Robert nudges Dad. Ten to one, they'll copy us. Priceless, chortles Eleanor, as she lowers herself down onto an upturned crate covered with a velvet scrap of curtain and observes the painted set, complete with a cardboard card table and drinks. Dad's right eye is a half-blink, or a thinking-about-a-wink.

Black has done most of the set-building and painting. I've prepared the room and written the script. Jessa introduces the show. Marlie, the eldest Rawson girl, and my little sister huddle behind the set and waggle a puppet each. Ten to one, you haven't cooked dinner, Judy, and *whap*, Punch (Marlie) thumps her. The set thunders and trembles. You punched me, Punch! squeals Molly.
A sideways dink of the head from Punch. That's the name of the game, Judy.
Aarrggh…for what it's worth, I made Steak Diane for supper, wheezes Molly behind the set, curling her puppet-hand open and shut in spasms. Your favourite.
Punch slips on a banana skin trap, and Molly makes her Judy-puppet shake with silent mirth. Oh dear, she says, wiping her eyes. That was a good trick, you have to admit. Priceless. And the puppet holds a stick-cigarette and puffs away, blowing out loudly.
My dad's friend Robert splutters with laughter, and the puppets both follow suit.
Judy keels over in a coughing fit. Oh dear.
Punch thumps her back. Mark my words, Judy, that 60-a-day habit will be the death of you.
Darling, you're as boring as a ginless tonic. All the adults erupt as she decks him back and I snort back a giggle behind the set. That's you, Eleanor, laughs Robert.
Here's a challenge Punch, says Molly (a.k.a. Judy): if you give up brandy, I'll give up smoking.
Oh dear, sighs Mum, wiping her laughter-tears, love how they put in your Steak Diane, Seán. She rustles out a cigarette from a new pack. Eleanor laughs robustly. Priceless. The smoke whizzes around them like auras.

A mauve bruise in the sky

Through my bedroom window, I can hear Mum and Dad in the living room. Do you realise, Seán, that in five years, we've had thirteen burglaries! Not to mention droughts, power cuts… You gone for weeks at a time…and now you're off training men in the bush again, for another six weeks? Their voices leave spaces, like a thread-less hem with a line of small holes.

The night suddenly bursts into crickets. Dad's murmuring tones, too low to hear the words. Then silence again. I hope he's hugging her. When he's back, she always dresses up like a film star and goes to the officers' mess with him, and they come home late, tipsy and happy. Mostly.

Sliding into bodiless

It's break-time. Jeannie and I sit on the wall, open our lunch boxes. Mine is cheese, cucumber and marmite. Hers is peanut butter and jam. We swap one each. Across the road from the school is the cathedral, with its vast door that looks like a huge mouse hole. You can see my new house too. I point, to the bungalow on the corner of Broadway. She looks over. Where did you live before?

I'm counting on my fingers, trying to remember. Our first home was on Sea Road, in a place called Salthill. Right next to the sea.
I've never seen the sea, says Jeannie.
That was in Galway, in Ireland, where I was born. Then my mum and I went to live near her family, in a place called Westport, which has a river and hump-backed bridges.
That sounds so pretty, she says enviously.
I had my mum all to myself because Ivor and Molly weren't born yet.
But truthfully, how could I remember? I was only a year old.
Where was your father? She's opening up the sandwich I swapped her, to push in the cheese slipping out.
He was in the army. They sent him to the Congo for the war. He was gone a long time.
What about here in Zambia, before you came to Ndola?
Oh I'm not finished with Ireland, I say. *Then* – I'm counting on my fingers as I speak – when my dad got back from the Congo war, we moved to another house in Galway. Then my dad was sent to Mullingar, on the other side of the country, so we had to move there. So that was four houses in Ireland for me, two for Ivor and one for Molly.
Four! And I have lived in one house all my life. The same friends since I was born.
My boasting grows speedier, as though I'm a runaway train.
And then, before coming here to Ndola, we lived in Tugargan Barracks in Broken Hill. I mean Kabwe. But, oh, I forgot, before *that*, we were in Arakan Barracks in Lusaka, or…maybe Kalewa Barracks …I pause and count on my fingers again. I think...
Did you like changing places and friends? Does it feel like being on holiday all the time? Not having a real life or home anywhere? Will you be leaving here too?

Her questions unleash a landslide.

Bedlam in the birdsong

The birds rouse me at sunrise, and I have to go outside. The pool, the orange trees, our green tin roof.

A *chongololo* toils through the red dirt in the flowerbed. How can it move along without all those legs crossing over each other? I lift it and put it on the flat of my sunlit palm. Instantly it coils into a spiral. *Playing dead.* I start counting the segments on its back, but stop at thirty. Not even quarter of the way through.

Black's voice rising through the open window of the dining room like smoke. Please *Bwana*, take me with you.
Dad's response is quiet, but I can just catch what he's saying. It's too cold in Ireland. You wouldn't like it.
What is he talking about?
I will give you an excellent reference. You will find another job.
I rush into the kitchen and stand in the doorway of our living / dining area.
Dad?
Not now, Itosha.
He's standing by the dining table, not even looking at me.
But Dad...are we *leaving* again?
Darling, my contract's up. They want me to renew it, but your mother wants to go home.
I wrap my arms around myself. But Daddy, *this* is home!
Life here is too stressful for your mum, pet, especially when I'm away.
But Dad, I say, you are important here. The president told me.
Your mother's wishes are more important. Now, off you go. I'll talk to you later.
Black's hand is leaning on the piano top at the other end of the room, as though he might fall if he lets go. His head is bowed, but he slowly lifts it to look at me.
Dad walks over to him. Take these, he says, laying his hand on one of the two elephant tusks arced across the piano. They were given to me by the army as a farewell present. Sell them. The money will keep you going until you get another job.
I cross the pretend wall between the two rooms too, and put the *chongololo* in Black's palm. His eyes fill. Mine too. Now he has no children at all, and no wife either.

Books and a ball

The S.A.Vaal, somewhere on the Atlantic Ocean. Dad says I'm permitted to buy one book from the floating newsagent's. I spend all day there, my eyes flitting around the wonder of all the books, craning my neck to read titles, opening paperbacks in the middle, in the thick real of the story, after the fancy whirly beginning and the jaunty ending, and the shop assistant lets me. I'll choose tomorrow, I say, returning a paperback to its gap.

*

Molly is with the other little kids in the Junior Mariners' Club on the lower deck. I prefer it up here under the sky. The only other person on this deck must be the most ancient person on the ship, and seems to be travelling alone. A steel-coloured bob and far-looking eyes. I rub my cropped head and, as usual, wish I'd brought a hat. I bet people think I'm a boy, especially as I'm living in shorts. Every now and then, I sneak a peek at her, and find her glancing back at me. As she shifts her chair away from the lengthening shade into another patch of sunshine, she's inching closer to me.

I plunge in. That's a huge book. Do you mind me asking what it's called?
Moby Dick, she says. It's about a man obsessed with hunting down a particular white whale. Ideal for reading while on the ocean, but it's rather an adult book. What age are you, about ten? I nod. You like reading too? I nod again. Only I don't have a book. Well, I think you're better off with something more fun. Look what I found abandoned over there. She reaches into her basket – filled with curious oddities – and pulls out a black and white football. Would you like it? She also gives me a white box wrapped in a pink satin ribbon. Turkish Delights, she pulls a face. They were a present. Maybe you'll like them. I loathe them!

*

A few days later, I'm dribbling the ball, kicking it up against the side of the deck, wishing Ivor were here to play with me. But he's already in Ireland, in boarding school. He'd love this ball. Aiming for a mighty wallop, I decide I'm going to give it to him as soon as I see him. But the ball hoops right over the mesh of the high perimeter net and down into the torrent of water. The wrench in my heart! As though it's my own brother who's been launched into the whip of waves. Anxiously glance down towards my new friend's deckchair. Relief! She's not there.

The ball is its own little island-self on the water. I watch it for as long as it's visible. But eventually it's engulfed, and I have to go inside to mourn my loss. When I finally rock to sleep, it's to dream about the ball following the oceanic flow around the sphere of the globe, like a small trailing moon.

Giving in to a wave

The S.A. Vaal, somewhere on the Pacific Ocean. Molly prefers the activities at the Junior Mariners' Club most days. I'm the only kid my age on this ship. I miss Ivor. But at least I can roam the decks unchallenged, swim up and down the salt-water pool; eat four-course meals served by a waiter under swaying chandeliers, visit the cinema and sit entirely alone among rows of sumptuous seats; spy on the adults in the casino, read on the deck, or watch the clouds, like bouncing Magic Roundabout creatures.

Sometimes I stare out at the water and remember Dad telling me that the planet has sixty four million square miles of blue sea. All those white-capped waves stretching out to a circular infinity.

Occasionally I have to grip the railings to stop the dizzy sensation of the ship falling off the round, turning world, into some cold dark abyss.

The big bang of terror

The plane
screams into walls
of wind,
your breath hyper
through the chattering.
Doug the instructor
nodding to Fynn.
He braces
in the blowy space.
Your feet feel
Fynn release
into the howling.
On the bench, Doug
slaps your thigh.
You grip his hand,
eyes telescoping down
through the open doorway.
I can't see him!
Fynn's behind us, he says.
We're moving
70kms per hour.
That roaring gape,
a yawning invitation
into the mouth
of death.
You flounder.
I can't...
You can! Go go go!
Go! Go! Go!
And he shoves you
into nothing
but pure
white space.

Bird of a feather

Hot and breathless at the equator. Let's go for another swim, I suggest to Molly, though we've had our bedtime showers. First she insists on brushing her hair, her teeth, looking for a swimsuit that's not wet. By the time she's ready, the sun has plummeted and darkness has swept in. We follow the corridors and steps up to the top deck where we find a live orchestra playing music, adults flicking ash, sipping champagne. Mum told us that, as Dad's an officer, they've been invited to sit with the Captain at his table. We spy army and navy dress uniforms, medals, gold buttons. Mum in a yellow cocktail dress with a swishy fringe. The Indians in their own corner: women in amber gold-threaded saris, or maroon, or peppermint or lime.

*

For the fancy dress ball, Dad is an Arabian prince and Mum, his concubine. Her costume is see-through chiffon, bare belly, hollow as a dust bowl. Dad has a fake goatee and a turban. When we go up to spy, our parents are the swirling couple everyone watches. *Twinkle twinkle.*

Mum scissors herself, as usual, out of the photographer's black and white photo. Why? All that's left of her beautiful, mysterious, exotic self, like a kindred in a possible other life, are two ringed hands cradling her side of the prize – a large Waterford crystal vase.

*

I droop to the pool deck in a flock of one. Water rolls off my skin in little pellets. That ripe moon, glistening, as though wet with salt spray. The night stars shimmer like a flight of fireflies, dissolving my gloom. The astronauts said the best part of going to the moon wasn't the moon, but looking back and seeing our beautiful planet. 'A brilliant jewel in the black velvet sky,' Buzz called it. I am certain we are not alone in the universe, and my kindred might be out there on some other planet, watching our blue globe, spinning in nothing but pure black space.

Arms extended, I whirl around, dizzying myself. *The world, the world, the world.* The motion hurls me to the deck, like a crash-landed bird. Later, my thigh is marked with a jewel-blue bruise.

3.

A whine and a solace

Limerick, Ireland. We have a short, blunt concrete driveway, and a pocket-sized garden, overflowing with soggy patches of rain-frayed, sun-grieved grass. Ours looks like every other house in the road. How can this ever be home? Home is wherever *we* are, says Mum.

The walls are onion-peel thin. Victoria Falls might come rushing through them when the neighbour flushes. Molly and I run upstairs, flush back. Mum, finger to lips, nods toward the wall whenever we 'raise the decibels'. At least in the kitchen there's the Aga cooker. Only warm room in the house.

The rest of the house wheezes and creaks, like a doddery tree on the verge of crashing. I imagine spectres escaping, like motes of dust, under the door of the huge, creepy room halfway up the stairs. Mum offers it to me, but the thought of being that room on my own is untempting. I follow Molly, a little hopping frog, into the smaller room in front. She's happy to share.

Our neighbour is a priest, the postman told us, called Father Galvin. He bangs against the wall of our bedroom with his stick. *Thud, thud, thud.* To think of that priest, so close, listening to us! I click my tongue like Black's wife. This sky is a bowl tipped up, emptying oceans. And our window leaks.

A gusto of draughts. The bottomless winter afternoon has drizzled into dusk and the priest is shuffling about, his clumpings and door-shuttings. Even under heavy blankets, our feet meet a hard chill.

On the plus side, my brother is home again. I can get back to being the person I am when I'm with him. He opts for the green box room next to Molly and me instead of the huge cold ghost room. We tiptoe through the glasshouse, long thready tussocks prickling through the broken panes. Seeping rust. We lie on the buttercups-and-mad-headed-dandelions side of the garden, watching the shadows of birds rippling darkly across the sky, like mobile ink-blots.

In the garage, we find a left-behind artwork, with a thousand nails hammered into glued-together planks, in the shape of a tree. Ivor pulls off one of the planks, still glinting with nails, to wedge in the apple tree as a reading seat for me. At every sunny moment, I escape with my book into the tree's green radiance.

Prickle

Maryville, Laurel Hill Convent, Limerick. Dad's new Jaguar, smart as the straight green arrow of his tie, headlights like the eyes of a powerful cat. He's always been obsessed with cars, my dad. If people see a smart car, they think you're successful, he says. That's how you get clients. So, first the car, he says, then a proper house.

I don't like it. The interior smell makes my stomach prickle into nausea. And it's not comfortable. He drops Molly in to her little school: St Philomena's. Then it's my turn.
From tomorrow, we have to take the bus.

But at least for this first day, I have my dad.

From the carpark, I step inside the Maryville cloakroom, a sea of hooded maroon coats hanging from named hooks. A nun, whose hand is snaking into one coat pocket after another. What are you doing? I blurt out peremptorily, in a Mum-voice, as though God has punched the words out of me. She swiftly withdraws her hand from a pocket. Are you the new girl? I nod, quelled. Her face has frozen into a coldness. I am the Principal, she says. Put on your 'indoor' shoes, she says. I pull them from my satchel, remove my boots. Whirl around to look at Dad, guiltily. To make matters worse, I'm an hour late.

She summons me to follow her to the classroom and waves Dad away. More prickles.

The feathery rain and the bus and the hiss

The red bus, with its full decks of passengers, trembles and steams along North Circular Road. Sitting in the clammy ribcage of the upper deck, I make a circle in the window. Birds baffling about, black or brown or grey. If only I hadn't behaved like a coward, instead of getting back up into the saddle. If only we hadn't galloped five thousand miles away from Black, from Jeannie and Kevvie, from sunshine and Christmas beetles, from the singing sky of Ndola. The bush, with its elephant grass growing up to seven feet. Those velvety nose days that dipped scent into our hands. That pummelling rain, like a thousand hands clapping on a thousand knees. The jasmine. Pomegranates. Dung-beetles. The sunbirds and lilac-breasted rollers.

Instead, I'm stuck in this clambering damp.

The bus shudders to a stop and the door hisses open. I look out the window, my eyes blurring. In a field, two horses running. I think of Ivor and me in Luanshya. And for a moment, this bleak world is beautiful.

Twist in the shame

Our drill teacher lifts the corners of her lipstick-bled mouth and claps. Dyed sandy thatch, bulky tweed skirt, blouse with a florid bow at the top. Talcum powder and pee.

In a circle, girls, she says. We shuffle forward, spread out. Now, everyone, hold hands.

The girl beside me glances at my swollen, enflamed palms. The dermatologist says I'm allergic to shampoos, lotions, dust, detergents, feathers, hessian, grasses, pollen, animal fur. Tells me to rub a stinking black tarry concoction on to my skin at night. A smell worse than pee.

The girls on either side of me give each other loud looks. My embarrassment is earth-splitting. Any moment now, I'll fall through the chasm.

Long black, waist-length hair swings across the room. A whispered hi. I'm Yvette. I catch a twist of girl-sweat. Her cool hand grasps my hot, weeping one.

From the interior of a cloud

Dad rarely comes to mass with us. Church is for women and children, he says. Why? God and the disciples and the priests and the pope are all men, I say to Mum. She bends down to whisper to me. Remember Jesus saying suffer the little children to come unto me? The prayers of children go more swiftly to God. Say a prayer for him. But there are other men in the church, I whisper back. She just flutters a hand to shush me.

As we are walking home, I pause to watch the roadworks, earth erupting through the tarmac. The juddering vibrates the ground under my feet. Mum and Molly are ahead of me, huddled under an umbrella. Ivor's probably reached the house already.

A fog has pulled its hood over the road. Out of the fog, a mirage floats across my path, small and wet as a cluster of soggy leaves. It starts barking. A muck-slashed workman shouts, aiming a boot, belting the small bedraggled creature. Mum and Molly, so far ahead now. That poor rain-drenched body, pallid as the light of the foggy air. One blue, blind eye, just like Dart. The brute kicks her again. Shut up, Chips! Her poor little ears, I scream hysterically at him, the noise is upsetting her! My words are snatched away by the colossal sound of the drill. Don't kick her!

Anger shudders through my shoes, my feet. My body moves of its own accord. The noise of the drill is acute. I scoop the frazzled creature up, hold her against me. 'Can I take her? He nods, flapping a dismissive hand. I walk and keep walking, not looking back. She shakes and silvery glitter-drops land on my sleeves. I grow quiet and mystified.

I just prayed in church for a dog.

When Mum opens the door, a tap inside my mouth twists open and pours out a stream of words, nuzzling rain and fur. Can I keep her? *Please?* Are you sure it was his? And he said you could have her? I nod furiously, trying to erase her dubiousness. Imagine, Mum, she arrived like a gift, out of the fog. That's what I'll call her.

Teamwork

Ivor finds a tomato in the fridge and chops it, frizzles the bits in the pan. An explosion from the toaster. I get buttering. Molly fetches a flower from the garden. By the time I'm ready, Ivor is sliding a perfectly fluffy tomato omelette on to the plate, triumphantly announcing, I'm going to be a chef!

We put the single tall daisy into a blue bottle. Ivor carries the wide tray along the hallway, beanstalking up the stairs and through Mum's doorway, as carefully as if the tray were dynamite.

Mum says Dad has to *dress for success* and *wine and dine* potential customers in Michelin-star restaurants, and tip the waiters lavishly so potential clients are impressed, so we won't have to live for long in this leaky, freezing house that's made her sick.

Mum sits up in bed and smiles. You've made me so happy. I cooked the omelette, Ivor says. By myself. It's a tomato omelette. Come here, she says, throwing her arm out as though flinging gold stars. And drops a kiss onto his head. Sunlight breaks into the room and the brief dazzle lands on them. Two thoughts occur to me at once; one produces a hollowness. I made the tea and toast, I say. Molly pipes up that she picked the flower. Mum looks at each of us in turn. Come here. She reaches out a hand as though to anoint us. I have the best children in the world...

The taste of rain and lies on my tongue

After school, Yvette, Caoimhe and I huddle at the bus-stop, stare at our feet. The clouds are a sodden quilt, like Caoimhe's mattress-spring curls. Her skin is very pale, with almost invisible freckles waiting in the wings for summer.

Two women stand out bareheaded in the drizzle, chatting, oblivious. Tiny pearls of water ease along strands of their hair. A ruthlessness of umbrellas. Traffic is a red peal along O'Connell Street. The tall redbrick office buildings loom up, brushing the low-flying sky.

Around us, Laurel Hill girls are milling about in a high, excitable babble.
I love your accent, says Caoimhe. Talk some more about Zambia.
Um...so I told you we lived in the bush, with only a security fence between us and wild animals, I say. Well, sometimes, we'd climb under it. We'd go tracking elephant and lion, prodding dung and guessing what animal made it, and what it had for breakfast.
Yeuch, says Yvette.
And sometimes we'd shoot guinea fowl with our catapults.
Oh, that's awful!
Story-telling is invention, Sr. Mark told us.
I had a pet monkey too, I blurt. I taught him to peel bananas and feed them to me.
A *monkey*! What was his name?
I cast about swiftly and recall Jeannie and Kevvie's little brother. Orlando, I say.
The more I talk, the more the real truth flickers off into the hummocky hills, like ghostly impala. And yet, the moment a lie is out of my mouth, it becomes as real as a secret form of communication.

Bicycles swim past us, their headlights flexing and quivering, things skidding from edges. Shiny after-wet. I lift my head, stick my tongue out.

Dream flying into the sky

Glenbeigh Hotel, Co Kerry. St Patrick's Day. Ivor is fidgeting and yawning and blinking and stretching out his legs and jumping up and pacing and putting his hands in the pockets of his smart new trousers and looking up at the chandelier, hanging like a silvery jellyfish in a white sea of ceiling. Mum tells him he's getting in the way of others and to sit down. Slumped back between me and Molly, his legs jiggle. Without looking up from the book I'm reading, I put a hand out to calm his legs, the way Mum does. Through the knee-to-ceiling window, clouds are striped with nail polish. *Cerise,* Mum would say. Dad is still queuing to check us in.

Mum turns to us. See that debonair man at the other side of the lobby? That's Gay Byrne, from the Late Late Show, she whispers. To our amazement, his radar seems to pick us up and he strolls over to where we are sitting. He's wearing what my mum would call an *immaculate* suit, with a shirt so white you could read by it. What a beautiful family you have, he says, flashing a brilliant smile at my mother. She smiles back, serene as a drifting river, and introduces each of us and he shakes our hands. Itosha, he says, glancing down at the book beside me. With a name like that, I can see you becoming a writer. Light shafts from the window, falling on him like the finger of God.

Dad weaves towards us through the thong in the lobby. His sudden towering presence next to us vanishes the famous stranger.

Why did they give you an interesting name, while I just get to be called *Molly,* my sister grumbles.

Dad says I have the sister of his teenage sweetheart in Donegal to thank for my writer-like name. A girl with charisma, he says.

A name makes its own sound in space. Maybe mine will bring me luck.

*

We're allowed to watch the Late Late the following Friday. A glow of stardust all around him. Feel a fizz when I think of what he said.

Counter

Limerick. At the back of the post office queue, a mum with a fretting baby. *Pick him up!* She doesn't hear my telepathy, which is blocked by the symphony of noises in her orbit: squeaking pram, whimpering-turning-to-wails, rattling charms on the hood. She frantically rummages through a kitbag of nappies and powder and wipes, then hauls out a bottle, shoves it into his mouth. *Poor thing.* I think of Zambian women, who carry their babies on their backs, and swing them round for a feed when they niggle. Always skin to skin.

An old man shuffles to the counter. How are things, Dónal? says the clerk. Clearing his throat, Dónal eventually gets his response out. All sorted, he says, voice thin as a string. He launches into a saga about his cat, Tsáile's, recent operation. Tsáile is sixteen years old, we all learn, but she doesn't want to die yet. Even in the night-time of life, I hear Black say in my head, it is worth being alive, just to hold it. He would say Tsáile's life is important, because it gives the old man purpose.

In a low voice, I try out the word. *Tsáile.* Further down the line, a woman with birdlike shoulders, cheeks rouged like luscious plums, tsks. There are people here waiting to be served, she says loudly. And did you get the phone bill sorted? All sorted, says Dónal. My brother's wife's cousin works for Telecom Eireann and she put in a word. Well now, that's great news, Dónal.

Eventually, the conversation at the counter winds to a close and Dónal dodders out the door. Mum moves up, says good morning, slides letters through the hatch. Sorry about that, says the clerk. It's just that I know Dónal lives alone and, until pension day, literally has no one to talk to. No harm in having a bit of a chat with him.

His smile, with a charm of dimple.

The fall

Whenever Mother Patrick casts her eye in my direction, it's with contempt.

I approach her desk. Please can I go to the bathroom, Reverend Mother?
You can, but you may not.
I am not told that what I am expected to say is:
May I go...
Instead, I fall into a chasm of embarrassment as the girls giggle. Wilt back to my seat and cross my legs hard for the agonising duration of the lesson.

*

In front of me, Ailbhe, pale blue eyes magnified by specs, shoves her chair back to stand, destroying *The Listeners* with her nasal, high-pitched voice.

The girl next to me whispers that it was Ailbhe, the teacher's pet, who reported her for smoking. Behind Ailbhe's back, she gestures an idea. Without thinking, I lean forward and pull Ailbhe's seat a little further back.

After Mother Patrick has complimented Ailbhe on her rendition, she gropes behind for her chair, already crouching to sit. Lands on the floor. The class titters. Ailbhe's strangulated scream: My wrist!

I'm sorry...! I didn't mean...the words tearing from my mouth.

Mother Patrick's eyes send a double shot of hatred in my direction. Pure evil is what I see. She hurries out with Ailbhe, leaving an uproar in her wake. I nibble anxiously at an ink stain on my index finger. A trace of toast-aroma.

*

My father receives a letter from the school reporting my crime, and a hospital bill for the broken wrist. He's considering my punishment. I feel the fall of a darkness over me.

He decides they'll ignore my birthday.

Control is an illusion

Your cylindrical
shape
drops
into the chute
of a rip-roaring
nothingness,
sun, packed
and coiled
behind a cloud
reservoir,
your arms
springing
up,
legs,
scissoring
open
like
an automaton,
words
tearing
from
your mouth
like an incantation:
arch
thousand,
two
thousand...

Less and more

1ˢᵗ April: For my eleventh birthday, my lovely brother secretly spends his pocket money on me. A beautiful diary, to begin my life of writing. First, I practise on a jotter, in case I make mistakes.

Our gate is only a small trip to the corner newsagents. Mum and Dad send us down for cigarettes or the paper, and we spend our pocket money on Taytos and Curly Wurlys. Yvette lives in a house just like ours, around the block, though theirs is much warmer and lighter. Seven brothers and sisters. She's in the middle. Their mother has silver hair, even though she's not old, and stands in the kitchen, cooking. Feet clatter up and down the stairs; fingers tap at the kitchen table by the window, while her father sits in the living room, reading his paper. Yvette's mum says to her: You are the one who's most like me. Take my advice: don't have babies. But I still love her. She is funny and kind. Even though she's like the old woman in the shoe, with so many children, she always welcomes me. And she's always there, rain or shine. Sometimes I wish I were part of this *family.*

Didn't know that I had that thought, hidden in a pocket at the back of my mind. But it's a true feeling. One that would hurt my mum if she knew. I climb on to a thinking box. Remember a collage we made at school recently, with pictures and cut-up words. Fetch a pair of scissors from the kitchen, chop text and fling them in the air like a cowgirl cracking her whip. Reassemble the words to make new meanings.

Yvette's mum says our gate is only twenty steps from her table. We get pockets and stand in them. The kitchen is kind. She has silver hair, even though she's not old. We buy Taytos and shine. She's always there, while he's reading his paper, rain in the living room. A house just like stairs, tap at the window, clatter up and down for cigarettes or the still paper, in the middle of the school bus. Take my advice: don't have feet at the Aga. She is always ours, a welcoming finger. She is funny, just a small trip. Our parents send us down for brothers and sisters. I have money now and Yvette lives with babies. I love her. You are most like me, she says. It's much warmer and lighter at the window, while her father sits by the shoe with so many children. Sometimes I wish Curly Wurlys.

A swell of glee. Sometimes I *do* wish Curly Wurlys. At bedtime, secret flowers float inside my eyelids.

The clock and the octagon

Westport, Easter. Joy when Mum steps out, stretches arms east and west. This, children, is *my* town. All feathers and spring sunlight. It's been so long since I saw her face gladden like this.

Joy to see, through *her* eyes, the Mall, with its trees like columns, the cathedral grandly halfway along. A wedge of sunlight, a row of Georgian buildings. The river with its hump-backed stone bridges. She points to a house in the crescent of the Octagon. That, says Mum, is where your grandmother was born.

The car wheels judder over a cattle grid, and follow a long curved driveway up a hill, firs and bulrushes hushing. Joy to see, in the misty distance, Croagh Patrick rising like a fairy-tale mountain, its point tipping clouds, which Mum says is snow-wrapped in the winter, like a Narnia mountain. Joy as we reach the bungalow, frog-ivy leaping across the front façade. This is where *I* was born, she says.

Joy when we hug a tumble of Ryan cousins and have tea and barmbrack, and Lala brings me outside to look at the mountain. Your mum, she says, climbed the Reek, barefoot, at least nine times, as a girl. From the top, Lala says, you look down on Clew Bay and beautiful Clare Island, which was home to the pirate queen, Gráinnuaile.

In Golden's chemist, a man in a white coat comes from behind the counter and gives Mum's little frame a bear hug. It's her dead sister Judy's husband, Gar. Callie Ryan, he says. As I live and breathe. And it's as though the hands of the town clock have whizzed backwards, and Mum is a girl again.

Window into a rock field

Carrabawn, Westport. Lala, cigarette wagging from her mouth like a finger puppet. Legs thrust out like two short gum poles. The draughts, explains Lala. Do you want the footstool? I ask. Oh no, this is exercise, she laughs. Did you know, she says, that my sister Julia caught your mum smoking when she was your age. Asked for a puff. It became their secret.
Smoking, when she was eleven??
Yes – she was trained by her older brothers. I only found out years later, says Lala, huskily laughing, puffing away herself. Julia was the reverend mother at your mother's convent. My mouth pops open. What else can you tell me about my mum? I say, exultant to be on my own with her. The lit fire, piano in the corner. I glance around at the cosy room, corner-cabinet-oddments, mantelpiece-clock, shaped like a jelly mould. She played the cello in the local orchestra. The tiniest member, with the biggest instrument, she laughs. And she often went with your grandfather on his rounds. Lala's sapphire eyes are so bright it's as though someone's holding a lantern behind them. She wasn't allowed to be in the way of a mare when she was giving birth, so she'd fix her eyes instead on his face, grimacing away as he hauled the newborn out by its ears, onto the straw. While your Pops and the farmer went in to the house to celebrate the birth with a bottle of whiskey, she'd stay to watch the mare lick off the lard – the birth-muck – and prod the foal to its feet. She'd be all whispery about it when she got home. Of course, Pops couldn't drive after drinking, so Callie had to sit on the edge of the seat to reach the pedals and drive them home. She *drove*?! At *eleven*?! Lala thrusts a packet of Silvermints at me. Things were different in those days.

Your mum was a wild thing, barefoot, roaming around the place. She ran away once. Got as far as the rock field. With nine of them in the house, no one noticed she was gone. So, come dark, she slunk home. Ahhh, poor Mum! I glance out the window at the hill – the rock field – above the invisible lower road. Oh, no need to feel sorry for her! She was very popular. Nine boys invited her to the Leavers'. Richard Harris, was one of the lads who 'walked out' with her. The actor? Yes, the very one. She might have landed in Hollywood, like her third cousin, Grace Kelly. I bet she's glad she got Dad, and Africa, instead, I say. Pulling her old Aran cardigan more closely around her, Lala smiles. I'm sure she is, love.

In bed, I suck on my pen and think of my mum, the same age as me, in the rock field, listening to silence. Nobody calling for her. Nobody noticing her not being there, or after she returned, that she'd even been gone. The dew-drenched blades of loneliness she must have felt.

Breakfast with(out) Czechoslovakia

Stella Maris, Limerick. While Dad drinks his tea, I pour cornflakes and tip in milk. A sprinkling of sugar. *Incomparable* pleasure, I sigh, lunging for the box again. Indubitable, he quips back. Intangible, I reply swiftly, feeling those bubbles of pleasure when my dad pays me some rare attention. Incalculable he responds, even more swiftly. Inaccessible. We stare solemnly at each other. Outside the window, a crow is being blatted about by a vicious wind, feathers whooshed like a blown inside-out umbrella. Incombustible. Dad gives a crescent moon twitch of the mouth as I blow a stray strand of morning hair. In…peccable, I snort into my spoonful and milk goes up my nose. Incorrigible. Dad lifts a brow. He snaps his Irish Times, parks it on the table and sweeps his palm over the creases. What do you know about Czechoslovakia? I know it's a country in Europe, I say. It was on my spelling list a while ago and I can spell it.

What else? he asks. Four other newspapers are staggered on the floor, Czechoslovakia in all the main headlines. Dad's always saying you have to check several sources to get accurate information. I giggle, because I can take a shortcut. What do *you* know?

But I don't get to find out, because the phone trills from the hallway. It's Robert Rawson, Dad's army friend from Zambia. I slide off to finish my homework essay, hunt for a way to weave in incalculable or incombustible; maybe even Czechoslovakia.

The fire and the fury

Stella Maris, Limerick. Ivor shuffles the Chance and Community Chest cards, lays them in their zones. Let's open the box of chocolates from Easter, suggests Molly. She rips off the cellophane, tosses the wrappings into the fire. It blazes up the chimney. We all gawp. It flicks long tongues out. We have no guard.

Commotion outside the window: Fr Galvin, our neighbour, in discussion with a scoutmaster, a tail of scouts behind him. They're pointing. We run outside. Clouds of smut are billowing out from our chimney, swelling like black balloons, and fire is charging into the air, stabbing the sky. A moment later, they're in our living room hunting for jugs and buckets, passing, pouring. We line the furthest wall and watch, as these strangers make the house safe again.

Fr Galvin has already hurried in to his house to call the fire brigade, but by the time they arrive, the crisis is over.

It's dark when Mum and Dad come home. The grate's been swept out and the whole house is as cold as an open freezer. Why did you let the fire go out? my father growls. We aren't sure whether to tell him about the Great Rescue, Father Galvin in a flurry, the fire brigade arriving, the scouts and their master even cleaning the hearth for us afterwards. Our house full of boys. Then Molly pipes up. The fire went big. And everybody came and put it out. Or the house was going to burn down.

In bed, my body is all wakefulness, thoughts snapping, back to the scoutmaster's warning, loud as a fractured plank: *a fire will feed on anything.*

Deep in conkers and bombs

Stella Maris, Limerick. Ivor, up to his ankles in conkers, which the wind has pushed up against the tree trunk like a stack of poker chips into the centre of the table. He selects a handful for his pockets, then scrambles up the tree and jumps across to join me on the roof. Below us in the road, a few lads, kicking gravel. They go to my school, Ivor says, looking down. Across the road, red brickwork, spiking grime, the folds of net curtains hiding interiors. They beat me up for having a tan and an accent. What?? I whirl round to look at him. I'd assumed that his collection of bruises, growing multi-coloured as an ice-cream factory, were caused by him falling off his Chopper after pulling practice wheelies.

One of the lads, with an overbite worse than mine, looks up, shoves another boy and mutters something. Fuckin' Brits, he growls, glaring at us. I'm *flabbergasted* (Mum's word) at hearing a kid swear like that. Hey, we're not English! I shout. Ivor fires a conker at the leader, and misses. They run into the building site next to our house, crouch down in the newly-dug foundations. Next minute, they are bombing us with *stones*. Oy, I shout. We duck behind an overhanging leafy branch. The minutes tick past. Perhaps the gang have retreated. Ivor puts his head up above the branch and catches a rock smack on the cheekbone.

His rapidly swelling face, turning plum.

Dad, I say as I burst into the living room, there was a gang of boys who called us Brits and fired stones at us. One hit Ivor.

But Dad is too gripped by the news to notice. A bomb planted in a pub in Belfast, the newscaster is saying, has claimed the lives of fifteen Catholics, including two children.

Dad...
Not now, Itosha.
Mum is out. An obsidian cloud wheeling above him, Ivor marches right past Dad, who is still glued to the TV. I follow my brother as he heads out the door, a noose of blood beginning to form around his throat.

Artful

Stella Maris, Limerick. I can see Ivor through the open door, turning into a crab in front of Mum. Look at me, Ivor, Mum says. He drags his eyes up. That perfume for my birthday? That tie in your drawer? You said you'd got it from a friend. And then a bucket. A bucket, says Mum. To fetch the coal, he mumbles. Ivor's hair has grown way long at the back, like everything he doesn't say.

I'm very disappointed in you. She flicks her lighter. This has to stop.

*

I'll bring him in to you, I hear Mum say. She's on the phone in the hallway. And if you could... exactly. She puts the phone down, sighs heavily.

Mum drives Ivor to Dunnes Stores to apologise to the manager. He tells Ivor next time it'll be a call to the guards, and probably borstal.

*

We're out in the front garden, lying on our coats. Why did you do it, Ivor? I say, flipping over on to my elbows. It was a dare, he says.

Under the whizzing clouds, he throws his words in the direction of the wind.
It was the only way those guys would stop...

A throbbing, mad-stallion rage when he tells me he was still getting beaten up every day on the way to school or on the way home. My little brother, the smallest in his class. He's always running to school, fast as a thought, and now I know why. You know that guy, with teeth like Bugs Bunny, the one who was firing stones at us that time? He's the one. The leader of that gang. Always punching me after school. But the other day, when he went to hit me, he kind of stumbled. Ivor's fringe, hanging over his eyes. He pushes it away. The others couldn't believe it when I punched him hard in the jaw and he went down. Ivor laughs and all the daffodils in the garden and I do too. Then his face changes, like a light dimmed. I'm going to get beaten tonight though, when Dad comes home.

It's raining nightmares

Stella Maris, Limerick. The wind, a river of rivers, whirling around the house like a furious god, scooping up all the bones of the dead and rattling them down the chimney. Panicked yelling. Rush to my brother's room. He's thrashing around in the blankets. Clumsy as a drunk, I slump down beside him in the dark and put my hand out. Shhhh, it's okay.

The floor around his bed is littered with comic books, like apples dropped under a tree. He sits up, staring wild-eyed at me. Touches his pyjama top in pop-eyed amazement. It's not wet. Why would it be wet? I say. Must have been my dream. I was tied down in my bed, and the room was filling with water, and I was drowning. Oh Ivor, what a horrible nightmare. And last week, it was an elephant sitting on your chest. Giggling. Tosh. I couldn't breathe! If you hadn't come in and woken me, I bet I would have died. His face. Do you want to come into my bed? He nods and follows me.

I can feel him staring at the wall. It's lucky that Mum is good at keeping secrets, I say. At least you weren't beaten. Mmm, he murmurs. Think of something else that would make you happy. Getting picked for the team, he says. Ok, now you can dream of scoring goals, I say.

He drifts off. Beside us in the other bed, Molly's a coiled shell. It's very quiet. Time melts. Mum and Dad are soundly asleep. Or maybe they're still out.

French disconnections

Stella Maris, Limerick. Dad comes in from the kitchen, cigarette in one hand, glass in the other. I'm lying on the carpet, propped on my elbows in the living room. I've been telling my new French pen-pal about your import/export business, I say, craning my neck. And about Mum's French fashion line. And my whole letter is in French! Dad grins. Good girl. Actually, I had a French fiancée once, he says. Her family owned a vineyard in Normandy. Really? I sit up. What happened?

He pulls deeply on his cigarette. Blows upwards. The smoke throbs against the ceiling. Her father wanted me to leave the army and move to France to learn the vintner business. What age were you? I ask. Twenty-one, he says. I face him, cross-legged, back erect. I bought the ring, then brought Françoise home to meet my parents. My father called me in for a chat in the front room. He lifts his glass, glances at the brown liquid and grins. He drank a sherry, I had a glass of milk. What did he say? He said: she's a lovely girl, Seán, but my advice to you is, *marry your own kind*. He was a man of few words, so I heeded them. A wink. Besides, if I had married that French girl, I wouldn't have met your mum, and you three wouldn't be here, so of course there are no regrets! He gives me his glass to refill, and I model-walk to the kitchen with my shoulders set straight as the bottom bar of a hanger, in case he's looking. *No regrets.*

Dad always says it was love at first sight for him and Mum, a flash of lightning in a dark sky. Mum retorts back that actually it was about an hour later for her, when he started playing Love Story on the piano, notes rippling like scintillas of light across water.

I hand him his whiskey. Dad, will you teach me to play Love Story? He spends five minutes showing me the first chords, then gets bored and heads out somewhere.

Later, while pouring the day into my diary, I try to imagine the other person my dad might have become. The other children he might have had if fate had not siphoned out that possible future and poured in another option. How Mum and Dad are both the youngest of large families, both with fathers who were vets, both Catholic, both from the west. *Your own kind.*

Risk wakes you

Blue-knuckled grip,
shot of fear through
your arms,
regrasping
a muscle memory:
clenching
half of a wishbone.

Bedfellow

Stella Maris, Limerick. Temperature of a blade. My chest feels pressed in, like flowers flatted inside a book. Rain gone mad, on roofs and walls, along the kerbs of North Circular Road, rain on the dark trees. Rain, like TV static. That melancholy rhythm. A depression of grey and brown. The walls give off a suggestion of damp earth. Another day of no outside. The nagging damp of our house seeps through my body, echoes in the weeping lumps on my wrists and palms and fingers. My days collapse around me as the swelling and loud pain and itching take over. Even when I have managed to soothe my hands by cooling them against a window pane, or by weaving a sheet between each finger, the dulled prickle remains, just barely holding its horses.

Still, my dog Fog continues to sleep with me, warm as a hot-water bottle. I cannot give her up. The feeling of safety she gives me when Mum and Dad are out late again, and I'm in charge, is worth all the itching. Or when they're back and the muted clamour through the wall wakes me up. And the tone of their voices – stalking, wobbling, flying, ferocious – is a risk that has me attaching even more tightly to Fog.

Road trip with car sickness and appendicitis

Leather and cigarettes, belting around bends. Endless fields, yellow-green bracken, stippled like a pawpaw. *Inconceivable* to hope they'd consider refraining from chain-smoking. But it's not just the smoke; the sickening stench of the car itself prongs my nostrils. Dad, I need to throw up... He swivels around in his seat, taking his eyes dangerously off the road. Can't you wait until the next pub? But no, I can't.

Hurtling along skinny, winding roads, some lanes extra narrow, some ditches too close. It's being shut up in this car, constantly at risk of hitting something, of going off the road, thinking maybe in a few minutes I'll be dead, or paralysed, be blind for the rest of my life. If it weren't for the nausea and the clutching fear, and the inevitable stop at Paddy Burke's in Clarinbridge, and two or three other pubs, and the fact that I know we'll end up skipping our visit to Westport and head straight to Donegal, I'd love this rainy road trip. Already the light is fading along the curved horizon.

Eventually, *finally, at last,* we arrive in Letterkenny. We crawl past the ribbon of shops along Main Street, veer right up a steep, narrow street. At the pinnacle, looming above the town like a great beached ship, the cathedral. This, Dad tells us, is where my appendix burst when I was ten. I'd complained to my mother about stomach pains, but she thought I was trying to skive off school, so she shooed me out the door. There, he points. Right there. That's where I collapsed. My brother Brennan carried me home. I woke up to poppy candles around the bed, the family chanting prayers. It was my father's cousin who gave me an emergency operation and saved my life. We've heard this anecdote before, but this time, he gives it physical context. For an interminable mile, I stare at the pavement, visualising a twelve-year old boy, the same age as his son Ruari, my wild cousin, piggybacking his unconscious ten-year old brother, staggering and stumbling and panicked.

We loop back around the town, past O'Boyce's and turn up the knuckle towards Cove Hill. It's 1am. We were expected eight hours ago. Lights go on. Auntie Jan rushes out, arms open *Incomparable* happiness.

Spark

Covehill, Letterkenny, Christmas. Nearly twelve, like me, Freya – opalescent skin, dark eyes, straight fringe, black bob – is directing the show we're putting on: *The Little Match Girl.* Molly is in the lead role. Ali, Freya's younger sister, thin and hollow-eyed, as though for want of meat, might have made a better match girl. Instead, she's part of the happy family within, along with Ivor, who's also ten, and Killian, Freya's long-haired seven-year-old wanna-be footballer brother. The rest of the extended family gathers in the room to watch.

*

Granny playing the piano, despite her topped little finger (after a disastrous encounter with a can of sardines). Auntie Jan's clacking speed-needles. Grandad's pipe and ahems.

The landing stairs lead left to bedroom number three, a dormer room, cousin-dormitory for Killian, Ivor, Molly, Ali, Freya and me. Pink wallpaper, two double beds. Three in each bed (*and the little one said...*). In Zambia, we'd see geckos laughing at us from the ceiling, I whisper to Freya once the others have drifted off. In Ohio, we'd have cinnamon pancakes for breakfast, says Freya. And like that, we paint pictures of our former lives in Ohio and Zambia for each other. They came back to Ireland just before we did.

A late-late Santa (our missionary uncle, home from Jeju Island in Korea) tiptoes through the flop of the sleeping upstairs, into our room. He lays down six red knitted stockings. Only our eyes open for the wink. Downstairs, the adults are calling up Lady Luck at the poker table.

*

Freya and I decorate the pushed-together tables straddling two rooms with holly and ivy, coil napkins in glasses, lay crackers. During the big meal, candles bloom on thirty four family faces.

Twilight; a Narnia lamppost, yellow moon inside it, apple tree goal posts. Snow swallows our voices and foot prints. Each flake a breath. Arrow-slit of light. Copper and blond and black heads; ruddy skin and sallow, or deathly pale behind freckles; the tubby and the lank, the disordered fan of a cow's lick, several with eczema. Accents keep us singular, but our DNA is a mantra of movement and skin and sweat. Blood ties. Slight breeze brushing the electricity of a new feeling.

The American Influence

Letterkenny, Donegal. Outside, old roofs, music of the rain, a percussion on the panes. Inside, a charm of blues and greens and yellows and reds, pouring across the floor. Freya's mum's workspace is the upstairs front room, a river of patterns and gauzy, radiant fabrics: silk and satin and pearly chiffon.

She gives us material remnants so we can experiment with sewing on her Singer. Freya's mum is as glamorous as Jackie Kennedy, like mine, and also like Mum, a lover of sunshine. It was Auntie Ellen who gave Mum the idea to set up a boutique herself.

Freya and I attire her mannequins and experiment with wigs. Two mouths, lipsticked red. I mean rouge, says Freya. We glimmer in stockings and suspenders, heels. We flaunt in bell-bottoms, like two hipsters from the sixties. *One for the money, two for the show…*Our feet thud on the floorboards. Auntie Ellen swiftly spirals up the stairs, hintfully with finger to lips, then points down: customers in the boutique. She gives us money to scoot out of her hair, up the hilly street to Dylan's, for frothy, milky coffee – my first taste of it – and chocolate cake. Bliss.

Out of salt and sand

Rutland Island, Donegal. Granny never swam, you know, says Freya. None of them did.

I'm sitting with Freya and her sisters. Grace with the cork-screw curls, all shake and toss, and Ali, their younger sister, a miniature of Freya, black-helmet haircut, chalk-pale complexion, dark half-moons under her eyes. We snuggle into picnic blankets with flasks, crusty bread, Dad's *Camembert de Callie*.

Salty wildness, the boys racing towards us. Ruari is blowing out salt-water snot. The wind, revved and half-starved, like a feral boy. Way above, in the dunes, our aunts and uncles having their own picnic.

The cloud above us is a bear scratching its back. At the other side of the island, two rows of twelve terraced houses, schoolhouse at the end, all fallen to ruin. I try to imagine my grandmother, one of fifteen children, growing up here with a few other families, sitting in the school-room by a window, sheep grazing the hill above her, wild sea all around.

A colossal white gull ow-ing as it trapezes over the dunes.

Pebble-and-shell-filled pockets, clacking gems from the pearly-grey sea.

*

A boat comes to collect us around five. From the water, I stare back at the dwindling island. The stern chafes its walls against the quay. We shudder up the ladder into a Burtonport cousin with a jeep and a sheepdog.

The wind is a snarler of hair, snatcher of words, a claw sliding under my jacket. In the pub, we play pool. I feel for the pebble-and-shell relics in my pockets, strum my fingers across them.

*

Back at Covehill, in the pink dormer room, I dream of my granny as a girl. She stands in the doorway of a terraced house, like a rock outstaring the black Atlantic, scanning for a boat.

Family strands

Gortahork, Donegal. Ivor and I have been sent up to Donegal, to the *Gaeltacht* to learn Irish so we can catch up at school. On the strand, we meet our cousins. Ruari, who's twelve, like me, is in the middle of a story, and has them all going. When I went wandering next door to tell Grandad we're off to Gortahork, to the *Gaelteacht,* he says, Grandad goes to Granny, can you get us two cups of tea. And she goes: Ruari didn't come in to see you. He came to see me. Poor Grandad, says Hugh, Ruari's older brother. Jaysus, she's tough. Aye. Granny can't stand him playing the fiddle, says Ruari. He has to wait till she's out of the house. Once, says Freya, I came over when Granny was out and Grandad was playing the fiddle behind his back. She pulls off her sandals and sinks her toes in the sand. I think Grandad's family home, Meenbog, used to be the session house when Grandad was growing up, says Grace, running fingers through curls and shaking her head vigorously.

Hugh lies back on the dune, under the big wheel of the sky, hands behind his head, hair the colour of the sand. His freckles are almost invisible. The day-moon has pulled the tide all the way out, leaving just the whisperiest hush on the sand, a thin watery skin. Light transforms the horizon of sea and sky into milk.

Remember, Ruari, Granny sitting in the porch, catching you drive past with Kim and Aelish on the bonnet. When you were only nine. Perched on a cushion. Wearing a wig, adds Ruari. Freya and I are collapsing. (Their sisters aren't here – too young for the *Gaelteacht*.) Ruari has a cow's lick, like me, which makes his fringe skew. And I thought Mum was ahead of herself, driving at eleven! I say, flopping down on the dune beside Hugh. Freya joins me, followed by Grace.

Ivor is comparing his footprints with others, stepping in circles. Dad told us that Grandad was always going to farms to help with cows calving, he says...only, because it was just after the war and everyone was short, he'd return with no money for his troubles, to a mad Granny. Yeah, nods Freya, she'd be shouting about the eight children she had to rear. And what was the point of winning a university scholarship to do veterinary, she'd go at him, only to be coming home with just a chicken as payment. Ruari pulls up a long grass and sucks on it. Chickens are nice, but, he says. Misty clouds are reflected in the thin watery screed; the water becomes the horizon, the sky, the universe.

Small white birds

Gortahork, Donegal. Our host in the *Gaelteacht* is a mustard knitted cardigan, tweed skirt. Orange hair freshly liberated from curlers. Sacred Heart over the sideboard. Do you have any Irish? she asks. *Tá cupla focal agam,* I say, thinking, she probably doesn't realise I'm being literal. There is a husband, but we don't meet him. We sleep in hard bunk beds, unhungrily face a hard-scrambled breakfast each morning.

After breakfast, we ramble across the huge stretch of beach to our classes. Large headless fish in the sand. Splints of timber, shreds of razorfish, nets, forensics of ocean life. Black sky on the horizon behind us, more solid than air, but the sun still falls onto our shoulders. We reach the community hall before the first drop of rain. No copies or pens, just talking and reciting and song. After tea, *cheilidhs.*

To make up for lapses into English, on the way back to our host homes, we practise what we learned during the day. *Tá se fuar. Tá se an-fhuar, mar tá se tinn. Tá se tinn, buachaois le Dhia. Anois teacht an earraigh, beidh an la ag dul chun sionadh, is tar eis na feile bhride, ardoidh me mo cheol...*

Dreams and magic, folklore and ghosts. Some of the kids we meet wish they were spending their summer elsewhere, but this is exactly where I want to be.

Back in Limerick, the girls laugh when I pronounce 'go mhaith' in the northern way: 'go my'.

The sense of happiness

Limerick. If you had to give up either seeing or hearing, says Yvette. Which would you choose? Not sight, I say.

Imagine not being able to read. I'd lose whole worlds.

Sometimes, my eyes get so tired, I rub them manically, feeling the hard marble shape of them inside their sockets, and then panic in case I push them – plop – right into my skull, and lose sight forever. Once I shoved my good eye off-kilter, like a golf-ball teetering from its tee, and for days felt this screaming-fear weirdness. Mum made me spend a day in bed, with a patch on.

*

There is no traffic. I stride into the middle of the pot-holed road. On high alert, start walking, eyes shut, take forty black steps. My aim is to reach a hundred. The road starts to feel as if it's puttering past me. My heart drums a furious bush warning. The whoo of a bicycle rushes by and my eyes fly open, heart pounding with fear and realisations. Falling blind would be like falling down a long dark hole, with no-one to catch you.

*

Dad is at the dining room table poring over accounts. I bring in his drink, ice clunking against the glass. Dad, will you answer some questions for my survey? I don't have time right now Itosha. Just one then? A quick one? What's the most important word in the English language? Communication, he says without hesitation. Can you finish this sentence: *Happiness is…* Dad grunts. You said only one question. This is the last one. I'd say: *Happiness is…* financial independence. That's a strange one. What would you say? he asks. I'd say: *Happiness is* reading.

Rag in a gale

The wind, tearing
tiny tears from you
and making
your nose run
as you slap
against the sky
so hard
your body goes
high alert,
a bush warning.
That single,
off-kilter
step — into
nothingness.

Invention of a big sister

Yvette's father inherited two unwanted mannequins when he bought an outlet. He gives one to Yvette, one to me. Mine sleeps on the double bed in the chilly ghost room, but assures me she doesn't feel cold at all. Sometimes, I put her in one of Mum's negligées. Véronique, when I grow up, I want to be a model like you, I say to her, catwalking around her room, twirling with a flourish. Ah, Itosha, I sink you will be a writer. Ees better. Eet is hard to be a model, always changing, smiling, changing, smiling. And then, you are thirty, and poof! *Le fin*! Better you are a writer and move to Paris, where all the great writers have lived. When you want butterflies you must sleep in the wheat fields, *oui*?

I think about this for a few moments, and throw myself on the bed beside her. Excellent plan! But Véronique, can I borrow your French clothes sometimes? She smiles at me. But of course! And you, will you keep me when I am old and broken? I smile back. But of course.

My mum's hands

Stella Maris, Limerick. Molly is still in the bath playing with the bubbles. As I am towelling myself dry, Mum enters the bathroom. You didn't wash your hair. Frowning. And now the bath water's too soapy. Okay, the sink it is. I fetch a chair from the bedroom, kneel on it, and half fill the basin with hot water. Press a dry flannel tight against my eyes, a suck of white blindness, bend over and start to lather my hair with lemony Sunsilk. Get some in my eyes almost immediately. Mum is just wrapping Molly into a fresh towel from the linen cupboard. Shampoo in my eyes! I yell. In my eyes! Oh, Itosha. Don't be so melodramatic. Here, let me.

I see stars bopping and sparking against my head. Feel the clink-clink-clink of the glass against the basin as she scoops hot water and pours it over my hair. Her fingertips as she rubs shampoo across my scalp. I hear her palm cradle my head for just a moment while her other hand lifts the mug and fills it one more time. Eyes tight shut, I can smell it: clink-clink-clink. Wish her hands could stay a little longer. But, swiftly, efficiently, it's all-too-soon over.

Hands and whispers

Limerick. We walk two by two, from Laurel Hill to St Joseph's. Up the steps we go, a line of girls like soldier ants, for confession. Most of us have already turned twelve, ready to be Soldiers for God. The hands of pedestrians, making a full stop on forehead, sternum, left collarbone, right collarbone, as they pass the church. I don't hug my arms, don't want to let the cold goad me. Even inside the cathedral, the chill remains, like water in a slow-draining bath. Into the box. After my usual litany of lies, disobediences, the priest clears his throat, like a car whose ignition is failing to kick in the engine. Do you ever have dirty thoughts? What do you mean, *dirty*? Do you think about naked bodies, do you ever touch yourself, you know, your private parts? Something feels sharp and jagged inside me. No! Body surges of heat. What is he talking about? My mother has always taught me to use a flannel when washing *down there*. Never to touch with my bare hands. Ugh! That's where you pee and whatnot.

I jolt out of the cubicle, shuddering as though I've just been attacked by a squad of hot fleas in the gulping dark.

Game-watching

Stella Maris, Limerick. Ivor whistles into the living room. Dad pauses from watching Wimbledon and looks up. Straighten your back, Ivor. Shoulders remaining hunched forward, Ivor glowers, spins and whirls out the door again. Ivor! Dad says harshly. I get up and follow my brother into the garden.

Ivor paces for a while, mouthing off about Dad, then flings himself down beside me. We sprawl on the grass, arms behind heads, staring up at the poetic sky. One bonus of this cloud-constant country. After a while, we begin to identify crocodiles and elephants. I hope they don't dissolve into mist or drizzle any time soon.

Checking to see how my eyeballs are working today, I shoot them swiftly ground-ward and skyward, sideways left at the car in the concrete driveway, sideways right at Ivor. Note his sallow skin, dark brown hair, recently cut short at the back, floppy fringe falling off his forehead. Usually, around Dad, his default expressions are sullen or mind-your-own-business defiant. His eyes, a black anger room. Outside, he gets to grow spacious, and the broken glass of his mood begins to warm up and melt together again, the way the clouds are melting now. Yvette says her little sister Emily has a *grá,* as she calls it, for my brother, whom she's seen with me at the corner newsagent's.

We lie for a bit, still as stones, under a gathering cloud forest, while the planet we're lying on is making itself dizzy with all that whirling.

Ivor sits up and pulls out a few long blades to find the best whistler. Momentarily, the sun beams down a pale warmth, and I notice how it changes the colour of the grass, as well as Ivor's irises, and I can see why Emily has a crush on him. Facing into its light, he is amber-eyed, a lion.

Everything's fragile body

Stella Maris, Limerick. We have no heating in the house. *Tá se fuar,* I say to my sister. Shiver voluptuously, probably due to the suggestion. Molly lies on her tummy, drawing. Weird that it's cold, and it's October, she says. The haunted month, I say. And suicide month in Zambia. Remember how hot it got? Yeah. Wasn't it October when Black's wife took her life?

As I wait for the kettle to boil, questions snare me again, the same ones that agitate my night-times. What had made *Amai* Halawa so unhappy, so deranged? Was it having no children? Wanting a bigger house? Not to be poor? For the weather not to be so hot? Did she dream of Malawi? Maybe her mother was old and sick and she wanted to be with her? Was she unhappy with Black? Black said she had *storms in the brain*. What did he mean?

And Black, poor Black. He's just flotsam now, no home, no wife, no children, no job, and he's not even in his own country. I wish we knew where he was, so we could send money. Maybe he went back to Malawi. Or he got another job. Or – imagine if he died from hunger and loneliness?

Reckless fits and non-fits

Stella Maris, Limerick. I can hear my sister mouth-breathing. She has a cold. Then Fr Galvin, doddering around. Banging. The shadow of Molly's arm jolting up, like a giant stick insect on the wall. What's that? she hisses. Just next door, I mumble. No it wasn't his kind of noises, says Molly, lunging over on to my bed. It was, like, maybe a sack of something dropping. And a sound like crackling. Like dry leaves. Someone might be in the garden. Molly, stop wiping your runny nose on my pillow, I say. Another thud. The sound spirals through me, causing a sensation of falling. Overcome with the jitters, we cling to each other. Tosha. You guys awake? The door creaks open. It's Ivor. Did you hear something heavy falling? he says.

We charge to our parents' room. Molly throws herself against me, knocking me into Ivor. We stare into each other's huge pupils. Now we all hear it, loudly. And then…Mum, giggling. Dad whispering *Shhhh*. We hesitate. Tiptoe back to bed.

*

The next day, Saturday, Ivor and I creep in to their room. Maybe they were wrapping early Christmas presents? He scans under the bed, wielding his torch like a weapon, skimming its light across cryptic objects. Hauls out a book. Maybe it's for me! Mum, of the rapid steps and the never-cease, isn't a reader. And Dad mostly peruses the papers. It has a foreign-looking title and … only pictures. Very, very strange ones. We pore over it. Pictures of acrobats, just, with no clothes on…silhouetted figures in different positions. Knees splayed and…and then, a figure kneeling over a bed, bum jutting. And I'm back in a room, with some boys and a bar of chocolate. I seize the book from him and push it under the bed again.

Queens

Stella Maris. Dad wryly observes that Queen Elizabeth the First considered herself a paragon of cleanliness. She was religious about bathing once every three months, regardless of whether she needed to or not. I giggle. Me too, says Molly. I'll have a bath next week. Mum swats her with a tea towel. Do I *have* to, she wails. Yes, you must, says Mum firmly. Up you scoot. Your turn first this time, I say. At least your bath will be hot. Satisfied with that, she saunters up the stairs, regal as a queen.

It's almost tepid by the time I curtsey in. A small wave crashes against my neck. Mum enters and perches on the corner of the bath. I cross my chest, stare at the cream tiles, a towel trickling from the handrail. I have a book for you, she says. I lean forward excitedly. It's about

growing into a woman. Oh. I glare at the soapy water. You'll be going through some changes soon, she tells me. When this happens, remember the Virgin Mary also went through this, and pray to her if you feel confused. Mum, please can I just have my bath? It's cold enough already. Okay. I'll just leave this here for you.

Last week, Aileen, an older girl from school, dawdled along by the Shannon with Yvette and me, and talked about something called periods. And also about sex. Alarm bells about men and their thingies. The shock, so visceral. Holes and swirls. Violent as a cat eating a bird. Surreal as the bird jumping out of its belly. All I wanted to do was go back to not-knowing.

So it's *not* made up.

Clamouring thoughts and images tumbling in my mind like clothes in a washing machine. The idea of blood-down-there happening to Mary. Feels sacrilegious. Although, if it was a virgin birth, who's to say she wasn't also blood-free? Unless she was a girl like me before the Angel Gabriel came along. Before she turned into Queen of the May. I wonder what Queen Elizabeth did when *she* got the curse, as Aileen called it. In any case, I just can't conceive of it happening to me.

Fish are jumping

I can see the notes, like fish, flowing up the stairs. Like birds lifting from a shoreline. Yvette and I sit on the fourth step in our nightgowns, listening. My dad's flourishes are so swift, the keys can barely hang on to his fingers long enough to respond. Wow, says Yvette. Her long hair has dropped forward, and she scoops it behind her ear. I catch a whiff of her particular Yvette-smell, musty and sharp and sweet, all at the same time.

More arrivals downstairs. Each brings a new, rippling vibration to the house.

After blue greetings and grey coat flurries, and a dark shutting door and a white necessary hush, I'm in story-telling mode, in a whisper. One time, we went to the Shelbourne in Dublin to meet our aunt. There was a grand piano, afternoon tea happening, the kind with sandwiches and cakes on a silver platter pyramid, and he asked if anyone would mind if he played. By the time Mum had parked, and followed us in, a famous opera singer was accompanying him. He played for hours, and in the end, everyone was up dancing in that grand tea-room.

My mum says your dad has *soul,* says Yvette. She heard him play in Hanratty's.

A shadow crosses the hallway, opens the front door again. Icicles of air smash up the stairs. After stepping carefully over the fifth creaking step, we scoot back to my room.

Black ice

Stella Maris, Limerick, 3 December. The living room door is half-open. I sit on the stairs watching my father through the banister, crouched in the chair by the fire. Although Mum has asked us to give him privacy, I can't bear it any more and stumble down the last two steps, rush over and put my arms around him. The fire is talking to itself quietly in the recesses of the hearth, behind the new fire guard. Sorry, he mumbles through the open book of his palms, pressed against his face. His voice is all breath-broken. Mum says crying is good for your eyes, I say. And your heart. Dad pushes the heel of his hand back and forth, like a windscreen wiper.
He nods for me to go back upstairs.

*

When Mum told us what happened to Dad's sister, Freya's mum, my glamorous Jackie Kennedy-like aunt, I felt a forest tumble down through me. On the way to Dublin for a day's outing, a frazzle of black ice caused my aunt Ellen's car to slide right across the road and into a ditch. Grace, only fourteen, beside her in the passenger seat, shaking her unmoving mum.

*

Later, Mum swoops into the room to say goodnight, the way she used to when we were in Zambia. She says let's pray for Auntie Ellen and the family.

No more life for her. No more sunlight. When my mum lays her hand on my head, hot tears peel down my skin.

*

We are not allowed to go to the funeral, to share the grieving with her family. I can't hug Freya, who has lost her mother. Or Grace, or Ali, or Killian. Or their dad.

Sitting on top of a hill, dense and bright

Castletroy, Limerick. We've moved again. I felt bad abandoning that cranky, dampy semi, holding out its chilly arms and saying don't leave me. I felt bad about leaving Yvette's mother's kitchen table, sun pooling on the red flagstone floor, shelves of yellow and white crockery, hooks swinging mugs. A kettle on the Aga, her apron looped on the rail. On our last day, she wiped the scratched surface of the table vigorously, plonked down a plate of hot scones. Jam and butter and cream. We dived in, munching and slurping our tea. I fixed on the images, feeding a future memory. It's not one home, it's two I'll be losing, I moaned.

Nonsense, said Yvette's no-nonsense mum. Sure you'll only be a fifteen-minute drive away. Yvette and I looked at each other. It may as well be another country

*

Our new front door has frosted amber glass. When you're standing in front of it, facing out, you can see all the way past a wood, to where the Shannon flows. Our three bedrooms smile onto a rockpool, which is lit up by tangerine lights at night. And we have central heating. I can throw all my clothes off and still feel warm. We have a den, with a ping pong table. Not one speck of damp, no mould anywhere. No Fr Galvin banging his stick on our wall.

Mum and Dad's French doors open on to a courtyard, with a fountain out the back, and a field above it.

Low-slung button-down cream leather sofas in the living room. Sunlight drawing honey circles on the pale carpet. A gigantic painting. In the right foreground, a fist-sized black bull, pawing up a great howl of dust, which flares into layers of orange whirled outward beyond the boundaries of the canvas. The cushions, two bright sparks of orange, perched on each end of the sofa, like tiny twin matadors. This outside beauty, conflicting with some inside apprehension.

The trickling water at night, the pond's hidden spongy mysteries, the lilies sighing shut, the glow of lights around the rock pool, the potential combustibility of the bull, all trigger feelings that are rangy, far-flung. This peaches-and-cream house, spiced with a dash of danger.

Groove

Castletroy, Limerick, July. Dad says it takes about ten years for a new house to settle into itself. In my dream, I felt the floorboards screaming for help, like a once-was-a-tree, out of range of human hearing. I throw off the blanket, my body in flames, as though I'm still in Zambia. And then remember it was *Amai* I was dreaming of, swinging from the mahogany tree, Black clutching her feet. Her body falling, then the tree falling, then Black's life in Ndola, the city itself, the whole country – falling and falling into a void.

Creaks and whines. The tongue-in-groove oak flooring. *Tongue-in-groove,* a term that gave me pleasure when I first heard it. A breeze gusting ghosts by the window. The amber lamp by the pond, a candle made of water.

The pealing shrieks are coming from Mum and Dad's party. Sometimes, the only way to escape is into torch-light.

Or, the next day, as the party is still ongoing, into the field.

*

Hidden by a groove in the long grass in the field above our house, I watch the exodus of tail-lights, at last, jangling like wayward trinkets. At least Molly's safely next door with Juno, her new little friend. And Ivor's at Clongowes, his new boarding school.

This field is my raft of waving grass, sailing across the warlike smoke of images that trample my brain. A torrent, parcelled in. Random inebriated visitors around Dad's bar, that end-of-the-bottle voice of his, wet and rounded and slurred. Not one but many words pressing themselves up against each other. And underneath them, some other meaning. Just like Mum's silences. Horrible messy Saturday-merging-into-Sunday house-warming, and now indelibly stuck in my brain, like veneer to wood, those, those falling-about leftover adults with their hands and their slurring insinuations! Before my head erupts, I try to follow the outline of clouds. They turn into a girl crouching behind a rock. My mum in *her* field. Has she forgotten? Promise myself that I will not forget this.

This. This *feeling* – of being twelve. Right here, in this field.

River talk

Castletroy, Limerick. After mass on Sunday, I meet the lads at O'Boyle's. I throw out a careless remark that turns me alien. Stop talking, Sofia winks. She is Dutch, fourteen, almost two years older and wiser.

We meander our way to the Shannon. Jamie and Timothy, two brothers, rosy-hued shoulders, fringes and freckles-on-milk, carroty frogs legging it, waving their arms like semaphores. It's swim or lie on moss and roots, inhaling the briny stench of the rowdy river. Unruly strip, dump clothes on a hillock of ox-eyed daisies and I'm right in after them. Hit the river hard. The water grows another current. I dive down beneath the opaque grey and re-surface gasping. So cold it feels older than time. Water comes rushing up my nostrils. Man, this isn't the Zambezi! Yeah, but I'm all for a river with no crocs, shouts Jamie. He spews river from his flatbed mouth, a water fountain. Oh, I say, but we had guides standing shotgun, keeping an eye out. My stories are growing taller by the minute.

Jamie's friend Barra has cruised over, and is dispensing iced lollies. Barra, blond, green-eyed, grace and power of a leopard. Sofia and her boyfriend Leo are swaying under the tree, tucked up in their bubble-wrapped joy-for-two.

We climb out and sit clothed in towels, under a motley sky.

I'm babbling about the Zambezi... The sun would be blitzing down, this brilliant light, and the river was three times the width of this. After swimming you'd lie like a lizard on a hot rock. They look at me blankly. After a spell of silence, I pull my knees up, leaf edges sharp-needly under me. I've done it again, *dropped a clanger*, as my dad would say, as I always do, whether we're shuffling through the dogs' graveyard scouting for the best names, or cruising the woods, pine needles crunching like matchsticks under our feet, or in the field above my house, collecting hundreds of rosehips from the verges. *Stop talking.* Sofia's wink is code now. I've always been one to appreciate a grey sky, she says.

I lean back against the oak. Stare at the pale, burbling, gushing chaos. Damp foliage tickles my toes. Quail-grey smoke splutters into the pale dome, gauzily joining a silvery scarf of cloud. In its own way, really quite beautiful.

Jellyfish

Jellyfish strip, blithely unconcerned about nudity and the afterlife. Those figures, bent over, nipples pointing at the ground. Curiosity, mortification, disgust. And a blackbird. Down *there*.

My body is rattled by this shaker, replaced by a fizz as soon as I dive into the pool. Only in the water am I really and truly at home in my skin.

Eat veg. Drink water, says Steve, our small, balding coach, after our session. Keep your body strong. Don't drink alcohol. (I've already signed a pledge at school to remain teetotal till I'm eighteen.) Don't trash your body. It's where you live. Eat fruit.

Can we just have another few minutes, I ask, and Steve nods. But Yvette hauls herself out, pulls off her cap, tumbles her long black hair down, like a rag, and tiptoes back through the small foot-bath. I follow.

In the changing room, two college students breeze in and again, nudity. Yvette and I take sneaky sidelong peeks. I'll grow hair *there*? White skin, awful hanging breasts that dangle like paw paws. The prospect of growing such things myself makes me nearly go off the deep end. From somewhere inside comes an oh! of pain. The thought lands in my mouth. Yvette looks at me in surprise. I put my chlorine-scented hands to my face, pretend it's a sneeze that was coming and now isn't.

Wheeling clamour

The sound
of your body
rattled by
this shaker.
Between huddle
and out,
what happened?
You check
your trust,
harnessed between
two trepidations:
this outside thing,
and the deep
inside one.

Prince of the meadow and butterflies

Castletroy, Limerick. July. Sometimes, the sun rips through the tall grass in the field above our house, and the soft green blades move like a sea. Whenever the sun shines, Mum drops the tea towel, throws on a bikini, and dashes out to the courtyard.

*

Sometimes there's a bull in my field – huge head, toffee-coloured, with white curls, horns – standing like a sentry, gazing towards the distant hills. I call him Caspian. The field is a no-go zone when he's around, claiming his domain. Occasionally, Caspian rubs his drooling jaws along the top of the wall that overlooks our courtyard with its little fountain. Eyes closed, basking on the sun lounger, Mum seems oblivious of the danger.

*

Mum's boutique, which she runs with her college friend, Beth, is in the front wing, halfway down the first aisle of the Crescent Centre shopping mall. Elizabeth Callie, it's called. When I wander in after school, Mum is whirling a silk scarf around my mannequin, Véronique, who is finally fulfilling her destiny. *Every creature has its own domain.* Perfect timing, love. Will you mind the boutique for me while I nip off for a smoke?

I meander around, adjust the flare on a polka dot dress. Imagine myself in Paris in this dress, a pair of sunglasses pressed to the top of my head like a tiara.

A woman flutters in. She lifts a blouse, holds it against her. What do you think? My mother's voice comes to me: *We don't say pink, darling.* I think cerise is perfect for you, with your lovely tan, I tell her shyly. I'll try it then, along with these. She speaks like the queen. In the end, she buys four entire outfits. I wrap each garment preciously in tissue paper, the way I've seen my mum do.

*

Goodness, Mum says, on seeing the cheque, she was a lady. I know, she was, I say. No, stresses Mum, I mean, she's a duchess! Mum lets me choose something from last season's rail as a reward. I pounce on a cream loopy jacket with a chunky zip. *Please* can I have a bra too? She laughs. But sweetheart, you don't need one yet. Mum, I'm the only girl in my class without one. Oh, alright. She finds me a set in the smallest size, AA, sheer. On the knickers and on one cup, a lilac butterfly. Joy! Now, when the girls look for a strap to snap, I'll have one.

Heart

Castletroy. Easter. Lala visits us in our new, warm house. Notices that Mum hasn't come back from the loo during dinner. Gets up to go check on her. Finds her on the bedroom floor. Calls the ambulance.

*

When Dad returns from the hospital, words are coming from his mouth but they take a while to reach me. Intensive, he repeats. Care. We must take care of her. *She almost died,* as he looks at me. Do you understand? That heart attack nearly killed her.

My heart, caught on a hook.

Sealed

Cove Hill, Donegal. Freya and I hug long and hard and say nothing. Her mother gone, mine nearly gone.

Two pyramids for our birthdays – Molly's eighth, my thirteenth. More presents than Molly and I have ever had. My little sister is particularly in love with a laughing doll, called Chuckles, which Auntie Jan says is from Mum and Dad. Mine from them is an Instamatic camera. Later, feel guilty when I realise that for the whole happy daze of our shared surprise birthday party, the bright decoys of presents, I had forgotten about Mum.

Freya and her family have moved too, into the house they'd been building right above Cove Hill. So they can wander over any time they like. Her dad has to work two jobs now, to make up for the lost income from Auntie Ellen's boutique. Grace is cooking the meals and minding her sisters and little brother.

It gives me a feeling of security, says Freya, having the family nearby, as back-up.
That's the closest she's come to talking about her mum's death.

I haven't talked about my mum and her heart attack either, though everyone knows this is why we have been sent here. Because Mum is in intensive care.

A cloudburst erases the sun, sealing it inside a crate. Abruptly, I am in two places at once, as though on both sides of a pane of glass.

In the key of family

Letterkenny. Freya and I write down our dreams and try to decipher them. One day, we promise each other, we'll travel to Paris together. I take pictures of her, casting about for the best light-and-shadow contrasts. She's wearing a lumberjack shirt, which she loves because it evokes cowboys and wide prairies and freedom. We rock 'n' roll. We write songs, drumming the curve of our guitars to emulate the sound of hooves while playing Ghost Riders. *Alors,* she says, *je vais chercher du bon vin à la cave,* and disappears to the loo. We follow stair-photos, the aroma of grilled cheese. Auntie Jan recruits us to help with the B&B. We use the inside of one the previous guest's pillowcases to wipe down basins, baths, mirrors. Hospital corners, says Auntie Jan, bending over a bed to demonstrate, the motion pronouncing the blue tributaries on the back of her hands. We serve and clear away breakfast. Our reward: her best-in-the-world caramel squares. You two are most like me. Take my advice, says my maiden aunt /godmother as we munch, never marry. Austrians and Italians, easy-come strangers, arrive for the folk festival. Gianni teaches us to pluck a guitar as though it's a double bass. Granny's deep red flourishes of piano notes, aqua and violet. Freya's little brother Killian's bended knee to Molly: 'I'm a sailor home from sea, to see if you will marry me...' One girl after another with Ivor in the wardrobe practising kissing. Just like the Loretto girls, who once queued to go into an old railway carriage with Dad, so Uncle Brennan tells us, puffing on his cigar. Out by the hump-backed garage (designed by Uncle Patrick on one of his trips home from Jeju Island), Grandad tamps his pipe, peering across the meadow towards the Oatfields sweet factory. Hidden behind the milky glassiness of his eyes, some inscrutable insight.

We visit Auntie Lynn and Uncle Brennan next door. But he's mostly away being a TD, or running the Grill. From their wedding photo on the Cove Hill stairs, we can see that she once looked like a film star. Her ephemeral beauty has been caught forever behind glass, like a butterfly in an exhibition case. Now, corpulent arms freckled and trembling, she plies us with cake and biscuits. Outside, their once-lovely swimming pool is smeared with a puddle of courgette-green water and decomposed leaves. Auntie Lynn takes Freya and me shopping in the North, along with her girls, Hugh and Ruari's sisters: Kim, who's our age, Aelish, the redhead, and Dorry, the baby. Stuffs goodies into our closed-up coats. We appear extremely over-fed. At the check-point, her boot is scrutinised. She turns to wink at us, rolls down the window, and dials up her famous smile at the guards when they approach to check the interior. They wave us through.

Covehill is the moss our rolling stone life has always failed to gather.

Another side

April. Usually, on a bus, neither space nor time exist between one point and the other, because I'm immersed in the intimate immensity of a story. But on this long bus trip back home to Limerick, I finish my book early. The hours left without something to read are intimidating. Without a book to distract me, buried thoughts flicker up, like white flames.

My body feels split by the wavering motions of the bus and my apprehensions about going home. How can I be a better person for my mum? Glance across the aisle at Molly, who is looking through a yellow string bag at all her new things. She's always an *angel* – Mum's word for her – while I'm *difficult*. I *try* to do things to please her, arrange daffodils in a vase, set the table, offer to take the coats of guests etc. But I can't seem to help the talking-in-a-blurting-rush. Words fly out of me without filters, the way a flame shoots out of a burner when you turn on the gas. For Mum, I'm the embarrassing harem-scarem, the interrupter. Her soft voice in my head. Try not to be so *self-centred*, darling. And don't be so obsessed with reading. One day you'll look up, and your childhood will have vanished.

When she says that, I feel an internal sensation like a pane of glass that has been struck by a stone and is growing cracks. And it occurs to me that my childhood has already ended. I'm thirteen, no longer innocent. Oh I wish God could put things back the way they were before… before when? These days, everything feels as though it might splinter into a thousand pieces and be swept away in a whirlwind.

I make a vow to myself. From now on, I'll *try harder.* Be an angel. Read less.

Stare out the window, watch trees sprinting past. Time-trees flitting by, each a fragile moment. So many, so swiftly.

My private neon

Limerick. Two-Mile Inn. October. I cross the foot-bath, stand waiting on the tiles, grip my shoulders. When the whistle blows, I dive into the lane next to the wall, and pull the water under me, flip at the other end, surfacing halfway down the pool. The movement of water against my body is silk as my strokes cut an arc. Though I was just average in Zambia, here I am easily the fastest of my age group. The thought of all the miles I'm swimming, with nothing to propel me but my own arms, makes me feel strong, as though there are all kinds of things I could be capable of doing. Or I get those eureka moments, an idea exploding suddenly into my consciousness, like popcorn kernels erupting in a hot pan.

And sometimes, if I get the lane alongside Barra, I become conscious of being inches from his skin. Droplets shimmering from his arms. His glorious grace.

A penny dropping and a pencil mark

Castletroy, Limerick. April. Blood, black as mulberry. Instantly think of the devil sickness that stole my mum's sister. Punishment. On the verge of going hysterical, trying to find something to stem the leak, I flash on those STs tucked at the back of my wardrobe, which my mother gave me a couple of years ago, when I was twelve, for…

and the penny drops.

Relief, followed by a fresh bout of weeping. Already, my accent snags against the ears of my Irish friends, and my disparate upbringing means that I'm foreign to everyone. But this, this is the threshold into adulthood, that alien, vast unknown. Which means the end of everything. Which means I'll become foreign, even to myself.

*

The pencil mark on the wall next to the kitchen door indicates that I've gained two inches. So now I'm taller than my mother. And that's not the only change. Now I know what my mum means when she says she has her 'friends'.

Mum says that change is good for us, that I should embrace this new stage. Change requires us to adapt, the way we would to a new country, new climate, new diet, new pattern of daily life. Change, she says, leads us to an *expansionist sense of self.*

I have started to think of my body as a new country. What will these changes serve up?

Ivor intuits a strangeness too. Gives me new names. *Lanky the Swanky. Tosha the Mosha.*

Yvette, Caoimhe and I walking along by the Shannon, slagged by fog so thick we can barely see the water, drifting away to the world's edges. Blurs of light from riverboats. Let's scream, I say suddenly, and one-two-three, we all let rip.

Now and then, a disappearing

Castletroy, Limerick. Dad got rid of the Jag just for me, he said. Because it made me carsick. Now we have a royal blue Rover. I'm just going to nip down to O'Boyle's for the papers, he says on our return from church. Give the car a bit of a test run. Well, hurry, says Mum. I'm just about to make breakfast.

The crackle of bacon, the aroma, has already sprung saliva in my mouth. We endure thirty tormented minutes of waiting. Well, that's his tough luck, says Mum, and we sit down at the table. Consternation when he's not back by lunchtime. She calls all the usual places. No sign of him. Rings their friends. Zero news.

It's four days before he returns. I turn on the light. Listen to his apologies, excuses: he kept driving until he found himself in Dublin; ended up partying with some journalists, an actress, an opera singer, and his reprobate friend, Greg. They went to Vi Lawlor's for one of her celebrated parties. When they got back, Dad couldn't find his car, offered a reward for its recovery. A twelve-year-old boy found it – right where he left it, parked around the corner from the Shelbourne. Dad's wry laugh rolls right over her four-day fury.

As usual, Mum's response is too quiet to pick up words, but I can hear her tone. Scissors conducting the voice. Come on Callie. The Dublin Road just unfolded in front of me, and the Rover cruised along it so smoothly, I...ah, Callie. We are bequeathed one very short life on this earth, and our mission should be to make sure we're living it.

Cigarette smoke coarsens the air all the way down the corridor. He gets louder. Why must you always misconstrue what I say? Of *course* it wasn't planned!

I believe him. I know those bees-in-the-chest elations that rise up out of nowhere and need to be acted on.

Currents and embers

I unfold myself from my cross-legged position, stand on the river bank and dive in. Submerge, count a dozen breaths before I surface and begin thrashing. Agghh, cramp! I shriek, then go down again. When I surface momentarily, I see Barra get to his feet. Abruptly, the current takes me *for real* and I am dragged downriver. A blood pulse bursting my head, a terror that I may never breathe again. Stars in my lungs, exploding. Ears roar; sinuses fill. And it's not Barra, but an adult, a big, hefty man, who ploughs in to rescue me, grips my chin with his butcher-thick hands and yanks me back towards the bank. He hauls me out and lies me on the ground. I splutter and fumble at my bikini bottom, which has been dragged down. My heart is a bird flapping in a confined cage. How could my own element have let me down? Twigs split underfoot as Barra crouches beside me, not touching, not speaking.

*

Two weeks later, a kitten is perching on the furthermost extremity of a tree limb. A lolloping wind swings it like a skipping rope. Barra shimmies up, creeps along the branch, lunges for the kitten, which springs away. He falls, lands on his back. A wince warps his face. His eyes land on mine. The others standing around. Aren't you going to give him the kiss of life? Heat climbs up over my face.

*

Halloween night. Barra says he'll skip eating and keep the bonfire going. Now or never. I'll stay too, I say. My bold brave impulse! Conscious of a tightrope between our glances, all we achieve are pale whims of exchange about our trip to Butlin's to swim for Munster in the Community Games. Your mum's pretty decent, helping with the training, he says. I noticed her at the poolside, clocking your times. Well done for getting into the Under 14s *and* Under 16s, he says. *Oh god. He must think I'm still thirteen! Should I tell him I've turned fourteen now?* Occasional wood-laying, while inside my body, a mad turbulence of blood. The moon, planet-huge, connecting continents but not us. As much silence between us as on that desolate pale globe. A series of loud cracks and a fountain of fire-flakes, conducting the immateriality of ghosts in waves. Because of course they're here, resting their cold cheeks against our flushed faces. During this oblique, fretful intermission, sitting on a shared log, our palms are pressed a hands-width apart. She's gorgeous too, isn't she, your mum, he says. Yeah, she's great, I say, defeated. Eyes stung with smoke. No help from the lost souls.

*Your mind
is an oar
trying to row
through an air
gone mad,
a hundred or so
storeys high,
now ninety,
now eighty...
not the time
to query this
long leap
against
intuition,
the girl's warning.*

Full tilt into red illumination

Limerick. Crescent boys swarming up the step of the bus, like soldier ants around a cube of sugar, coats and long scarves flying. I'm still a hundred yards away. My hands and wrists prickle as I run. The bus heaves off. The next is in half an hour.

Too impatient to wait, I decide to walk.

By the time I've reached Castletroy, I've succumbed to that out-in-the-country feeling, the wide stony-green river. Dense foliage, long-fingered foxgloves, high grassy meadow on the other side. A gossip of white, pebble-dashed bungalows. High hedges. Nearly there.

Sanding by a lorry up ahead, a cat-faced man, looking towards me. Hello, I say when I reach him. His eyes, wan, jelly-like. Do you have the time? With a half-smile, he glances down, mumbling something. Clutching the straps of my satchel, I look down too. In his palm, a pink, bald-looking thing. Curious, I peer closely. *Aileen's warning about men.*

And then I start to sprint. Past the old big house, past the woods, past Plessy. Finally up the steep driveway, through the front door, into the living room. Stand in the doorway, shaking and breathless. Dad, a man flashed…

Humanity is incapable of perfection, my father is declaring to four of our new neighbours, who are sitting in a scooped circumference around his bar, which he had made specially. We can only strive towards it, he adds. The session is already chatterbox gurgling, sloshing and babbling, a head-wreck.

Humanity is incapable of perfection because of that ruined tower of adulthood.

The expression of clouds

The field is slung low, stuttered with dew. I'm in my nest in the long grasses, tall enough to hide a body and loneliness. Watch clouds curl and stretch and move like cats across a blue carpet. Sometimes, they are strung out along the horizon, like rosary beads. Sometimes they sit quietly on the brow of the hill as though polite guests at a dinner table.

Sometimes, clouds are disguised as dragons or starfish. Or a possible face.

Sometimes the sky slides into the doldrums.

I ponder about circularities, the way air lifts moisture into the clouds, and vapour grows heavy, falls back to the earth as rain, or snow, or sleet or ice.

But don't want to think about ice.

Quivers

The day is wavering and greenish, magnifying scents and feelings. We are reeled out, like a cast line – Timmy, Jamie, Barra, Leo, Sofia, me – right across the estate road, alongside freshly-cut verges. And we're walking towards the tree with the letters B.S.L.I.M etched into the bark, at eye level. The tree right next to Barra's house. The letters Sofia pointed out to me yesterday. *Barra S. Loves Itosha M...* maybe? I notice that the wind has thinned and shredded to nothing. The silence beyond the loud crunch of our footsteps grows enormous. My heart is in a chaos. Will anyone else notice, say anything?

Jamie whispers to Barra, who whispers to Leo who whispers to Sofia, who turns to me. Jamie wants to know if you'll go round with him. Jamie. Jamie? Not Barra? Not... Oh no. No. No, I say. And back it goes, all along the line. Far from me, Jamie's gaze drops to his feet. But I didn't mean... But... it's too late. It's too publicly, humiliatingly late. Will Jamie ever talk to me again? And now, of course, of *course*, Barra will never ask me.

Lonely bird

Dingle, June Bank Holiday: Floating across the sunset, a lone seagull. My shadow is talking bird language, trying to lift to join it. On the vast beach, I open my wings, drink pink light with my hands. The wind pulls me between two of its invisible fingers.

The adults have evaporated into a pub. I am in charge of Gerald and Donna Butler's seven-year-old daughter, Juno. They're our new neighbours in Castletroy. They've invited us to their holiday cottage for the weekend.

Last I saw Ivor and Molly, we were making caramel in the kitchen of the holiday cottage before I went to tuck Juno in. Where have they gone?

Filaments of light stand up in the air, so you can almost see the wind. The emptiness, a shipless blue sea, endless as eternity. Then I see the bird again.

*

Later I write a song about the seagull. *Skimming down across the sea...lonely bird, just like me...*

Freak Wonder Sky

Dingle. Before I turn and see the smoke running from the house like a scared dog, before I remember the caramel in the pot, and the stove plate I might have forgotten to turn off, before I think of Juno asleep in the last room at the end of the corridor in the cottage fifty metres away, before I birdfly the dune, the strand, the road back to the Butlers' house, burst through the front door, before I lift my t-shirt to block out the fumes, slam the kitchen door with its long tongue of fire, shut door after door after door to hold back the smoke, sprint my hair loose, yank at the knob, which won't open, which won't open, *which won't open* until I twist the other way, and stumble in, gasping, and lift her out of the bed, nestle her face to my chest so her green eyes are covered, the way they bring horses out of a fire, and Juno's legs grip around my waist as I plunge back through the reek seeping from door chinks and fractures – before all that, I stand on the brow of the sand dune and say *this is the end of the world*.

The moon blown up, like a balloon

It wasn't the end of the world. The damage was mostly smoke-related, and a destroyed pot. I blame the surreal setting sun, for distracting me. The way the moon is distracting me tonight.

That night in Ndola, when I felt the urge to get up, go outside to gaze at the impossibly huge moon, and Black appeared. His strange stories and proverbs. How sad he got sometimes. *The night cannot be like the day. The moon cannot dry our washing. Just as a child cannot be an adult, and we blacks can never be white. Just as the man who is warm cannot understand what it is to be cold. But the moon is magic, Black, isn't it?*

I switch on my little radio to Luxembourg. It's in mid-song: Frankie Valli's *My Eyes Adored You*. Today on the bus, it was as though a derelict garden has just been lit up by daffodils when Barra boarded. A free seat beside me. But he just nodded and continued on down to the back, to his mates.

Now I'm floating between two hemispheres, and under the African moon, Black is telling me that a warrior princess would never chase a boy she likes. She would hold her head high, and wait for him to come to her. And if he doesn't come, he is not the one.

Strike against the leviathan

Because I still crave his favour despite everything, clutching to his approval like a hot water bottle, it's a long time before I challenge my father. It finally happens as he is heading down the corridor towards the bathroom and hears us awake. I am reading to my sister, and have just hopped out of bed to switch off the light, then jumped on to my bed, when he storms in, his shadow projected on the empty wall, huge as a grand piano – I gauge him at the fifth of his seven stages – eyes red-rimmed and leaky, the growly words slithering out like a leaky pen blobbing onto the page: whahareyoudoingssschtillaaeee....as he takes two staggery steps, reaches me, lifts my nightie and wallops me on the bum. I have my period (the third) and there's the bulging ST, sticky with blood and that iron smell. I am both humiliated and enraged, all the way to my outer edge, primarily because it means that I will now have to inform my little sister about the facts of life. She is staring, horror-stricken, at the bulge in my knickers. On the other hand, any other time of the month, I would have been bare under my nightie, which would have been worse. Standing on the bed, I am taller than my father, eyeballing him. You will *never* – and I pause to make sure he is paying attention – lay a hand on me again. On any of us.

Milestone

Geography tour, Kerry. Hurtling around bends, our single-decker lurches from side to side. The sleepy mountains turn grey. Some of the pelicans – as Caoimhe calls them – take out their rosary beads and begin praying aloud. I can hear girls muttering all up and down the bus: *we're going too fast, too fast.* I touch the nearest nun on the shoulder. *Please ask him to slow down.* But instead she suggests we pray the rosary. We swerve into another bend. At the same moment, a lorry bursts, like a roman candle, around the corner and our driver veers violently, and the bus swipes left, and the front wheel skids right off the road, tipping over...over...over...over the precipice...

and I am flung on top of Caoimhe and Dorothy lands on me,

and below us, the valley opens its mouth...

and we are half-hung in mid-air; suspended, unfallen...

and the radio continues playing

and the driver lurches up the aisle towards the emergency exit, rocking the bus,

and a scream wrangles from Jasmine's throat, prompting others,

and a nun slaps her, and Jasmine puts her palm to her cheek, gasping,

and the driver reaches the back, where we are sitting,

beer on his breath,

and lifting a hammer, he swings it and the glass shatters

and he jumps onto the road

and the coach seesaws again, to unanimous shrieks...

and one of the nuns takes charge, saying *Everyone, move one by one, to the back. Slowly, no rushing, or the bus could go over...*

and as I'm at the back, I'm one of the first out, and see that a milestone is jammed underneath the front wheel and the bus's backside is jutting up to the sky, like a baboon presenting her blue posterior, and each evacuation causes the bus to pitch again, and the air feels thin as paper... and each time a girl or a nun drops from the height of the exit, the coach is more susceptible to the push of the wind and I'm watching for it to go over any moment, and then: *my medication,* wails Marian, who has spina bifida and, without hesitation, Clare climbs back in to fetch her satchel, while Marian rubs her crucifix...*Ohmygodohmygodohmygod...*

and for long minutes my heart is thudding so hard it might break my ribs, and *HolyMaryMotherofGod* pray the nuns, and when Clare finally drops back to the ground, Marian hugs her long and hard, and I think, that's what it is to be a hero.

Between the notes

Sofia is Dutch, pale from lack of sun, with a sting like a scorpion. Her father works at Ferenka, where my father also worked before he left to start his own import/export business. Belinda lives in the estate across the road and is in the class below us at school. I like Sofia. But I don't think the other girl's a good influence, Mum says. Influence? I know she means *not our sort*. Belinda sings Daydreamer, and links arms with us as we're walking along the Dublin Road. I'm not really the arm-linker type and subtly try to shrug her off as soon as possible. Often her lips are wide open, as though she's still singing a silent song. A gushingly sweet scent is pasted on to her throat and hair and clothing. She is plump and Mum would call her *well-developed*.

*

I arrange a plate of grapes and orange slices on the breakfast table. Belinda's hands are flung up to her face, which is a bit like a melting strawberry ice-cream after the walk up our steep driveway. She is in awe of our rockery and the trickling waterfall. I'm in awe of the fact that although she is only thirteen, Belinda already has a boyfriend. And *he* is eighteen!

Dad, behind his bar, is talking to our neighbours, Gerald and Donna Butler, about Tiede Herrema, his old Ferenka boss, who's been kidnapped by the IRA. Mum's not back from the boutique yet. Hello, he stalls us, as we're heading back out the door. Who's your friend?

Ignoring his other visitors, he asks Belinda to *make a statement*. Your house is the most beautiful I've ever seen, she replies. I grin at her. He loves her for that, of course. A dozen questions follow – about her family, her interests and dreams. Relays his usual mantra: the most important word in the English language, he says, is communication.

Before he can get too intrusive, I ask him to play the piano.

I look at Belinda gazing at his hands flying like birds, and hear him though her ears, see him through her eyes. The piano is my father's truest medium, vastly more communicable than all his stories.

Waiting for the sky to fall

Castletroy, Saturday. Belinda's leaning against the kitchen door. Her dead-straight red mop seems plastered by water. Her shiny face. I'm sipping coffee, still in my slippers. It's morning all day on a Saturday, because Mam's at work.

Can you keep a secret? Belinda waits until my head is a cascade of nods. She moves the empty mug back and forth between her two palms as she tells me.

Outside the window, the grass is still straggly.
Oh Belinda. How? How? I mean, when did you find out?

The grandfather clock in the study ticks like a steady accusation.
I was getting sick every morning. Mam worked it out.

She folds her arms under her embarrassing cleavage. I'm a year older and my breasts are still as small as apricot kernels. She glances out the window, and I follow her gaze. The soil is pretty boggy, that's why the grass is so poor.

She'll be imprisoned for months, she says, like the kidnapped Dutch boss from Ferenka. And then she'll come home with no baby.

*

I keep her secret, of course, but it gets out anyhow. A scutter, Sofia and I hear them say at the back of the bus. I blaze down to them. What about *him*?! And they laugh. Fuming, I flounce back to my seat. Better to say nothing, says Sofia.

Mam isn't surprised, which burns me. When my father finds out, he has opinions too. There's safety, he says, in virginity. Promise you'll wait till you marry. And Thackery agrees. *Be cautious young ladies. Be wary how you engage.* Oh I will, I think. No scaly lizard is going to dribble near *me.*

Once Belinda's gone, Sofia and I sit in my room and whisper about her situation. Pregnancy must be so scary, she says. The inevitability. Like when you can tell it's going to rain. Imagine, I add, your body making another one inside you, at thirteen.

Inside out

Castletroy, Limerick. I've just spent four days in hospital, with a theatre gown on, waiting to have my appendix removed, after searing, siren-wail pains. Days in a queue for the theatre, and then the intensity subsided, and they let me go home, appendix intact. We'll keep an eye, said the doctor.

*

When Mum and I arrive back home, Dad is talking on the phone, his Robert-voice on. Forty, hey? It'll soon be time to prepare the tombstone! Robert, on the gin and tonic, he whispers to Mum, hand over mouthpiece. Right now, booms Robert, I'm sitting out by the pool. A mango tree for shade. Life is really rather good here, he tells Dad. Really rather good. His voice, so carrying, we can all hear what he's saying. So, any news? Well, Itosha almost had her appendix taken out and Callie had a dishwasher put in, quips Dad. That's about it. Not much else to report. Oh, and a fire. The company warehouse burned to the ground. That's my business up in smoke. Well then, you need to book a flight, Seán.

*

Two weeks later, Dad is back. He flourishes a snapshot of a sprawling bungalow with a wide verandah, sunlit pool, terraced garden, tall trees, flower beds bursting with blossoms. Wow. Is that where they live? He lifts his half-smoked cigarette inhales deeply, then mashes it into the ashtray. No. Not them. Dad's pauses are always as dramatic as the ones in the Pinter plays he likes watching. Mum flies off like a carrier pigeon, then reappears from the bedroom with her totems: a bikini bottom and top, one in each hand. I'm ready, she says gleefully. And that's when the penny drops. But our new home! After all this – why?

This is a feeling worse than my appendix pain.

Ivor:
Dad arrived at Clongowes out of the blue. Then and there, I had to pack my things and leave with him. That warehouse fire almost made Dad bankrupt. All his imports. We had to leave.

Spiralling

You are falling
and twisting
through a wound
of white sky-walls,
a high flapping noise,
the downward velocity
stupefying,
strap cutting
into your shoulder,
body twisting
like a vine,
internal voice
asking
Why?

The box

My mother has packing down to a science. She loves blank slates, bare interiors to be recreated. Other people cherish objects handed down from grandparents: books, clocks, spoons, pictures, rugs, lamps. Our possessions have always been transient. We may as well never unpack, or treasure anything.

Mum, I can't bear to leave anything, I say. You'll have to go through my stuff and decide.

At school, a thought thunderbolts through me. Oh no no no! My treasure box, under the bed! I run for the first bus after the bell; run, run up the drive, charge into my room, like a burst water-pipe.

She is sitting on my bed, a spread of envelopes, open. Yellow envelopes for my letters, green for Barra's. As he wants to be a doctor, illegibility seemed appropriate, so I wrote his letters left-handed.

Feel as though the skin and bones of my secret self have been ripped apart. She tenses, fabricates an apologetic expression.

I bolt to the refuge of the field, where the sun is a sliver, like the peeping curve of an egg. Time passes more slowly in a field when you are lying in it. Watch the silvery sun being pulled to the horizon, as though there was a secret magnet. Of course it's not the sun that's moving, but the earth. The thought makes me feel contrary, like the Fool on the Hill, whirly with *the world spinning round.*

When the sun has bleared all the way down, I catch sight of Mum and Dad in the new Rover. It's creeping up the driveway of the Butlers' house next door. Now an apricot cloud is floating through the tusk of a crescent moon.

Ivor and Molly are in the den, playing ping pong. My mother has returned the box to its original hiding place in a far corner under my bed. I drag it out, haul it to the fireplace. Crumple up the greens and yellows, make a pyramid, set a match to humiliation and a lost fate, page by page.

Crisps and spikes

Castletroy, Limerick. At the bus stop, cigarette butts on the pavement. A sapling has begun to knuckle up through the concrete. Faces whirl past like confetti.

You have a way, you know, of shoving your friendliness right into people's faces, says Sofia. She is standing beside me, a head taller, head cocked, looking down. Sleek bamboo-coloured hair newly bobbed with a fringe. Don't be angry with me for saying this. But for the first few months, I found your friendliness too – aggressive. Too much.

The pebble-dashed wall presses into my back like a torture implement. Shadows zigzag into cat's fins, bird's tails. But then that day, when Emily threw up, and you fetched a bucket and got mopping, I decided that I like you. You can be kind.

What kind? Leo asks, returning from O'Boyle's with three packets of Taytos. Sofia's laugh is a single note. This girl in our class – her mother died last year. She always wears dingy tights, loose at the knees. Bad odour. On her birthday, Itosha went out and bought toiletries for her. I'm heat-smacked with embarrassment. Just wanted to be a hero, like Clare was, on the teetering bus.
We all chipped in, I remind her.
But it was your idea.

Others have begun to arrive at the stop. I nod at the cheese and onion and Leo thrusts a bag at me. The bus pulls up. I pinch the collar of my shirt up, where the wind is trickling in. The usual scrum to board. By the time we're inside, the conversation's changed.
You must come and visit me in Holland, Sofia says.
You're leaving?
Yes. Soon.
A spike of surprise. I haven't told anyone yet about us going, because I know people tend to withdraw from you when they know you're emigrating. It's a kind of betrayal. You're no longer worth their *emotional investment*. But now, I may as well.
We're leaving too, in a few weeks. Heading back to Africa, to a different country this time.
So we're the same, she says.
No, we're not, says an internal voice. *You're going home. I'm leaving home.*

One thing always leads to the next

Castletroy Youth Club, Limerick. I sit watching the slam dancing, pogo, jiving, flying skirts. And then, my chair, tipped back, lips against mine, pushing them open. Instinctively, grabbing him to prevent myself falling. Closing my eyes; an unfamiliar musk. First kiss. And then he stops, wicked grin, inches from my mouth. I stare beyond his close, cryptic expression, to the ceiling. Floor throbbing under my chair from the bass vibrations. My eyes flit nervously back to his face. Blond, green-eyed. But not Barra.

His cheek bones are more defined, face is narrower. And he transmits this nervous energy, like Ivor. I think of a frog about to leap, a fox about to fly. We've never spoken, but I know his name. Alex. He's about sixteen, two years older than me. He jerks his head, takes my hand. To my left, Bay City Roller half-masts. White cheesecloth shirt. To my right, shimmering silver eye shadow. Two-tone platforms, flared, high-waisted jeans. Dim fairy lights twinkling.

Be My Baby. Two minutes later, we're slow-dancing and his hand has slid to my chest and he's copping a feel and I'm slapping his face, running out of the hall, into the bathroom, a wounded rabbit. And the lights of the youth club have been switched on by some adult. I'm glancing down at my cheese cloth crop top, handled by wrong boy, lifting the silver crucifix that Sofia and the lads gave me as a farewell present. I rub it like a genie's lamp, wishing that wrongness away. Wait until the hall has cleared. Until I can't hear any more noise. Until everyone has gone.

Well, almost everyone. I'm guessing Sofia thought I'd left. But Jamie waited. Jamie of the furiously freckled face and the dark hair that won't sit right. Jamie who makes everyone laugh. Jamie, whose presence has never been more significant to me than a casual thought. Jamie who asked me to go round with him. And I turned him down.

He takes my hand. Not a word about the incident, just points out all the stars streaming a sash of liquid silver across the night sky.

Wrongness righted

As we walk, I sense the shadows dripping and hiding, and let his hand remain in mine, for that, for comfort, for gratitude. We talk, with no direction or aim, but no hesitation either. He ruined my first hop, I moan, finally bringing it up. There's more to the night than just that eejit's dodgy move, he grins, swinging my hand up to the starlight, and the moon's a far-flung dumpling, and all at once I'm able to gloss over it. And when we're standing under the amber streetlight below my driveway, and he turns me to face him, I'm standing on a raft built of rushes of emotion, and never would I have found myself here but for the earlier incident. An owl's transit, animal paths twisting through the thicket of our awkward kiss. My second, but the first that's given.

All the dandelions

The patio wall overlooks my field. Freya and I scrabble over it, sit cross-legged on feathery green pillows, polka-dotted with unblown dandelion heads. This is her first visit to our home, and it'll be the last too.

She's tall, isn't she, your mum's partner? Nearly as tall as my dad, says Freya. Think your dad and Beth will like each other? She nods, shrugs, looks at me, lifting her hands. Does it bother you? No. He's so lonely. And she's nice. Your mum's sweet to arrange a blind date. It could work as well as anything. She's a widow too, you know, I say. Been alone for years. We grow quiet, unsure whether the same thought has twisted through us both.

And then she becomes her animated self again. Apparently Indians have more faith in arranged marriages because they think western romantic love is a come-lately, make-believe concept. Wonder how you recognise real love, I say, whirlpooling some daisies into a dance with wind and finger. Maybe, I say, inspired, it's the way you might sense a ley line. Some mystical flutter. Or maybe you know, says Freya, when his thing doesn't repulse you. We laugh. I'm kind of with the Indians, she says. I reckon it's more of a decision you make. Bet I could marry any of the random males we passed on the way back from the shops, and the odds of it working out would be the same.

A breeze flushes by, the meadow tosses its head and dandelion seeds launch into the air. Words are veils but tone is a peeling of skin. Can you imagine doing it? Cross-legged, hands over ankles, shaking my head adamantly. Me neither, she says. Have you ever seen a penis?

So easy to tell her about the driver lurking by the open door of his lorry. I had the shudders for hours. Maybe, she says, he just hopped out to have a pee and you caught him in the act. We laugh and laugh, though I know what I saw was deliberate.

Ah Freya, who's going to discuss the great questions of life with me, and share my endless consternations? Though it's frightfully sad, we giggle again.

All this while, *I haven't been paying enough attention* to how you become Irish in your head and heart, as well as your blood. And now it's too late.

4.

White lie

Salisbury, Rhodesia, Africa. Welcome to The Sunshine City! Our driver beams.

Dad's moral crime at the airport made me queasy with shame. This is a catastrophe! he'd roared, in front of other passengers reporting lost luggage. You will have your bags on Monday, purred the Lost Property attendant. But we've come all the way from Ireland for a wedding *tomorrow*! A hasty cheque as compensation.

The whites shop, our driver says, in Barbours. And – pointing at some vendors – that is where you can buy ice-cream. We're safe in the city aren't we? Yes *sah*, the taxi driver smiles at my father sitting beside him in his derelict Renault.

The car tremors as though in a minor quake as it rounds a corner and shudders to a stop. My father tips generously, as he always does.

Safe from what? I ask my dad. From the war. What war? I ask, my voice shrill. Don't worry; it's far away, in the bush.

The bright city is laid out like a grid, but bodies and gestures are fluid. Mum and Molly follow a tree-high fountain spray to flower sellers in front of Meikles Hotel, a gladness of colour, already demising in metal buckets. Don't worry, we're very safe here. Mum opens her arms to the heat. Vast-as-an-ocean blue sky, hot chairs on the pavement. The Monomatapa Hotel, a sweeping, crescent-shaped building, soaring high over us, shrouding us from our old life and from the war, far away on the border.

Master of the house

3, Corser Close, Salisbury, Rhodesia. My new bedroom window is splashed with scraps of leaf-light. All the way down the hill of our new driveway, out the gate, a queue of swaying figures, like the tail of a kite. They are dressed in their best, melting in the heat, like butter in a frying pan. I watch smiles, hands holding references, a handbag, smoothing gesture down a freshly ironed dress.

Mum is in the living room, on the couch, interviewing them one by one.

My parents' friends from Zambia, Robert and Eleanor Rawson and their three girls – the Jane Blonds – moved here a couple of years ago. They have already told us it's an unwritten law that we have to employ at least two people, who between them will support about fifteen family members.

How did all these people find out about us?

Ivor, Molly and I go to the kitchen to hunt for a snack from the grocery bags. Next thing, the back door opens, and in strides a towering man, wearing white, with a real chef's hat on. He's probably in his forties, with a Macleans smile and the deepest rumbling voice. A big shiny dome of a head. Tell your mother she can stop the interviews now, he gleams at us. She has her cook. I'm Wilson, former head chef of the Monomatapa Hotel.

We run to share this bizarre piece of news. When we come back with her, he's already started baking scones. On discovering we don't have enough butter, he whips cream until it turns yellow.

We only arrived three hours ago.

Heat and ripples

Oriel Girls' School, Salisbury, Rhodesia. September. In Ireland, this would be a heatwave on steroids, although it's officially still winter here. At least school begins at 7.30am, while the morning is still cool, but by break-time of my first day, I am weak as an egg and dripping with sweat. In a cloudless blue sky, the sun is a boiling mass. Sand-coloured dust lifts off the parched, scrubby ground, prickling my nose and throat. A flurry of little scuds every time someone crosses the quad. The yellow lawn crunches scratchily when we walk over it. Because of rationing, it can't be watered.

During break, I wander down to the school pool, and find the entrance gate un-padlocked. Light particles trampoline across the shining water. I totter dizzily, let myself fall in. When I surface, someone is standing at the edge, mass of curly hair, gurgle of a laugh. What are you doing? Using my palm as a propeller, I whirl a circle of ripples around me, noticing how the movement refracts the light. I dare you to jump in too. You're crazy. We have French in five minutes. I dip my head under and emerge again. A squelching into my brown lace-ups. My checked white-and-sky-blue dress slips up, and floats, like cloth water. Oh please, I say. I'll be your best friend if you do.

She plunges in.

When the bell goes, we climb out, strip off, giggling, wring out our uniforms and put them on again. Shake out our hair. Drip our way into class.

Lois? my new French teacher, Miss Moore, asks, with a cocked head and active eyebrows. Just helping her settle in, says my new ally hastily.

Babeurre

Oriel Girls' School, Salisbury. Miss Moore is completely different from all the other teachers because of the air she carries around her. It's oxygenated and expanding outward. Almost as small as Anna Pavlova, she holds herself with the same grace.

Babeurre is French for buttermilk. Miss Moore is *babeurre.* Her hair is very straight, blond, in a pageboy cut to her shoulders. Milk skin, almost never exposed to the sun, I'd say. I guess by her calm demeanour and the way her voice carries a crystal note in it, like a large-bowled wine glass, that she is entirely in control.

Her attire is unobtrusive: knee length A-line skirt, blouse, cardigan. Cream, amber, jade are her predominant colours. Despite her diminutive height, she wears flat, comfortable shoes. Lois, whose mother wears them too, says they're called Birkenstocks.

English-born, Miss Moore has the persuasively-French accent of someone who's spent a chunk of time in Paris. If she is occasionally the sting of a nettle, she's also the dock leaf nearby. Her tongue is swift and witty and her green eyes could penetrate walls and heads.

Swapping cross-signals

Eve's party. December. Figures flickering across a mole-tunnelled lawn with crates of beer. Boys roaring in on motorbikes. Perturbed, my father is on the verge of reversing when Eve, the party-host, bounces up to the car. Hi. I'll take care of her. She bustles me out of the back seat. In the kitchen, a guy shakes my hand – Howzit, I'm Maro. You're the Irish girl – and hands me a beer. I don't drink, I say. The silence of the room doubles. A guessing mood. Oh. Ok. Through the doorway to the dance room, jeans and t-shirts, shadow-leaning. My lime green flares, white crop top and platforms seem chancier by the minute. Supertramp, dominating the dark...*she's the only one I've got*...Dance? Well, can't talk or drink, so...When he gets leather-jacket close, at first, relief. Now we're reeds together, flowing synchronously. Aftershave and tallness and boy. Then it starts, a spit-logged swapping of tongues and a clacking noise in my head. His little fish darting rapidly and repeatedly, my own, confounded. In-and-out, then round-and-round. And then, belatedly – how did I not notice earlier – the emerging bristles of a moustache. Oh no. No, no, no. Retreat, retreat! Tongue definitely not in groove.

For something to do, I throttle the tops of bin bags already boggy with paper plates and cigarette butts. At midnight, just as the party's at its whomping peak, my parents do the double-flash signal from the road. Maro is smoking on the verandah. In any case, I could never be with someone who smokes. Clouds are sculling the moon, but too swiftly, they scurry off, as though aware they're crashing the ambience. I am Cinderella, slinking away, suddenly caught in the moonlight. Hey! Where are you off to? I wave without looking back, truckling through the gravel to the gate.

The next day at school, Eve plies me with curiosity. What did you think of him? He was sweet, I say. Behaved like a gentleman. A bit older than us, isn't he? How do you know him? He's my brother. Eve shrugs. What?! But... you have different surnames. Her wrist dilly-dallies the space between us. We didn't grow up together. My parents and their best friends swapped partners at one of those key parties. And that was that. They split up the four girls and two boys too. When they remarried, he got Dad. I got Mum.

Key parties? Her words seem like some coded message winking ambiguously at me from a mirror, flash after flash.

Countdown

There's no time
to try
and work out
the prelude
to this
uncharacteristic,
act,
your real reason
for wanting
to jump,
or the coded message
winking
ambiguously
at you,
in the mirror
of the river below.

Monkey's wedding

The drought is over. By noon, the animal and vegetable worlds are beginning their anticipatory rustle. At 1pm, we are out of the school bicycle shed, like racehorses from their stalls, to try and beat it. The restless breeze makes me feel a little wild, a little migratory, weaving along the sloping cycle track.

Then down it comes, swift as a whip. The dusty ground jump-starts. Raindrops sheeting and pleating onto corrugated roofs. Monumental torrents blinding our path. Thunder, like a ghostly gallop of zebras, scent of steaming dirt.

We speed past the red-brick walls of other people's houses, invisible inside their private worlds. Past films of clouds in puddles. Rust mud and wet sunlight. Bloody rivulets joining larger tributaries.

We shelter under a jacaranda, crossing fingers we're not struck. This country, I've learned, has the world record for deaths by lightning.

Every journey home, we become the wet colour of rain; by the time we reach the back door, ratty-tailed and dripping our tracks, it's over. Wilson is laying down newspaper. The sky is fresh with sunshine, residual drips and a rainbow.

And the living is

12, Pemray Drive, Salisbury. December. Mum and Wilson have fallen out, and he's quit. Mum didn't like him giving *her* orders, lists of what to buy, telling her *he* would decide what to cook for dinner. And he didn't like it that Mum also loved to cook. So, he had to go. We all miss his lavish meals and huge personality. But he was wasted on us. He needs to be king of his own five-star kitchen.

That's not the only change. We're moving again. The sensation each time is like pulling yourself up, like a plant out of the earth, weakening the roots that are so hungry for familiar soil, whether black, red, sandy or loamy – anything to latch on to.

But this time, when I see our new home... well, I am a bell at its most ringingly euphoric. The pool! A sauna! The garden! Mulberries and pawpaws, prickly pear, bougainvillea. Best of all, a willow slouching in a corner at the bottom of the lawn, stirred by the bullet shots of thunder and spot-lit by forks of lightning, though the rain hasn't started yet. The sweeping green gown vibrates in my direction and pulls me over. Bags the *rondavel* shouts Ivor. I've already got what I want.

After the storm, the air is loud with insects and the sky is radiant. In Ireland, rain was often a kind of grief. Here, it's a joy, leaving gifts: the earth's breath, tendrils dipping and swaying; the shrieking choir of thin-fingered frogs.

We discover a putting green at the bottom of the garden, and even more fruit trees: mango, banana, lemon and guava. My father approaches us, a green weight in his palm. He hands it to me. This avocado, he says, has fallen from our very own tree. I rub my fingers over its rough, firm texture. And though we're about to have a summertime Christmas and I'll miss Covehill and snow, the jasmine trailing the patio trellis has a scent that attracts sun-spun butterflies, and the whippy interior of the willow is a haven, like my old apple tree.

Pretty smoke and glass

12, Pemray Drive, Salisbury. I'm lying on the flagstone floor of my room, enjoying its lithic coolness, my feet up on the wall, reading, when the door bursts open. Wolf air, boy-smell. Ivor goes into full flight with a little Johnny joke. His post-punchline knee-slapping chortle vaguely penetrates the mental glass barrier of my elsewhere, destroying my book's timelessness.

Hey, you used to be fun, Ivor complains to my silence. Now you're just a bookworm. Sorry, I mumble. Sit up and earmark my page. What were you saying? Forget it, he scowls, blocking the trapezoid of light that usually strikes the bed mid-afternoon. Molly skips into the room, singing *Who loves you pretty baby*? Chocolate-melt eyes, fall-of-syrup hair, wearing an apricot ruffled skirt and her bikini top. Ivor picks up my guitar and starts playing *Smoke on the Water*. They slip into a dissonant harmony, like an interviewee with a hostile journalist. Ivor ups the tempo. Molly waves long seed pods she found under the flamboyant tree. She twists arms and body, rattling the air. Arrgh, guys, I shout. Desist. Ivor throws down my precious instrument.

Tell you what, he says, you guys can teach me a few moves. Got a disco tonight. There's a girl I like, and I'm a bit useless at dancing.

Molly trawls through Mum and Dad's LPs in the living room and finds Jerry Lee Lewis. *Goodness gracious, great balls of fire...*and, laughingly awkward, jiving it is for the next half hour.

A low V

12, Perry Drive, Salisbury. Out of Ivor's *rondavel*, a girl. The one he mentioned the other day, I'm guessing. Jailbait, the guys at school would call her. *A brazen hussy,* Mum's expression says, as she watches her totter on heels into the living room. Mum and Dad are gobsmacked into silence. Ivor mumbles something about her having to stay over because she missed the curfew as he follows her into the living room. She lives out in Ruwa. It was too late for her to get a lift, he adds. Mum glances at the skewed crimson lipstick, the lushness of her cleavage. Just like hers. And just like Mum, I can see that she's already used to male attention.

Good morning. The girl spots the piano. Can I? Sure, says Ivor.

Next thing, her fingers are flying over the keys, lifting and swooping, aerobatic as swifts. Possessing more self than any senior at our school, though she's only in second year, Ivor told me. And the morning explodes into frangipanis and blazing galaxies. From his position on the sofa opposite the piano, Dad's eyes lift above his newspaper. That's remarkable. How long have you been playing? Since I was five. Her smile is shy, and suddenly she's fourteen again. And you play Mozart. Not what I would have expected from a young girl like you, he says.

I look at Ivor. He shrugs.

Mum goes into the kitchen and talks to our new cook, Moses. Small, quiet, unobtrusive, very polite. Moses, says Mum, we'll have a full fry this morning. Mushrooms, tomatoes, etc. And we have a guest, so please can you cook for six. At breakfast, the girl responds to Dad's interrogations, until all muddy thoughts have gone underground.

For the next week or so, Dad sits at the piano and plays Mozart, Schubert, Chopin, Tchaikovsky, and those in the room listen in questions, and the music is an answer, and when he looks up, birds are crossing the sky.

Harmonics

Christmas. Rita and Bert's farm in Raffingora, Rhodesia. I float out to the poolside after the Christmas dinner. Jack – sinewy torso, jet hair, peacock blue eyes, Cupid's bow, all the clichés – is sitting on the edge, legs in the water, his calves and feet magnified. A staring-into-the-water-to-spot-the-fish look.

He drops into the pool, dislodging clouds. He's about sixteen or seventeen, a year or two older than me. *Bet he's a real Jack-the-lad.* He reaches to rescue a dragonfly fizzing dustily on the surface, wades to the edge, lays it on the concrete and watches until it shakes its wings and totters off. *Maybe not.*

So, you guys know Rita and Bert from Ireland? he says.
My dad knew Rita in Dublin when they were both young, I reply. Apparently she asked him to dance once, and he snubbed her.
Jack laughs. Shame, he says.
What happened to your right hand? I ask.
He spreads his crooked fingers, flexes them. I was cycling down a steep hill. Reached the cross-roads. Brakes failed. I went straight into a passing lorry. Broke all 27 bones in my hand.
Feel my own bones quiver.
So, how come you and your brother are spending Christmas here? I ask. Where are your parents?
He doesn't answer, but pulls himself out of the water and flumps beside me, both our legs in the water. Remains silent for a bit. Eventually a narrative grows into the tree where he found his mother hanging when he was eight years old, after his father hadskipped to Australia with the au pair. Jack and his brother left behind, to a life of boarding school and holidays with the neighbours.

I take his hand.

On the back foot

Oriel Girls' High. Sitting on the school verandah step, munching on iced buns, a row of legs stretched out across the dusty ground to collect the sun. All tanned, muscular, silky smooth. Except my own – which are pale, bony, fine-haired.
The others are giggling as Iria, from a different class, describes her date.
Well, it *was* my fault that his thing was so sharp.
I'm as confounded as a Bedouin might be, staring up at falling snow.
What do you mean, sharp? I say.
You know, he had a hard-on.
What's a hard-on?

For the next ten minutes, after the uproar, Iria's an instructor, demonstrating the best way to manage a guy's needs.

Drunk luck

Wedza. We skid in at the Jamaica Inn, startling a fluster of dust. A drink for Mum and Dad, Cokes for us. At the turn-off, a man lies sprawled in the dirt, haloed by flies. Alarmed, I rush over to check on him. A rankness. But not dead. Just dead drunk. Appendage visible below his Bermudas, surely as long as the arm of a tree. His lips look parched. The heat is something brutal. Dusty bicycles weave around him like streams of water. A guy pushes a Dairiboard ice-cream hand-cart filled with bananas, blown chip wrapper jammed under the wheel. Selling like bananas, smirks Ivor.

I can hear my father inside the store. How is the season going? he asks. Eh, the drought destroyed our crops, *baas*, several people chime in. It's too hard these days. Dad has told us how some farmers fire off salt pellets in the desperate hope of carting down a few drops from a lone cloudlet.

I wrap the unconscious drunk's fingers around my half-drunk bottle of Coke. Ugh – away! flap my hands and rush back to the car – bluebottles? Horseflies? Buzzing fiendishly around his bulbous…

*

The farmhouse is rustic. Screened doors and windows, the floors polished to a high shine. On the wide verandah, a scurrying cockroach. Ugh! I upend a glass and swiftly dome it over the shiny flat-back. It goes still, seemingly as unperturbed as a fish in an aquarium. Dad commiserates with the portly manager, Langton, about the lack of rain as he opens a bottle of brandy. Six ginger ales. Ice. Mosquito screens in the windows and doors. Bouquet of Cobra polish. An old *Cosmopolitan* in the loo. My mother's cigarette, spiralling smoke like a genie out of a bottle.

I can't believe your old boss *gave* you his grand piano *and* his vineyard, says Mum, *sotto voce* so Langton, doesn't hear. Our new manager is guffawing at something Ivor just said. Maybe I won his heart with the Napoleon brandy I gave him! Dad laughs. In any case, who's going to buy a farm at the height of a war, in one of the hottest contact areas? he says. Especially when the grapes are so poor? And who else could he have given it to? Well…Mum nods towards Langton. We could give him a stake? she suggests. And we could try marketing it to blacks? I know they don't traditionally drink wine, but there are eight million of them. Crazy to ignore such a huge potential market. I inch closer to eavesdrop on their whispered conversation, hummingly reaching for one of the sandwiches Mum has just unpacked from the cooler bag. What if we sell it in dumpy bottles, as a more alcoholic alternative to beer? Mum is saying now, leaning close to Dad at the verandah picnic table. You're always saying alcohol is essential in a war! Dad chuckles. I was thinking of marketing it as a cooking wine, getting Wooty the chef to use it on TV ads, demonstrate recipes. I like your idea. Mum clutches his arm. We can do both!

Langton's bicarbonate-of-soda-on-a-stick scrubbed teeth flash a smile at my offer of sandwiches and a Coke. Coca Cola brings life! chants Molly. Or, as the Chinese would say, Coke brings your ancestors back from the dead! chortles Ivor. Let's hope we can bring this vineyard back from the dead, hey Langton? Dad spies a bullet hole in the wall. Did I do that on the last visit? No, *sah*. It was the terrorists. That one just missed my ear.

God made the little green apples

12, Pemray Drive, Salisbury. Mum and Dad are having a party. Robert Rawson, his friend from Zambia, who lured Dad to this country, bursts in the door followed by his tall wife Eleanor, and their three Jane Blonds, Marli, Jessa and Antoinette.

The older girls sleep in Ivor's *rondavel* – he's gone to Ruwa – while little Antoinette sleeps in Molly's room.

Through the wall, tones converge, growly, flirty, ingratiating, shrill, bellowing, defensive. Laughter, growing more leery, through the long lost night. Voices bloating and collapsing. Music. I thrash around in my bed. Press my pillow over my ear.

A tap on my door. My little sister enters, holding eight year-old Antoinette's hand, her long, white blond hair a tangle around her shoulders, fear twitching their faces.

The priest climbed into our bed between us, Tosh. I grabbed Antoinette and ran.
Maybe he was just drunk and groggy and looking for a place to sleep? I say.
He touched me, Tosh.
I stare at her. Where?
Down there.

The distant drunk voices getting louder through the wall. I drag my wardrobe across the floor and jam it against the door. After making room for Molly and Antoinette in my ship bed, I get in beside them. Want me to read you a story? I flick on the bedside switch.

When Antoinette drifts off, I whisper to Molly, who's only eleven. Adults are not to be trusted. Not even priests. Especially not priests.

Three ways

Salisbury, August. Molly is practising her dance, all coltish legs and wafty hair. *Wiggle wiggle wiggle.* I am sitting on my bed reading, and from time to time, look up to watch her talking gestures. Slap away a whining mozzie. The mozzie sings in a higher pitch. Even the buzz of a mosquito is a communication, Dad would say.

I bite off a piece of sellotape and stick it between my eyebrows. My mum's favourite sister, Auntie Iris, suggested this trick to prevent frowning. I get up and peer close to the mirror to see if it works. Tosha! You're in my way! I'm practising!

Oh my deep and desolate adolescence!

What works

Mum peers round the door to say goodnight. I'm sitting at my dressing table, and the mirror is gazing at me, trying to catch the attention of my swervy eye. Frustrating as a leaky pen, it only behaves when I shut the good one.

Mum, can I go to the movies with Lois this evening?
She comes into the room and stands behind me. *If you promise to stay alert,* she says. *When I was your age, a stranger grabbed me and pushed me up against a wall.*
Oh God, Mum – what happened?
I kneed him in the balls, like this. She raises her knee sharply to demonstrate the gesture.

Shocked, I take in my mother – whom I always perceive as carrying a luminous calm around her – and try to visualise her at seventeen, all wide-eyed effort and arms and legs and flurry.

She looks hard at me in the mirror and the shock of her full attention makes my swervy eye shoot straight. Then, she says, *I ran,* like a greyhound.

No wishbone

If only this air
was a glass ladder,
and you could climb
back
up to the plane.
Or you could
reverse
to when the girl
with the seagull earring
said
don't.
But you can't jump
out of a plane,
then change
your mind,
half-way down.
You wish
at least
you had been paying
attention
when the instructor
was demonstrating
the best way to
land.

Time takes the morning off

Easter, Wedza. While Mum and Dad do a tour of the vineyard, the three of us go to the church in the local village. We arrive just as the women are opening the double doors of the small, white-painted building, surrounded by dirt ground. One comes to greet us, and shakes our hands the Shona way.

There is no clock to dictate things.

The service begins only after the women have swept the dust from the mud-hardened floor. After the men have laid the benches out on the left side of the room. After the women have spread their colourful kikois on the floor on the right side, for themselves and their children. After the American priest, arrived from the city, has lain a cloth and a cross on the altar. After he has sneaked a slug from his hip flask. After he has greeted every member of the gathering congregation with a triple handshake and a chat. After he has asked Molly and Ivor and me – the only time he speaks English and not Shona – to stand up and introduce ourselves, the curious newcomers, the only whites.

Time has a different shape and rhythm here, especially during the hymns, when the women dance, swaying their buttocks, waving their arms. The children too. I feel the impulse to photograph it: the men, wearing black trousers and white shirts, standing still on the left, while their wives and children are all moving bodies and lifted hands, red-green-yellow-blue joy, on the right. And the harmony flows out the open doors, through to the market across the street, where goats wander freely among fruit and vegetable stalls, vendors. And at the end of the mass, out pour the Sunday worshippers, becoming shoppers.

So far

The Chop Chop Shop, Wedza village (an hour south-east of Salisbury). On the verandah, a tailor straddles a stool in front of an old Singer, with some Java print, feeding the green-yellow-coral-orange-white-patterned material past a whirring needle. From within the dim interior, a cascade of coins on to the concrete counter. Dad, getting rid of small change. An overhead sign: *Best hot chips in town, only $4 a bag.*

Someone thumps a crate onto the wooden floor of the store. The metal burglar bars catch a ray of sunlight. A quick, twisty *chongololo* skitters on the red dirt, shuddering slightly over corrugations. An eruption of laughter from two guys leaning against wafer-thin walls. Froth smearing their upper lips. The tailor is treadling with a lever at his feet. A nervy spider weaving a handkerchief web between bars. Because it's always mid-project, I could never kill a spider.

Someone is squatting against a tree in the shadows. *Plinkety plink.* Iron-grey tufts of cotton-ball hair. A *madara.* His fingers are wrapped around a tiny musical instrument. Lines on his face, as deep as cuts. I open the car door wide and swing my feet on to the dirt ground to listen to the twanging melodic sound. Molly has picked up a stone and is drawing a house in the dust.
So far, says the *madara,* we have a family.
He looks over at me.
The father directs traffic through his legs of steel. His tongue is a current. His sight is hooded.
I get out of the car and walk over to the tree, standing within a few feet of him.
The mother walks lightly and swiftly, lit with the gift of the sun.
The *madara* plucks his miniature instrument.
The girl has stories, rising like wings.
He plucks again.
The boy, he says, looking at Ivor – who has got out of the car too and is kicking stones in the dirt – travels his anger into a power.
The *mwana* balances a house of dreams in her head.
More notes.
So far, they have come.
And I suddenly realise he is talking about *us.*
When Dad comes out of the store, I beg him for coins to drop into the storyteller's custard enamel saucer.

Razor edge

Drakensburg Mountains, South Africa. We are sixteen, two years from the end of school, on a geography tour. Abigail decides to deal with my hairy legs. Shakes Johnson's Powder along my calf, glides a razor up. The radio is playing Afrikaans songs. The bus sways around a bend, and there it is, the canyon dropping far below to the right. Remembering our Kerry school tour, my stomach snarls. I grip the seat in front of me and suddenly hear Miss Moore, my French teacher's voice in my head, saying *a little alarm keeps life from becoming too stagnant.*

We stop for a picnic. While the other girls clamber close to the precipice, Lois and I find a flat rock a safe distance away. I run my palms along my unfamiliar, smooth, satiny calves. Lois's curly hair is jammed under a floppy hat. I pull out my journal. Very schooly, says Lois. No such word, I say. Besides, it's my diary.

Miss Ferreira, our geography teacher, is pointing out flowering vines and cycads and cabbage trees growing out of the face of the escarpment below us. I won't go close enough to look. But from where I'm sitting, I can see two little girls walking along a narrow mountain track on the other side of the gorge, a jerry-can of river-water on the taller one's head, her smaller sister trotting beside her. They must have climbed all the way up from the river below. I feel a dart of alarm shoot to my feet.

The bus driver hoots at some scrawny cows, flanks blazed by the sun. In the yard of a small *kraal,* chickens peck at maize kernels despite their proximity to a tethered goat. The hairs on the back of the driver's hands, orange as an orangutan; the way he feeds sections of the steering wheel into one of them, then back, turning the wheel into a snake reversing out of its own skin. *Don't lose your grip!*

The road is mountainous, sheer and narrow. Not a bollard in sight. Barefoot kids roll bicycle wheels with a stick. Churning dust and clammy hands. The ravine, plummeting away below us. *Don't look don't look don't look...*

At the lodge, where we're staying, I linger on the verandah, stare up at the huge sudden darkness. Those two little girls, alone, their heavy vessel, that sheer, narrow track high high up in the Drakensburg. Did they make it safely home?

Not cricket

A boy asks me to dance. A couple of songs later, *Let's go for a little walk, under the moon of love.* We laugh, swing off the dance floor and sail out through the open doors of the sports club into a night lined with silk.

Oops, no moon. Can't see a thing on the cricket field. Here. A hand. His voice. Here. And I am being kissed. Very fast, many times. We move and sway and twirl tongues. It must be the way he pulls me. I trip over something and ram hard against him. Ooh, *you're* ready for it, he grins, yanking at his buckle. I push against him. No, no, please…All the muscles of my body are wrestling in terror. The mind with its innate logic of cause and effect. If it happens, I'll throw myself off a cliff.

Suddenly remember, and do what my mother taught me. When he crouches and clutches and groans, I burst through the horrors, sprinting back through the black to the clubhouse. The sound of my heartbeat is all I can hear.

Wingtip to wingtip

Rude slash of passing cars, slapping wipers. Green army lorries vibrating the road, wheels rumbling. Wet earth and steaming tar. I fast-pedal past workers, still in their overalls, hunched over handlebars. Soaked by the time I reach Lois's. Her mother opens the door. A baking apron, floury hands.

Lo and I sprawl on the living room floor, listening to Fleetwood Mac: *Thunder only happens when it's raining.*

Lois is my lightning rod.

Up the flagstone steps to the mezzanine, and on up more stairs. Lois's room is as cool as pearls. Pasted on the walls, quotes from Kahlil Gibran's *The Prophet* and Omar Khayyam's *The Rubiyat*. On her balcony, I gaze into the face of a very tall sunflower, which has popped its head over the railing, rustling against it like the brush of a silk dress.

Lois has lots of books. You're so lucky, I say to her wistfully.

Three weeks later, she hands me a birthday present. *Jonathan Livingstone Seagull,* by Richard Bach. I open a random page and read: *Your whole body, from wingtip to wingtip, is nothing more than your thought.* Then turn to the flyleaf, where she's scribbled a message: *Stay forever young.* I settle down to read by the pool. With each page, a shutter opens in my mind, and then another and then another.

Cul-de-sac

Club Tomorrow, Salisbury, 1ˢᵗ April. For weeks, Josh and Matt, from Oriel Boys', have been calling over, teaching me songs from Dylan and Young, but mostly drinking with my Dad.

Josh is white-blond, with a wide, crescent moon smile and jutting ears, and when he laughs, I feel something pass from his body to mine. His aftershave is a pull too, like his tallness, broad shoulders, fluidity, as we swing and flounce and tip and spin. An intimacy magnetises during a slow song. *If you leave me now.* His tongue thwacks into my mouth as though it were a clumsy driver careening into a *cul-de-sac.* This is our shared birthday celebration, his, two days before mine; we're both seventeen, and Matt, his wing man, is always nearby; dark and intense and taciturn.

As Josh is fetching the car, Matt, too, introduces his tongue to mine. I pull away. First Barra-and-Jamie, now Josh-and-Matt. As though nothing ever happens just once. Now what? But now nothing. Neither of them asks me out again. Some kind of friends' pact? Another ruffly echo.

More wounding than a bullet

On TV every night, on the radio, in newspapers, the war grows. Curfews. Call-ups. Bag searches in department stores. Camouflage uniforms everywhere, pounding with male energy. People with missing limbs. Everywhere you look, *damage done.*

Gossip eventually trickles through the school about Sebastian, Abigail's brother, who came home on R&R. Sat down to dinner with the family.

When she finally tells us, I'm a gecko on the wall, seeing and hearing it all:
You're very quiet, love. His mother. Is everything alright, Seb? In general?
Her only son looking at her for a long moment before speaking. Sebastian, with his long, angular body, blond hair which used to coil into his neck, before he had to shave it off when he received his call-up papers.
I have something to tell you, he says. Don't know how you'll take it.
Son. His father, gruff. We understand.
Do you?
I imagine him trying to find the words to tell them, bravely, finally, how he'd worked out what had been wrong all these years.
I'm just going to say it straight out. I'm gay.
Jesus Christ, his father spluttering. I thought you were going to say you'd killed some *terrs.* Not, not – this. *Jesus.* You're no son of mine.
Getting up and storming off.
His mother, looking at him in horror and bursting into tears.
The wild Abigail, who shaved my legs on the bus, staring into her lap, unable even to make eye contact.
Excuse me, Seb saying quietly, leaving the table. Seeking refuge in the garage.

The tentacles of taboo and prejudice winding through the car window, strangling all his future out of him.

To name a place is to manifest it

Dry, crackling, yellow *vlei*, east and west of us. Dad turns on the radio. Joy Cameron-Dow is giving the road report. *On the route from Salisbury North towards Kariba, road shoulders are being tarred…* Dad consistently reminds me about Ireland's endless rawky dampness. *Darwendale… Salisbury to Darwin…Gatuma the Que Que Road…*the cold so cold it feels alive, stabbing legs and cheeks, pinching fingers and toes, biting your teeth at the root. *Gwelo…Bulawayo…Victoria Falls…Beitbridge…*The summer wind so sharp and brisk, it strips the clouds into ribbons, erases the pale heat of a weak sun. *Marandellas…Headlands…Rusape…Inyazura.*

But Joy Cameron-Dow's blend of colonial and RP has me missing the lilt of Irish accents. Those weathers that would weave in and out endlessly, full of mystical, lit-up surprises. Those slow autumn days with misty beginnings. Maybe what I'm homesick for most is that sack of familiarity that I had managed to fill: expressions, soft weather, green world, the ocean, winding roads and the hills. The feeling of safety. *West Nicholson…Plumtree…Eastern Inyanga… Ruwa, Melfort, Bromley…*

Limerick, I think: *Galway, Dingle, Westport, Rutland, Gortahork, Letterkenny, Rathmullan, Derry, Dublin, Kerry, Wicklow, Cork.* Sometimes feel as though my *real* life is going on thousands of miles across the water, without me, while I'm on pause here.

5.

Chasers

Ok, Mum and Dad say finally. We'll send you home for the holidays.

*

Letterkenny, summer. Uncle Brennan nods Freya and me into his venue, though we're underage. Inside, we meet up with her older sister Grace, our cousin Ruari and two of his friends, Liam and Richard. The music is bright strokes of colour, dancing reds and yellows, blues and greens. And the northerners, arrived by the busload, wear out the dance-floor with The Boys are Back in Town, the drinking, the joyousness, then standing still, hand-to-heart, for the anthem. The mobile chipper outside in the car park, cheerfully mobbed at 2am. Afterwards, Ruari's suggestion: How about we all go to the island?

And he hot-wires a pick-up, and off we go, away from the lights of Letterkenny, out past the cemetery. Everyone, except me, is scuttered, four up front, two in the open back. The road flanked by the rugged Errigal slopes. Once past the valleys, we spy turf piled at the roadside. Skid to a halt, tumble in clod after clod, until we spot the furious farmer and his sons giving chase. Congested hysterics. I feel wicked, like a grave-robber. For twenty long miles, the farmer's lights in the rear view, until at last, he veers off. We breathe at the sight of the open sea. The island, a bone bulging from the water's skin. A boat waiting.

*

In my uncle's cottage, a freezer filled with loaves. Chocolate digestives, tinned sardines, Barry's tea, brown sugar, powdered milk. Freya, Grace and I get busy, dropping frozen slices into the toaster. Ruari squats at the fireplace, until the turf fire crackles. We pull up, guilty and warm. Liam unscrews a half jack. Richard puts on Horslips. *I try to chase trouble but it's chasing me.* I begin to pick at one of the moons of candle wax left on the table from a previous visit. In the reflection of the un-curtained window, I see my lumberjack shirt, rolled up jeans. It's like watching someone else, some tomboy who takes off with dangerous lads.

Ruari finds a pack of cards, shuffles, deals. Liam taps out a cigarette. Freya takes a slug, passes the half-jack to Grace. Smoke barrels around the small room; alcohol fumes topple towards me like an upended chair. Think I'll go outside for a bit, I say.

The climbing drizzle, how soft. Lit cottages on the nearby island. Below the tussocky shelf, white sand slopes steeply to the black water. From behind, hands clasp my waist. We go toppling down the small incline.

Complicated rain

Iniccoo Island, Donegal. The night rain slips between his warm neck and collar. We are breathing the same breath. Explosion through my cells. Wet eyelids and cheeks. Inside our closed eyes for hours, or maybe minutes, not speaking at all, except with our hands, our mouths. My heart like apples thundering onto a slate roof. Time is a saltwater cave winding complicatedly through my body, looping all my selves and my memories into a single cubic structure. There is no correlation for this feeling. It's a first. Every atom, every hair, every portion of my skin knows this moment will hold everything I know of myself hereafter.

The cloaking drizzle lopes away, exposing us to each other. Hand in hand, still silent, we head back.

Inside, the rest are still playing poker, still smoking, drinking. A laundry basket full of oddities. I find a kimono. Of our extended absence, no mention.

Patterns

Below,
a blur of granite,
loud as Georgia
O'Keeffe's
giant petals.
Spiky greens
stabbed
into the dirt,
and you're
remembering –
what?
This is a first.
And the sound...
like...like what?
Do we always
seek correlation,
even as we are
shuddering
closer
to the unknown?

In the gap before doom

Iniscoo Island, Donegal. That there's a fine size, says Ruari, as I pull the wild creature from the agitated water. Thrashing the light, droplets plopping. I can feel the charge of its life energy screaming up the line to my hand. He takes the rod from me, and I get my two hands around the cool muscle of its whip-energy. About ten pound weight, says Ruari. The king of fish.

Almost home, after the perilous odyssey from the Norwegian Sea, the salmon flips frantically, exposing its pale stomach. Fire in its mouth, flames in its fins, smouldering coals in the flip of its body. A wind sound, like an ambulance siren, coming straight at me. The air drowning him. *Sacrilege.* (Mum's word.) *The salmon of knowledge.* All the tragic stories from around here, drowned cottages and sailors and runaway girls and returning ghost soldiers, their wails like church bells overlapping with wind, the white hiss of waves, and *quick,* I shout, *throw it back*! And Ruari smiles, unhooks and releases it. The fish flashes once in the open grey field of the water, then vanishes. He's away on over, points Ruari. He can move, hi?

And I know both the fish and I have just wriggled away from doom.

Bailing out the sea

Motor snarling. Ocean and rain storming, whirling manes anti-clockwise, like an obstreperous sea beast. Shit! shouts Richard. As we bear down along the wave, I squeeze tight. Wallows between swells and tipping precariously, and water sloshing and filling, and us bailing. You alright back there? Can't hear each other shouting. Pitch and slam and hands scrabbling like a pair of frightened birds, another wave hurling over our jittery laughter. We stagger up again, my weight pressing down on a beach bag containing my drenched clothes, Ruari, up front, spectral in a wet-suit. From under a shabby blanket, I feel a hand take hold of mine, casting an octopus shadow across my thoughts. Who is close enough to be my hand holder? Still, it's a comfort in the face of a mighty wave, sudden dip, the gale flinging us again.

We missed the radio warnings.

Roaring draught in my ears, other sounds, faraway-muffled. A lurch almost sucking us into the sea. Exertion of the boat tilting dementedly, long moan of a foghorn. Up the side of another wave, wait for the plummet. The record player glides into the water. Sea snorting, tall as a glass ladder. *Oh god, we're going*, gripping a leg as we spear, and albums and towels, and the hours tipping over. Until at last, there's the pier.

Edges and guardian angels

Burton Port, Donegal. We load the boat into the pickup. All of us pile into the front seat, except for Liam who takes shelter under the umbrella of the vessel.

Ruari pulls over to buy cigarettes, and the front tyre slips and skids down into a culvert. Fuck, he mutters before jumping out and heading in to the shop. Freya and I are in paroxysms. He seems to have forgotten he's wearing a wetsuit. A Garda car has pulled up across the road. Shite, murmurs Richard. We're tipped at an angle. Our driver without a licence. The turf we robbed on our way here. Boat possibly stolen too. Ruari strolls out of the shop and crosses directly over to the Garda car. Leans his elbow on the roof. I try to read his gesticulations, work out which way the conversation is going. They get out and help us to lift the pick up out of the ditch. Thanks lads, he calls out. Waves as we drive by.

Jesus and holy Mary, breathes Grace, what did you say to them? Ruari's beautiful, wicked grin, like Marilyn's skirt flying up over the vent. Ah you know. Bit of a chat about the weather.

This out-smarter of gales and guards. He lifts his chin, twitch of lips, so red I think of tomatoes. Freckles, a pepper spray. Voltage and glitter of stars.

*

Back at Covehill, I tiptoe up the stairs. Sit on the very edge of the loo seat, so my pee hits the side. Two fingers cross my lips. Hands along humming thighs, across pinkly-tipped breasts, flat belly. Alive.

6.

Dog tags and heat

Airport, Salisbury, Rhodesia. Straddling a suitcase, using my book as a fan. My body's got used to Irish temperatures, and my pulse is a horse trotting inside my skin in this heat. Mum smiles apologies as they pull up directly in front of the Arrivals entrance, an hour late. Their new Merc, white as the streaming, seductive sun.

A plane floats across the impossibly blue sky, its vapour trail like a water-skier's wake. Ahead of us, a military truck packed with new recruits.

At the lights, fragments of their conversation click and skit, like shrapnel. *Howzit bru...hey china...You too, hey...* the accents so blunt, after Donegal lilts. Head out the window to escape the reek of my parents' smoke, I crane to see if there's anybody I recognise but the lorry veers into Cranbourne barracks, insults belching from its exhaust.

Flash on what I've left: those fluent skies, otherworldly fog; the mobile sea.

What kind of somebody

Tea on the lawn at Lois's, she and I on one side of the tray, her older sister Mara and her friends sprawled out – mad long hair, ragged jeans, brown skin – on the other. No one is pouring. Wonder if I should do the honours. These whites, shopping, eating out, going to the theatre. It's like there's no war going on at all, smoulders Ish. Ignoring the fact that their white privilege is predicated on the exploitation of others, says Abs.
They are both Indian, the first I've met.

All is rotten in our sweet state of Denmark, says Mara, a surprisingly low voice for someone so petite, huge dark eyes, curly dark hair, flamboyant gestures.
I don't even know any blacks, I say. Well, except for our domestic workers, and my Dad's manager in Wedza. Strange, isn't it, considering there's a population of eight or nine million, that our worlds barely collide, except at the garage, or in shops.

*

Later, writing in bed, guilt creeps over me like a shadow slowly cast by a grey cathedral. Abs is right. It all feels so blurred, beyond the bubble of my sunlit, privileged life. Mum's right too. I *am* self-centred. How often do I think of what it must be like to be black in this country? My thoughts drift to young black boys, just like the boys I know, fresh from Oriel. I try to imagine them right now, in the faraway bush of soundless deaths, crawling on their bellies, creeping and slithering, waiting in ambush, flies buzzing, the bush eating itself, dark pushing in from the edges of sky. The boys' eyes peeled for a tremble of leaves, AK47 by their sides, believing that what they are doing is morally justified.

Hatching and skinning

12 Pemray Drive. Cheep cheep from the garage. Ivor has spent his saved pocket money on day-old chicks. Dad told him it's never too early to go into business. Unfortunately, now he's been expelled from Oriel for 'insubordination' and Dad has decided that he should switch to Plumtree, a hard-core boarding school in the bush, near the Botswana border, where teachers have rifles and the boys learn to shoot. So Ivor's asked Mum to feed his chicks while he's away, and he's promised to split his profits with her.

*

Mushroom hearts opening. I watch my mother peel the velvety skins. Mum, did you know that domestic staff can't have their wives living with them, unless they also have work?

The pad of her thumb under the hem of a frilled mushroom, she looks up at me, then out the window towards the double garage. Hmmm. You've given me an idea. She chops the denuded mushroom head into the pan.

At the table, she shares her idea with Dad, who has just won a contract to supply salt for the army. Dad consults Moses.

*

A week later, Dad has employed ten wives of the domestic workers in our neighbourhood. They sit at trestle tables in our double garage – a makeshift factory – scooping salt and stapling sachets to be added to the soldiers' ration packs. As the women have jobs now, they are legally allowed to be in the northern suburbs and to stay with their husbands. And Dad doesn't have the problem of having to arrange accommodation for them.

*

Our day starts with the sounds of dozens of chicks, a percussion to the women's harmony. They sing often throughout each day. Meanwhile, far away, in Ivor's new school, boys are flogged daily. In his weekly letters to me, Ivor says they are practically skinning him alive.

Evolving a theory of the smell of my future boyfriend

A wind edges around the willow, within which I'm idling away the afternoon. In here, it's almost as dim as a room with drawn green curtains. Drifting aroma of soil and chlorophyll and roots. The bodyguard leaves decline entry to my sanctuary, and the wind sulks off. I watch a stork landing on the squelchy, recently rained-on lawn. Black wings, white front, long narrow beak, angular jolting movements. It circles the garden, then drifts off. Siesta silence.

Sitting in this green basket, I open my journal.

I want my kindred other to be spinnerets and wing bars and tail feathers of boy. I want sizzles before dark. I want to feel like a bird riding a thermal when I'm with him.

And if soil and chlorophyll and roots are earth-smell, then boy will be essence of salt spray and weather.

Codes and cocoons

Radio on. Sally Donaldson with the Forces' Requests. '"For Noah in the RAR: what's the matter with your right hand? Lay off the little brown bottles...love from Lucy." And here's another one: "Pete, in C squadron, we're all missing you stacks. Love and kisses from Mum and the kids." And now over to John Edmond...'

Moses is refreshing a salad with some wooden spoons. Sunlight is tapping its fingers against the French doors. It's almost combustibly bright. The programme ends with the familiar song: 'We'll keep them north of the Zambezi 'til that river's running dry...' My face goes hot. Discreet as a breeze that takes its leave at just the right moment, Moses finishes the salad, lifts Dad's shoes from the scullery and takes them out to the *stoep* to polish them.

Through the open kitchen window, the salt women's voices, singing in a secret language. I think of coded Irish ballads, like *Four Green Fields*. Maybe Moses leaves the radio on as camouflage.

I take my unfinished fruit from the fridge and walk out of the kitchen, without saying anything. The best spies are probably those polishing the silverware and catching their reflections in a knife. Except, Moses is a Malawian, like Black was. Mum and Dad figure immigrants are safer.

Sit on the pool steps with my mango. The slurp and suck as I try to control the juice. My mother's voice in the distance. Can't hear the words, but I know it's her. The scritch-scratch of Fred's long claws ticking on the concrete slabs of the patio. I run my sticky fingers through the water.

Silver words are jumping

14 February. Jack, the boy from the farm in Raffingora where we had our first Christmas, the boy whose hand was smashed by a bicycle crash into a lorry, has been visiting our house a lot lately. Flirting with me.

And today, a poem on my pillow, with a single red rose. Molly gets twelve valentines. But I've never had one. For hours, I devote my gaze to his forward-slanted, exuberant writing that suggests a headlong scramble for some exit. Recite the words over and over. Potent as a kiss.

the voice of your eyes...

Ohmyohmy, the sky, the sun, the happy golden world. I stand on the passenger seat of Jack's red Alfa Romeo, and wriggle the upper half of my body through the sun-roof, bare arms outstretched. *This is it,* I sing along to Melba Moore, at the top of my voice.

Pedestrians wave as they saunter alongside the botanical gardens. I love the poem! I scream down to him from the sunroof. Did you write it? Jack shouts back up to me: No, I opened a book in the jacks at a friend's house, and jotted down the words. It's written by someone called e.e. cummings. Thought you'd like it.

Oh. Not Jack's words. Still. He chose it. And wrote it down, my first valentine gift. And he's all Irish, blood and sinew. We tear round a bend and he pulls over, jumps out to rescue a chameleon from the middle of the road. I rush over to catch the miraculous *crypsis metamorphosis*. All along the swift-changing skin and prehensile tail, its colours mute to the grey of the road. As Jack lifts the creature to show me, its bulbous eyes swivel to mine. He lays it safely in foliage away from the road. The gesture sweeps the whole shoddy war into a far away corner.

Arms like a bird's wings

A discus of light,
the earth's
hemisphere
encircled
by this perilous
blue,
fragile as confetti.
You are fighting
with your pocket-voice.
Bet Fynn
isn't feeling
these eruptions
of terror.
Bet he's a bird,
riding a thermal.

Hatred is a weapon

May. They say the SAS aim to dismantle you, strip you down until you are nothing but a shell, then build you up again, into a fighting machine. About 90% of applicants fail. To my amazement and dismay, Jack gets in. Then signs up as a regular. For three years?? Why? I ask him, throwing my arms up, dispersing an armful of freedom, safety, sanity. He was obviously expecting a different response. Should I congratulate him on his achievement, even though the SAS is the riskiest unit in the army?

The way he looks at me is a game of chess. My father never thought I'd amount to anything, he says. This'll show him.

Side-step

June. Jack has asked his friend Benjamin to look after me while he's in the bush. Quiet, blond, chivalrous, safe. The kind you wouldn't normally notice. He takes me to *Saturday Night Fever.* Later, we get coffee at Europa and, after banter, ease around to the looming black mouth of the war.

Any day now, he says glumly.
Would you consider taking the gap? I whisper low and fast, glancing around at the Italian men in their rolled up shirts, sitting at a table near the counter.
Course not. He looks at me, surprised.
Why not?
Because I wouldn't do that to my parents. Leave the country, while their friends' sons are fighting and dying to protect our way of life. Besides, I believe in the cause. The gooks are being backed by the commies, you know.
He fiddles with a red paper serviette. Imagine living in a communist state.
Imagine being second class citizens, I counter, unable to vote or even choose where to live in your own country. They're fighting for their freedom, for democracy, I say. And if it's communist countries who are willing to support them, well I guess they'll take the help no matter who's offering.
He is staring at me.
The last sip of my coffee is lukewarm, intensely sweet from a leftover bit of undissolved sugar cube. I'm being reckless, speaking like this in public, even though my voice is low.
You do know, he says slowly, eyes drilling in to mine, that they use narcotics to brainwash kids into becoming terrorists? They use torture tactics such as hacking off a hand if a civilian refuses to give information...?
A physical sensation travels through my body. My pulse drums in my ears. The saliva in my mouth dries up. My chest tightens against my lungs. I scan the room again, to see if anyone's within earshot.
Jack didn't tell me you were...
Quick as a hiccup, I dissemble.
Oh never mind. Just feels horrible that you guys have no choice in this. I mean, what are the options of war? Kill, or be killed.
I wince at him and he shrugs.
C'est la guerre.

Slash

12, Pemray Drive, Salisbury. The communiqué comes on at 8pm: 'The Security Forces regret to announce …' We hold our every-night breath for the downpour of names.

I follow Dad and Robert out to the bar on the patio, slide onto a bar stool and rest my chin in my palms. Quick question for you, Dad. Go on then. What do you think the outcome of the war is going to be?
Robert – bombastic, blunt, loyal, good-humoured – laughs heartily, so we laugh too.
Oh, I'm looking forward to your *quick* answer, Seán.
We share a sidelong glance. Grin. My father will never take a short cut if there is a longer, twistier route available.
Glad you're showing an interest in the situation, Itosha. Dad takes a preparatory sip of his drink.
In an ideal world, there would be a gradual transition to black rule, with Smith directing things for the first term. But sadly, that won't be tolerated, either by the blacks or the Brits.
The glass shelf on the wall blurs behind the drift of unremitting smoke from their cigarettes. With each breath, a streamy feather of nicotine assaults my nostrils.
But do you think the war will end soon? And the blacks will get the vote?
Well, we have the strategy, skills and machinery, but they have the numbers, the support and, let's face it, the will.

A gesture of drizzle on the wind. Scrape of chill across my bare shoulders. Still in my spaghetti-strapped summer dress, I cast about for my cardigan.
Itosha, you asked me a question. Do I have your attention?
His eyes, two lima beans, bore into mine. Corralled, prodded, easier to nod.
I can't understand how Smith ever imagined that, without outside political support, 200 000 white Rhodesians could contain the passions of eight million or so Africans, who are already inspired by all the decolonised states to the north of us. Britain has washed her hands of this country. Frankly, I don't think they have any more energy. It would be wise to settle this politically rather than wait for the inevitable. So, to answer your question, yes. One way or the other, it's only a matter of time. But if The Talks don't result in an agreement soon, it'll turn into a bloodbath.

*

Soap my legs, slide my father's razor firmly from ankle to knee. A small bleat of shock. The slash along my shin bone. Red Sea.

Invisibles

*Repteens class, Reps Theatre, Salisbury. Close your eyes and fall backwards...*Turns out I have trust issues. Can't fall backwards into Lois's waiting arms. Instead of being hurt, my kind best friend is intrigued about excavating the complexities that cause such distrust. But that's a conversation I can't even begin.

We're cooling off on the patio with a Coke, after our drama class.

I got my call-up papers, says Abs, who does lighting for the Repteeners. Exotically brown against his white t-shirt, he is tipping his chair back against a huge white urn filled with wild red roses.

But I'm not going. Why should we fight for the whites when they treat us Indians like second-class citizens too? I'm going to be a conscientious objector.

Spectacles. Smart. Blunt.

But that means you'll go to prison. Why not just leave? I ask.

He drops his seat forward again, leans his elbows on his knees, clasping his hands, and looks at me. You take the gap and you're branded a yellow coward, vilified for trying to save your own skin.

It's not cowardice, it's sanity, I say.

Lois's brother, who is standing near the door as though ready to exit any moment, smiles at me. Light catches the edges of his Afro, like a halo.

I won't take the gap, but I'm certainly not fighting either, continues Abs. I mean, the numbers alone...The more objectors, the sooner the war stops.

*

I scrutinise the papers and never come across any mention of conscientious objectors. They are the invisibles. If you don't see them, they don't exist. Just like those trying to scrape out a hazardous living on those faraway, barren tracts of land called TTLs – tribal trust lands.

One day, Abs isn't at Repteens anymore; he's been jailed.

Close your eyes and fall backwards...into the dark abyss.

Drive

I am reading *Wuthering Heights*. All the voices in the room disappear. I am swept away from the ticking and twitching, into the wild moor of Emily Brontë's mind. But Ivor's insistence eventually becomes a drone in my ear. I come home for the holidays and you can't even give me an hour of your precious time? Subliminally, I sense his haywire mood, the way you can tell on a flight, even with your eyes closed, that the plane is banking. To leave off reading feels like tearing myself away from my very own Heathcliff. But I lower my book. Ok. Let's drive.

Driving is our secret, subversive act.

Dad refuses to teach me, after the first attempt. I saw a dog accosting a tree, about a hundred metres ahead. Pulse screeching with adrenalin, I let go of the steering wheel as though it was burning me. Jesus Christ, Dad yelled, lunging across me. That's it! I'm not doing this again. My nerves are wrecked.

Mum and Dad are out in the Mercedes. Ivor hot-wires Mum's Austin Cambridge. As it starts up, all the needles leap. He gestures me into the driver's seat. Once you can handle the clutch, it's easy, he says. I ease slowly out of Pemray Drive, past all the walled properties with their elegant screens of trees, turn right up North Road, left into Dulwich, and right onto Arcturus, towards Lois's house. The butterflies shuffle and settle.

I was in the Mercedes once, when I was fourteen, Ivor says. The car broke down halfway up Ridgeway North. Next minute this elderly man stops and goes, 'What seems to be the trouble?' And he's glancing around for an adult. Don't think my voice had broken!
I'm laughing. What did you say?
Oh, told him I thought it was on empty. I can run you to the station if you like, says the guy. Do you have a canister? There was one in the boot. But I had no money. So he goes I think I can stretch to a fiver to get you home. Cheers, I say. Hope I can do the same for you one day.

Ivor's stories drive me into a natural, bending my elbow out of the window, flying through the suburbs, past the snarl of buses. With my brother so relaxed in the passenger seat, I could drive through the night, all the way to Mozambique.

Cross my Heart

October. Nature is my goddess, Lois declares. Not some patriarchal god. That's just some invention by men in power, to keep women and blacks subjugated and endorse their call to war. I vehemently object, of course, maybe by default. The nuns have drummed doubt out of me.

But no one has ever told me that trinities and virgin mothers and resurrections are known in faiths other than Christianity.

Our break-time debate spills into the next class.
Do share, Lois, calls Miss Moore, green eyes lively, chalk poised. And for the rest of the class, our discussion is all about religion.

It is only as we are leaving the room that I notice, for the first time, light catching on a gold cross dangling from a thin chain around Miss Moore's neck.

*

As I am leaning to whisper something to Lois during class, Miss Moore spins around from the board and fires her stick of chalk in my direction. My left hand flies out, like a frog's tongue catching a fly, and seizes the chalk. She laughs.

Nice catch, Tosh. Now stop talking and read out your Pagnol translation.
Um, I didn't do it, Miss.
And why not?

She seems to find my excuse entertaining. There and then, she brings me next door, to Mrs Smith, our English teacher, to whom I have to repeat it in front of her Form 2 class. The storm was so terrifying yesterday, I thought the world was going to end, and I didn't want to spend my last day on earth doing homework. The girls snigger.

Miss Moore lets me get away with it because she doesn't really believe in homework anyway. After the bell goes, as we are all cramming out through the door, she calls me back.
Incidentally, what did you do with your last day on earth?

Wrote a poem, I tell her, called *The Last Day*.
Really?
Promise.
Oh I have to see that, she says. Bring it in tomorrow.

The porousness of war

A flurry of birds erupting from a tree, like a small gang of black bullets shooting into the sky. Avocados dropping like bombs from the tree by the kitchen

*

Simeon, the gardener, pushes a mower that fountains grass shards and diesel fumes. Later he sets the sprinklers. *Kitchaah, kitchaah, kitchaah,* then *ti-ti-ti-ti-ti* as they flip back to start again. Simeon has one of those calm, implacable faces that have been walled up. I think of Black and the *chongololo* playing dead. *That is what he does to keep safe.*

Or maybe it's so that none of the humiliations of servitude enter the quiet of his inner sanctuary.

*

And mines are laid in the bush and borders are crossed and villages raided, but in the city, glasses are filled nightly with lemon and ice, and sundowners come with canapés.

And while lorries carry off youths, urban dogs growl only at shadows, and that scuttle is just a gecko skittering across waxy leaves in a flower bed. *We are safe in the northern suburbs,* Dad reminds us. The news says what it must and no more. And we cycle to school in our freshly starched uniforms, cinched at the waist with a belt. And if we hear the sound of a gunshot, it's only the backfire of a car, and our laughing untwists with a high glassy note of relief. And every night it's a few drinks too many, and the same old stories rise to the surface, like worms after rain.

War flowers

November. Jack brings a fellow SAS solider over to the house. Bruce recently lost a leg to a landmine. After a few stiff drinks, he starts doing party tricks with his prosthesis. Twists the foot backwards then asks Molly to dance. Jack enthusiastically pushes chairs out of the way. Barry laughs at her downward-glancing shock. Cackles from everyone, and Bruce grins too.

I think of what Jack said about phantom pain, and touch my own leg. Is Bruce relieved that the randomness of his body's flung trajectory spared his life? Does he feel lucky? I suspect not. Somewhere in his tone, I can detect a buried miasma of futile rage. Camouflaged grieving.

How would I feel, really? Our minds are one thing, but what lashes us to life if not our bodies?

So, our new normal is this endless presence of soldiers, swarming into our house like the profusion of roses clambering over our wall. Molly calls them *war* flowers.

Minding

Molly's friend Zoë, sitting at our table, startled by our regular eruptions of mirth or just-as-swift outbursts. Itosha! as I lunge and jab my knife into a butter curl. Oops. Sorry. Ivor pats his belly. Full. Molly: Couldn't eat another bite. Me – gazing at the apple pie – Me neither. Dad: I'll have a piece. Me: Me too.

I know Mum – with a new hairdo, waved like a twenties movie star – is thinking about the cig she will have after everyone leaves the table.

Zoë is tawny-skinned, prematurely shapely, with a chestnut afro, eyes glowing like candles, tiny, an only child. I never have dinner with my parents, she says.
That's a pity. Dad looks at her. Families need to spend time together to learn the art of conversation. Because that's what it is – an art, not a whim. And it's an art a family learns at the table.
Yup, says Ivor. First lesson, Zoë: a good conversation is like a miniskirt. Short enough to retain interest, long enough to cover the subject.
He cracks up, and we laugh at his own self-amusement.
That was a cracker joke from last Christmas, wasn't it, says Molly.
If you ever end up in solitary confinement, Ivor, I grin, you'll have no problem entertaining yourself.
I wish I was part of this family, says Zoë, looping her stare from one of us to the next, as though seeing a ribbon that connects each of us.
Stay for the week, says Molly. Stay forever! Can she Dad?

Zoë looks down at her lap. Molly has already told us that her new step-father beats her for the slightest infringement, such as leaving her squash racquet on the bed. Her French mum, pretending she's still thirty, is not dealing well with her daughter's prematurely shapely body. Plum grows from Zoë's collar to her forehead.
Would you mind if I stayed a few days?
We would, says Dad.
Pinter pause.
We would mind you.

See-saw

Robert is got up as a nun. Mum, in camouflage, clambers under his skirts; Eleanor, dressed in full military uniform, is attempting to interrogate Robert, while Mum peeps from under his petticoat. Dad does a Dave Allen impression with a tumbler of whiskey, the top of his left forefinger hidden. Marlie, Jessa, Antoinette and I cheer enthusiastically. The three Jane Blonds have grown taller and skinnier and blonder with each year.

*

Everyone has just been hooting after Mum's pithy remark. We can always rely on your one-a-day, darling, Dad declares magnanimously, lusciously kissing her. Mum smiles secretly, folding her cleverness away under bright-coloured wings. Robert leans close to me, and I catch his brandy-whiff. If Seán dies before me, I'm going to divorce Eleanor and marry your mother. Fond of him, I laugh uneasily despite a suspicion that he means it. His bald head, ape-hairy arms and chest. His combustive guffawing that always induces a laugh of my own. And yet, the things he says disturb me. All *munts* look the same, he announces cheerfully. Unless you know them, it's impossible to tell them apart. Well, I retort, from their point of view, we probably all look the same too.

*

The crash and the scream has me rushing out to the patio in my nightie. A flung barstool lies two inches from my mum. A smashed glass on the floor. Robert's arm curls protectively around her shoulders. What happened? No one speaks. A shrill tension, like the whine of a saturated, glittery bee. Robert ushers Mum through the French doors into the house, and Eleanor follows them. Dad slumps back into his seat behind the bar, diminished as a used up candle. His default position when there's no one left to perform to. Sometimes I want to tear him open, check to see if there's anything real and true and heartfelt in there.
I lift the whiskey bottle.
Put that down, he barks mutinously at me.
I twist off the cap and spill the entire contents on to the lawn.
Whiskey makes you aggressive, Dad. No more.
My father's stare is a black tank bearing down on me.
I scram back to bed.

Trap

Why is Jack here? He looks at me and says just one word. *Benjamin.* My legs go jelly and I drop to the floor.

*

A sun shower – monkey's wedding – at the gravesite. Had Benjamin begun to battle with the 'official' truths versus the visible facts? I think of what I said to him during our last conversation – *kill or be killed.* Pointing out all the propaganda about 'fighting against communism', hardening, spreading, becoming more entrenched, when the real reason for this war is to hold on to white power, pure and simple. Oh God. Did I trip him into doubt? Benjamin was one of the good hearts. Feel myself moving inexorably towards a bulky black thought: was it my fault?

*

Jack parks beneath a tree. Come on, Tosh. It would mean a lot to his parents, to hear you say lovely things about their son, Jack pleads. No! A tumultuous bird is pressing its wings against my chest, pushing, pushing. I can't, I repeat, just can't face them. Yank my arm away when Jack tries to coax me, yet again, out of the car. He stomps off without me.

In front of me, a last raindrop aches slowly from a drooping leaf. The words I should be saying to his parents. *He never allowed me to pay for dinner, drinks, movies. He was always a gentleman. Gentle, in fact, is the word that would define him for me.* Bang my head against the dashboard. Use up my dress as a box of handkerchiefs. Shift it, so the snot-covered bit doesn't rest wetly against my legs. Haul out my notebook and write *coward* over and over. I circle the 'war'. And I know what he'd say. *C'est la guerre.* Maybe he thought this was more honourable, more of a statement, than taking the gap. What a trap. At least this way he had control over the time and place: he chose the beautiful botanical gardens, raindrops on leaves glowing like starlight beside him.

The bird pushes harder, deeper, into my muscles and organs, creating a heaviness that my bones can barely tolerate. Too heavy for me to leave the car and go and speak to his parents, though I'm full of shame at not being brave enough even to do this. I begin to write a letter to them, which I'll leave in their letterbox. A wafer-thin mongrel dog trots along the roadside, past the car, panting and agitated. The kind you wouldn't normally notice. His eyes, slate black, turn in my direction.

Mutations

This wind,
scything
through
your parachute
as though
reaping a field,
your body,
a chair
rocking
in it.
Only,
no edges.
just you
in the middle
of all
this
height.

Birds and bottles

12, Pemray Drive, Salisbury. New Year's Eve. On the piano top, a large silver platter of smoked salmon and capers on fingers of brown bread. Everyone is holding crystal tumblers of spirits. Some people are outside, looking up at the star-filled sky, or at the bar, but most have gathered around the piano. Like an aristocrat, Dad requires an entourage. The night is sultry, and the French doors are ajar.

Molly's had her hair cropped. Jack laughs. Hey, Bottle Top. When he sees she's miserable, he strokes her new smooth helmet. Honestly, it looks great, he says, sliding an arm across her shoulder. In fact, call me when you're eighteen. She blurts a shy laugh, and flicks a glance at me. I give her a wink.

Even when Dad has been drinking brandy by the ocean, his fingers touch ivory and ebony like feathers landing on a pillow. Standing next to him, I offer a challenge. Bet you a bottle of Napoleon brandy that you can't compose a piece of music right now. Despite the slack mouth, the drink-bleared eyes, he places his pliant fingers on the keys, goes into a kind of trance, tinkles up and down between the white notes and the black, playing a melody with a haunting delicacy, building up to a soaring ache that reminds me of that day in Dingle, when I was alone on the beach with the seagull.

There you go. *Itosha's Theme.* Jack and I look at each other.

Delta Echo Alpha Romeo

Jack pops the top of my Coke bottle and fizzles it over ice cubes into a long tumbler. A slice of lemon. I feel a rush of tenderness at that extra gesture. *Dear boy.*

He swigs his beer direct from the chilled bottle. I am lying by the pool at his place, the sun poised to bestow golden tans. He sprawls beside me, drops a hand in the water, lays a cool wet palm on on my sun-heated calf. I lift my glass. A kick of dark sugar-rush.

The phone blatters from the hallway. Damn, he says. Pulls himself up and goes inside.

His voice carries in the still air. Sharp-sharp, bru.

Standing in the doorway, he waits till I look up. I've gotta leave. They only gave me a couple of days for the funeral.

I drop my glass. Small wicks of dread flare into being.

This I know

January. We have to write a self-portrait for Miss Moore. I start small, and in English first. Feathers are my favourite doodle. I munch food noisily – like a horse, my sister says. (I'll never be like my mother, who eats thoughtfully and reverentially, as though receiving communion.) I blow my nose inartistically and sneeze like a plate crashing to the floor, unlike my sister's polite little gasp. I love collecting new words. My head is usually immersed in a fictional world – until I'm on to the next book, and forget the last one entirely. I can be melancholic (My mother would say *melodramatic*). But I'm forever rearranging my moods too and feel euphoric at a moment's rainbow. Feel sure that I'll be alive for the end of times. Can't figure out if that makes me an optimist, a pessimist, an egotist or in denial about death. Miss Saitch has given up all hope of me ever getting a handle on maths. I feel like a child chasing after an untethered balloon, trying to understand new concepts at the speed she teaches. My family are *perpatéticiennes* – wanderers. *Per mare per terras* is our family motto and we live up to it. But I want to *belong*, to have my own terrain. So how can I claim the spirit of a wanderer? And how can I know who I am, when who I am keeps shifting? Just like truth, slippery as a raw egg underfoot. The careers guidance teacher has suggested journalism for me. But a journalist needs to have conviction, surely? While I'm oh-so-fickle – even when I think I have arrived at a firm decision, some other new thought comes along and makes me change it.

Dad's friend Robert laughs at what he calls my *naivety,* when I say that from the point of view of a Martian, all humans would look the same. Why can't they vote? What's the big deal about skin colour? *It's not the colour but lack of experience in governing, my dear. They're not ready yet.* But whatever he or the radio, the other adults, soldiers, girls at school – that is, most of the whites – say, I know something is horribly wrong with the war this country is fighting.
I delete the last few sentences, because, as she plays the devil's advocate in every discussion we have, I have no idea what Miss Moore's real opinions are. *Coward!*

It's only when listening to extracts from the essays of others that I realise I clean forgot to describe myself physically. Miss Moore says without self-knowledge you are walking in a narrow twisting labyrinth without a fuse to light the way. The assignment has made me realise that I engage and empathise with characters in books more closely than I do with actual people. In the real world, I feel as insubstantial as a cloud.

Watch-goose

Dad ran right over her on his way back from Wedza, he said. But Gertie – as Dad has inevitably named her – seems uninjured, except for her psychotic personality. Her daily clickalink rings in our ears every morning as she propels her body across the parquet flooring. Every now and then, she rubs her beak against the leg of the grand, as though to sharpen it. Come to think of it, the greying beak is not very gooselike at all. More like a bullet that she fires at select visitors. Fred and Moon, our two rescue dogs, are petrified of her giving them the goose-eye.

She reminds me of the first animals I ever loved – Spot, who was wily with fences, and NoName, who slithered through the burglar bars every full moon. Both outlaws.

More than that, she is all the fire I wish I had.

Contact

January. I know what black ops are. He would have parachuted into a camp beyond the border. But Jack didn't die. He didn't die, although the rest of his stick did. All the bodies at his feet, sprawled bulls-eye targets. His friends, comrades, brothers.

It's an SAS mate of Jack's who contacts me. He heard from the soldiers who found him. Jack crouching / lifting / holding. Five bullets, ending five not-so-long lifetimes. Then another, whistling through Jack's grimace, disintegrating his teeth. Jack unslinging his AK47, tapping his magazine, howling bullets at the trees. Five hits, five score settlings.

Because the bulge in the ditch

February. In my wing mirror, the man shaking his fist. Fucking *munts*, Jack snarls. I wince. Ever since the last contact, he's been mental. Now he's driving the car directly at a mother balancing a basket of avocados on her head, baby swaddled behind her in an orange *kikoi*. She topples into the ditch, becoming a parcel of soaked orange cloth. I scream at him. Did he do it just to scare her, to see her jump? Or did he actually intend to hit her? Harshly, he laughs.

*

From our hallway, I can see a few soldiers on the patio, a few blonds draped over them. I'm not going out there. Aside from my row with Jack, those women are a different climate, and in their presence I diminish, like a goldfish turning white. From a distance, I spot one of the guys deftly flipping the top off a Castle lager with another bottle.

I hate this war that distorts people, like a pebble through murky water. I curl on my bed, each shuddering exhalation longer than the last, flattening me like an airless balloon. *It's over with him.*

A tap on the door. It's Mum. Come on now. Be sociable. Jack's friends are here with their girlfriends. When I tell her what happened on the drive home, Mum's voice softens. Remember what he's been through.

Eleanor, Robert's Amazonian wife, introduces Johan, an Afrikaner Dad met at The Blue Room and brought home. He's a mercenary, she bellows. We shake. Jack pulls Eleanor to her feet. Slap-happy, burlesque, arms flailing above her, she stamps her feet with the rhythm of an African, everybody cheering: '*Ipi tombi, tombi yam,*' until finally, puffed, she settles back on her bar stool.

Eventually everyone disappears. Only my father remains behind the bar, a dark curl flopped over his forehead, cradling his brandy, savouring its oesophageal journey of burning snow, mumbling to invisible companions. I try to persuade him to go to bed. He promises he's declaring an ABF – *absolutely bloody final* drink – and tries to cajole me into keeping him company until he finishes, but I escape with the reasonable excuse that in two hours I have to get up for school. Sleep is not going to happen though. The distractions gone, all I can do is rock, knees to chest, thinking of the woman and her baby tumbling into the muddy ditch. The whole country falling inexorably towards its own magnifying shadow.

Playboy of the northern suburbs

12, Pemray Drive. Johan, the mercenary's legs hang over an arm of the sofa he found to collapse in. He sits up, bleary-eyed, blinking at the rush and thunder of our panicked last-minute homework, lost ties, spillage of cornflakes. I sit on the patio step and lace up my shoes. Zoë, Molly's friend, is pretty much living with us now, to escape from her step-father. Mum appears, in her cream and cerise satin dressing-gown, and asks Moses for tea.

Molly, Zoë and I rush out to our bikes, and soar down the hill, flapping our wings.

*

My father doesn't mind at all that beardy Johan's conversation is duller than the tick of a clock. Because he's usefully practical. My father can't even put a fuse in a plug. Johan can fix the cars, repair the pump in the pool, drop and collect, fetch and carry. He is allocated Ivor's room. So now we have Zoë and Johan too.

What about your childhood, Callie? We're all sitting around the bar. The moon is a crescent, accompanied by a planet. Dad, who has been talking about *his* life for the last hour, immediately replies for Mum. For the first twelve years of her life, she thought she was born on the 1st January 1937. Her mother altered her birth by a day, so she could keep her last-born back from school for another year.
Seán, don't be ridiculous, says Mum. Sure I'm only twenty nine. How could I be born in 1937? 1936, Callie.
I think you look amazing, says Johan.
She beams at him, offers him another drink.

*

We slag Johan for the endless women he takes out. I can't figure out what they see in him. What can I do, he shrugs innocently, in his strong Afrikaans accent. On my last date, a girl at the next table slipped me her number when I walked past her on my way to the jacks. It would be rude not to call her.

Every lift eventually plummets

You are not flying
but falling
level
by level
from some alto-stratus
high
the way rain
has to do,
wind-battered
towards houses
and cars
and golf balls
and insects
the wavering line
of your invisible
path
moving inexorably
towards
your magnifying
shadow.

7.

Secrets

Spoil Lala, said my mum, after I persuaded them to let me go home to Ireland again for the holidays. Bring her tea in the morning. Do the dishes.

*

Westport, Ireland. But of course Lala of the gleams won't let me lift a finger. Especially when, the very first morning, I'm coiled in bed, sniffling, suddenly needing STs. Lala has something else in her cabinet. But won't I break the hymen? With all your running about, it's already been broken. Throwing back her head and laughing, husky after my *what if I lose it inside*? That's what the string is for, she says. In properly and you can't feel it at all.

She gives me eucalyptus for my chest.

I shake out the cereal box, cornflakes rustling like leaves, into my bowl, her tame robin on the table, nibbling at toasted crusts, We talk all day, drizzling honey and lemon on pancakes, and keep talking, until the moon has over crossed the cottage. Shedding her Aran cardigan, Lala steps up onto a low table, shows me the steps of the Charleston. It's good exercise for the legs, she winks.

Gives me a hot water bottle for my cramps.

My Irish self, hidden like a bird in back streets, collecting these precious crumbs.

Wet expectations

I want adventure. I want to go camping, something I've never done before. It'll only rain, says Yvette, and wreck everything. We can check the forecast and cross fingers, I say. We can go to Kilkee, so we have a back-up, in case, says Caoimhe.

We tootle along in Caoimhe's Beetle, through green patchwork fields, Ireland's best postcard self. On one side of the car, curtain rain; on the other, silver bursts of light through cloud. I recite the small towns to myself: Shannon, Ennis, Kilrush, Moyasta…till we reach Kilkee. Despite the rosary of clouds clenched low above our selected hill, we erect our tent.

Of course, within a couple of hours, rain is sloshing in by the bucket-load, battering the saggy nylon. Our kit is drenched, Amazingly, Yvette is still sleeping, slumped wetly. Caoimhe and I whisper hysterically in the dark. We listen to the sky until it soaks Yvette awake. Plop-plop-plop snorts the rain. Like the sound of a pond thrown onto stones, says Yvette sleepily. We cackle at her malapropism. Actually, says Caoimhe, it does feel as though a pond has landed on our tent. At around midnight, we cave, unzip the door-flap, lurch to Caoimhe's holiday home.

*

I sniff the house. A musty, unlived-in cloak of dankness. Caoimhe lights a cigarette. They drink cider. I drink a Coke. A dog's hollow bark, far off. The night pulsates around us as we whisper stories of romantic escapades. My god, I spent so long mooning over Barra, remember? I look at Yvette. And I've turned my memory upside down, shaken it like a snow globe, but can find almost no particle of that crush left. I obviously just had to have somewhere to put my feelings, and they happened to land on him.

Next thing, we're blinking into the wan light of midday. Advertising leaflets rain through the letterbox, spooking us into more paroxysms.

Familiar and strange

Covehill, Letterkenny. My Donegal grandmother's quarried-out blue eyes are a shock. Who's that beside you, Granny? says Freya. She nudges her. A hint: she lives in Africa. Granny arrives back from her vacant staring. Africa. That's where our Seán lives, she says. Aye, so he does. This is his daughter, Itosha. Your granddaughter. I watch Granny's hand, the fingers opening and closing, curling around emptiness. You need to eat something, Auntie Jan says. The front doorbell tinkles. Granny rocks her chair. From the kitchen table, Auntie Jan glances out the window. Mary Crumlish is here. Your oldest and closest friend. She brought you a Victoria sponge last week. And her granddaughter just got married.

Mary! says Granny as her friend bustles in. We loved your cake. How was the wedding? The secret-wink family collusion, making light of this frightening thing.

What's left of you after your memory is just broken fragments of a precious plate?

Ambushing memories

Sometimes, when I'm writing the previous night's dream into my diary, I'm aware of an urge to *snatch* images before they speed off, into impenetrable mists, as though the conscious mind is not allowed to enter that forbidden territory.

You have to creep up on dreams, like a terrorist, catch them unawares.

Maybe the act of remembering is like dreaming: once you describe a memory to someone, all the elements you omitted to mention evaporate. Dad repeats the same memories over and over, almost using the same words for each event. What is he omitting?

Maybe memory is something you should practise, like swimming, to keep it strong. When Mum reminded me about being trapped in the garage as a toddler, I had forgotten. But as soon as she said it, there was the memory, like a pocket with a long-forgotten pebble in it.

Miss Moore says we are shaped by ten key events of childhood. But are we shaped by our *experiences*, or by our *remembered* experiences?

I spend the afternoon making a list.

Dream-language

From the soaked ground, a ladder leans against a tree. Some crows flap on the uppermost branches, screeking, tripping me into alarm too. It's a sign. Freya and I walk past it, alongside the flat wide ribbon of a river, behind a long queue of other people. Wind hustles our hair into tatters. We lag behind and sit on the bank, our legs dangling above the water. I look down to see what is written there. Tosha, she says, you don't need to catastrophize everything. The worst might not happen. I laugh, lifting my hand to my mouth, the way my mother does. When I look into my palm, it is full of teeth.

Relief, when I wake, to find my teeth intact.

Green and white and gold streams

Donegal, Ireland. My uncle Brennan's venue can take five thousand, but everyone still calls it The Grill, because it started out as The Golden Grill, a small diner.

Tonight, it's packed, but I see him straightaway, leaning against the plane of a pillar rough as an emery board. His carefree eyes. An imperceptible movement of the head.

As he and I wend our way through the jammed crowds celebrating my uncle's re-election into the *Seanad*, our fingers interlace. His warm hand, my cold one, a sultry breeze plaited with a cool stream.

Much later, we tiptoe through the quiet house where his mother and sisters are sleeping. On his bedroom walls, I notice several Republican posters. Maybe to deflect a potential question he sees forming, he asks me about the likely outcome of our civil war. I'm guessing we'll see majority rule soon, which I'll be glad about, I say. I mean, if I were black, I'd probably support the freedom fighters. We have something in common. *No blacks, no dogs, no Irish,* right?

He shushes my mouth with a kiss, and it's as though we're in a cathedral. I feel his hair rush through my fingers. The walls swing, ceiling shadows wheel. Minutes become hours. A slow crawl into intimacy.

And then, it's almost morning. I'll be leaving for the airport at noon.
Wait, he says.
Ties a woven strip, in the tricolours of the flag, to a belt loop on my jeans.
To remind you of your roots.

8.

A new social order

Salisbury, 17 March. Dad's tip for the driving test: *Check the rear view mirror every eleven seconds.* Rear view: girl, slumped in a seat at a pavement café. Parallel parking: perfect. Hill start: perfect. My final instruction: turn *left* at the robots…Rear view: stray tree branches reaching into the road… I cross three lanes and turn *right.* But it's St Patrick's Day, and my examiner is Irish. I hate to see a grown woman cry, he sighs heavily. So I'm going to pass you. Well, of course, I hug him.

Mum wipes her eyes as I recount and the Rawsons are raucous, especially when I repeat: *A grown woman.* Dad gives his Dave Allen smile.

*

Next night, Mum and Dad let me take the car. The girls and I head out to the cinema. Lights flash. A siren. Nerves grind the gearstick. The whiff of sweat and cigarettes is a swarthy, stocky policeman leaning in. All the girls, hooting with laughter in the back. I quaveringly hand over my day-old licence. You don't have your wipers on. So, he says, I need to breathalyse you.
Sir, I've never drunk alcohol in my life, I say, giving him the full beam of my innocent eyes. Nor have I driven in the rain before.
You were also driving without your lights on, he says drily, glancing around at the five of us in the Austin. Never driven in the dark either, I assume?
I shake my head. But to counterbalance that, I tell him, my parallel parking is perfect.
The policeman peers in the window again as Jade is whispering *Show him your last-minute cut across two lanes,* and the girls are splitting their sides.
Sweaty and all as he is, he's a softie. Grinning, he waves us off.

*

You are *so* lucky, Jade says in the cinema queue, twiddling with my cardigan buttons. Not just with the test and the cop, but your parents too. Mine would never let me drive their car.
Your folks attend every parents' evening and every sports day, I say. We're both lucky in different lights.

But she's right. And my popularity at home has just leapt into a different stratosphere. *Itosha, be an angel and nip down to Bon Marché for some Bols brandy and a carton of Kingsgate. Tosha, can you run these letters to the post office? Itosha, will you drop Molly at her modern dancing class? Tosh, when you drive to Lois's, can you pretend you're dropping me at a mate's? I'll take the car from Lois's and pick you up later…*

Memory's crevice

Freya writes to me about Grandad shuffling out of the bedroom, bent and woeful, in a daze of loneliness. Granny had lifted my cousins from their beds with her terrified screams about the stranger beside her. Freya's sister, Grace, curls in a dishevelled just-out-of-bed heap, putting her arm around him, leading our Grandad to his rocking chair. Tucking a blanket around him, trying to console him. Just a nightmare, Grandad. She'll remember you in the morning.

Granny wanting to leave her bed to catch the train to go *home*. Grace repeatedly reassuring her that she *was* home. There were no more trains. Granny staring out the window, past the meadow of mazy, veering flowers, all the way back to Rutland Island, to her mother, who would be fretting about her.

The night, heaved from its orbit

Pemray Drive, Salisbury. The loud words, the horrible words, tones turning harsher, more menacing. And finally, finally, the cutting-in clip clip of Mum's heels on the parquet. Mum in her satin nightgown, five-feet-two-and-three-quarters, standing still, till they notice. Then her stern voice, her cold voice, her scary voice, ice. Even though she never raises it, it cuts through all the smoke and cacophony, the music, the moving of furniture, the hands in wrong places, the toppling of glasses. *That's enough.*

And then you know there'll soon be respite, because hers isn't a drunk voice, it's an in-charge voice, a you're-keeping-me-from-sleep voice and the visitors will be jolted out of their excessiveness, their loudness, their never-endingness. Even though she's usually the most gracious and courteous, the most hostess, she's not at all scared to send these strangers packing, these randoms, these party-seekers, these spongers, these we'll-never-see-them-again pop-ups that Dad found in a bar or a meeting, or a street or a car park and brought back to our place so he could be king of his castle with his subjects all round him.

After glugging back the last of Dad's whiskey, his vodka, his brandy, his gin, gradually, they all troop to the front door, sheepish, muttering apologies, and they'll drive home, wheeling from one precarious ditch to another, and I'm hoping the rest of the world is asleep and no trees get in the way, but I don't really care because now they're gone and the house is dropping blissfully into silence, though my head is still scrambled because out there, everything's a mess, strewn with half-filled crystal tumblers, over-spilled ashtrays, melting ice, the sad sorry end of a night which, bedraggled and soaking, tottering, confounded, with that what-just-happened here query in its voice, shakes its black petals, only minutes before the first waking bird trills the opening note to say it's now the next day, and we've missed it again, the tree-wafting, world-sleeping nightness of night.

Eyes on tomorrow

13 February. The grandfather clock clearing its throat in the hallway. Above us, stars are birdlike markings flaked across the night sky. Josh and Matt giving each other that 'time to go' look. We haven't so much as strummed a note. Again.

Molly feigning a need for the loo, and not coming back. My father cajoling me to stay with him. Just till I've finished my drink. As long as you don't pour another one, I say grumpily, sliding back on to the stool. I like your friends, he deflects. You're lucky you've grown up in an open house. Sinatra crawling across the air. *And now, the end is near...* We couldn't have friends over, says my dad, unless my mother knew and approved of the parents.

Tasting the crook of my elbow to block out the smoke. Dropping my eyes to half-mast at the repeat story about how she was a fierce snob, though it was my grandfather's family who disowned their son for marrying an islander.

I chip in with a memory of my own: I remember her saying *I was once the most beautiful woman in all Donegal, with an eighteen-inch waist.* Laughing, speedily, last-burst energy. I blunder on, despite his blank, switched-off face. I asked Grandad if that was true. And he said, *She wasn't bad looking.* Dad blocks me. Is this your story or mine? tartly. Sorry Dad. You have this habit, Itosha, of interrupting. It's very annoying. Always hunting for a pause in someone's sentence to kidnap the attention...

I blithely babble on. She must have had her disappointments too. Once Granny told me that old age was the most unexpected thing that could have happened to her, and I should spend my time well. Soon enough, it'll all be over.

Maybe I'm trying to tell my dad something.

His silent response, crooked steeple of fingers, a glare. Did you hear what I said? Do you ever think of anyone but yourself?

His comment crushes me, echoing Mum's *try not to be so self-centred*. Instantly I compose myself in the attitude of a listener, like my mum, receptive as a table set for dinner.

I am full of resolve as I whirl off to bed half an hour later. Ok then. Tomorrow is the day I begin my new self. Consider others. And dish out lava heaps of kindness, unprompted.

Making a choice

14 February. At the Interact meeting, remembering my new resolution, I tentatively raise my hand to volunteer as chairperson for the last, least sexy charity: Hopelands, for the physically handicapped. Cause and effect. What will happen next?

My raised hand is followed by Josh's and Matt's, and the last straggle of Interact members who haven't yet joined a committee.

Afterwards, everyone heads off to Gremlin's, the drive-in restaurant in Newlands, abandoning two hundred and fifty mugs and cake crumbs. *Do the good thing.* I start clearing up. Two of my new committee members stay behind to help. Lionel right? A single nod, solidity of an affirmative. And Fynn: supple movements, mossy eyes. Body and height of a water polo player. Aura of amusement, self-possession. Deeply and glowingly mysterious. Swivel-handed wrists, not a single wasted gesture. Laconic. The kind of person, I'm guessing, who follows his own sun, veering away from the crowd. He fixes his gaze on mine – green, talking eyes. For the next hour, laughing, flicking tea towels as we wash and dry and stack. Fynn's long tapered fingers adroitly tapping droplets from a plate before he sets it on the metallic draining board. While Lionel's out emptying bins, we talk subjects – his are maths, physics, chemistry – and exam results. Two ones and a two, says Fynn. Laughs ruefully. Still trying to get over the two. My Dad says I suffer from kakorrhaphiophobia, rolling out the word lusciously. I look at him: *Che?* Abnormal fear of failure, he grins. What a word.

Afterwards, realise I saw him first in a dream: languid, remote. In the dream, charged with electrical vibrations, I put my hand on his chest. A reckless act.

Blunders and butter curls

Use the butter knife, Mum says. Hastily, I dig into the soft, then smear, while relating my good charity deed. Itosha. Slow. Down. The. Delivery, intones my father. Mum lifts my napkin, coiled into the shape of a swan, and lays it on my lap. Dutifully, I tend to half the roll, though half of anything is so pointless.

We've learned not to butter our rolls at all in Plumtree, says Ivor. We get beaten for the smallest wrong manoeuvre.

I can't imagine being beaten over butter curls. Over food.

Dog night

Friday evening. Ivor cruises in to our parents' bedroom, where the TV lives. He scissors his legs, tipping my plate with leftover crusts of toasted cheese, tomato and onion sandwiches. After unearthing a few crusts from under his bum, he stretches out next to Moon, the rescued-after-his-family-emigrated keeshond, and feeds him the crusts. Fred, the basset, whom I've claimed, is sprawled at the end of the bed, in line with a packet of cool air from the French doors. Oof, what a pong. Ivor, you need to start using deodorant. *Ja* well, you've got halitosis. He goes to the en-suite bathroom, and scrounges around. Underarm wash first, I yell, just as Columbo is starting. Molly is sitting on the floor at the foot of the bed. Surreptitiously breathe into my palm. Fred is still snoring, loud as a generator, lips billowing like shirts on a line.
It's 10pm when their car lights flick across the walls.

Oh no! I forgot to feed the dogs!

A flicker of indecision. Own up or lie? *Yes, I fed the dogs.* An image of them happily munching would be created instantly in Mum and Dad's minds. The others wouldn't tell. Job done. Only, I *can't* leave them hungry for the night.

I race to the kitchen. Plonk their yellow enamel basins on the counter. Grab tins of chunky chicken. Shake out cubes.

Too late. My mother swings the kitchen door open. *Why must they drink every night?* Accusations of selfishness and other combustibles. A hand is lifted. A blaze of reckoning. Such power in one so small. I am knocked halfway across the room. A doorknob collides with my head. Booming pain in my ear. Mum has never lain a hand on me before. But her words, more than hands or fires or hurricanes, make smithereens of me. Clamping my mouth to stop bottled-up burstings. *Hate* is a word that can never be erased.

*

There's no action I can take, except to barricade myself in my room. A wardrobe across the doorway. Itosha. Itosha, I'm sorry. A bowling ball in my throat. Ignore the knocking. Owl sounding a panic outside my window. I curl into a foetal position, feeling as if a train has just punched through me.

There are rustles and scritches, crackles and sudden loud pauses. The physical pain has stilled, but the emotional hurt keeps leaking from my body, salt slithering into the corners of pressed-shut lips.

Tip and pivot

Flying fast
below you,
the jade blades
of a
forest,
and there's no
action
you can take,
unless...
what if you pulled
the emergency cord –
would a second chute
slow the plummet?
Or would it implode
the main one
and lance you
into the ground?
Indecision
whirls you
into a spiral.

Echoes in the muffled corridor

Saturday. A wardrobe for a lock. The fireball sun breaches the barricade of the window. I watch pods fall from the tree outside my window, like parachutists coming in for a landing. Leaves flounce and skim the wall. Yesterday, the euphoria of the endless weekend ahead. Now, empty hands; leaden feet; unuttered vowels; greasy hair. Outside my door, still no Ivor, the only person I could bear to talk to. I crumple across the bed, like a wet sheet being shaken out. Spend the time writing, until my pencil's a nub. Rub out sentences, create charcoal clouds. I have seen how alcohol distorts. She didn't mean me. She doesn't hate *me.* She meant Dad.

Haul myself up again, to inspect my cacti menagerie on the sill. Morning heat has glassed into them. A bulge of sudden growth from one. They prickle and wait for me to tell them what happened. When I do, they stare, remain silent. Out in the garden, birds lift from a dog rush, into the immensity of sky. Even Fred has abandoned me. There he is, outside, lapping at the pool's blueness with his long flapping tongue. Gloomily, I reflect on a found owl's feather, recently added to my collection. My glass of clear water. I lift it, gulp ten times.

Is being in this room an action, or is it a feeling? A statement? There seems to be no good answer. Eventually I lie on the floor, do my homework. Write a letter to Freya, although what I say to her is only what I want her to know.

Outside, everything is in full motion, summer at its blooming height. Molly and Zoë and the Jane Blonds are splashing and laughing. I stare at my three selves in the three-way mirror. I look shattered, aggrieved.

Oh, my injured pride, stretching me all the way through the long morning, longer afternoon, twilight and darker night.

Boxed

12, Pemray Drive, Sunday. Voices and laughter and splashing and clinking. But it will only climax in another showdown as usual.

Fred whines outside my door.
Mum knocks. Itosha, come on. I've said I'm sorry.
A tight ball of closure. Outside, smoke wavering sideways past the sun loungers.
Suit yourself then.

Stomach growling like the day coming and going. Aromas of char-grilled meat wafting through the blurred ribbon of heat. But even that temptation will not open my door. I drink the remaining water in my pint glass, squat, then pee into it. Approach the window, slide urine out.

The feelings still won't diminish. Sunset is a bloody spray-painted mess against the wall of the sky. Outside, I can see my mother dropping ice into glasses. My mood is a bat click-clicking.

The innumerable times Dad would bore his eyes into mine, ignoring everyone else, as he told a story at the bar. I would glance east and west, trying to get him to connect with others too, make it a group thing, not some *tête-à-tête* between the two of us. The innumerable times she left us at the bar, Dad cajoling me to stay with him till he finished his drink. I'll come to bed straight after this ABF, Dad would call placatingly after her. And then, because I'd be waiting for him to finish his vodka, he'd sip so slowly it would seem as if he didn't need the drink at all.

In the mirror I stare at my face, my body, to see if there's anything of her there. This body that used to live inside hers.

At around 8pm, Ivor at last. He taps on the open window. I sneaked a plate for you. He slides it under the burglar bars.

And the limp leaves waited for rain

6am, Monday. I walk straight out the front door before anyone else is awake. Fetch my bike from the garage and cycle to school. Find a shady spot in the quad and settle into my new library book, *The Wasteland*, which suits my mood. *The wind crosses the brown land, unheard.* I stare up at a tree-top, the sun rapidly rising above it.

Tosh? What are you contemplating? Miss Moore, appears, and there is a breeze of wings, a river of butterflies in the air. She swings her arms, walking purposefully towards me, the second person to arrive at the school.

She doesn't ask why I'm at school so early, but her eyes on me suggest that she somehow knows. I show her the book. We've been studying *J. Alfred Prufrock* in English, and I've fallen in love with Eliot, I tell her. Good choice. He's one of my favourites, she says. I feel a rush of elation that washes away all my simmering rage and hurt.

When I look at my watch, there's still half an hour to go before the first bell rings. Still no one else around. I've learned something new about Miss Moore too. A falling leaf beside me. I lift it, study the veins.

Truce

Molly, bolting out of the Form 1 classroom at break-time.

Tosh, you know how Mum and Dad say never let the sun go down on your... Mum feels bad about her row with you because it was about something so...And Tosh, what's the point, if... she stops dead.

I can always see her unspoken thoughts before they rise into voice. Even though they often don't conclude. This is a typical Molly habit: she starts sentences and then stops half-way through, as though her batteries have run out. Maybe it's because she's so used to me impatiently finishing her sentences. Maybe she becomes lost in her insecurities, her sense of inadequacies. I force myself to listen, conscious that she's trying to make things better between Mum and me.

Molly, I don't think I'm ready to see her yet, I say. I'm going to Lois's after school.

*

I cool my feet in the shallow end of Lois's pool. A sunken dragon fly is squirming on the surface. Before I reach to lift it out, my eye is drawn to its enormous winged shadow, staggering across the tiles.

Raging against someone only keeps you tied to them, says Lois. Holding on to that anger is not good.

I know my mother tends to simmer those black clots. And I don't want to be like her.

I arrive back around 7pm. Mum walks into the living room and sees me.
Supper's almost ready, she says. It's your favourite. Piri piri chicken and chips.
Yum, I say, then head towards my room.
Tosh, Mum says softly.
I turn, and make my own offering. Want me to set the table?

And the days gradually go back to their usual size.

April is the coolest month

12 Pemray Drive, Salisbury. 1ˢᵗ April. 6am. My prints join the twisty zig-zag footnotes of birds on the dewy lawn. Nightie off, flop my body into the pool. The water feels soft as a Persian cat against my breasts.

A bicycle bell rings. It's Lois, wobbling down the driveway. She is balancing a plate of chocolate éclairs sprigged with daisies (my favourite flower, sunny yet unflaunty). How beautiful she is. Happy birthday, she calls. Haul myself out, wrap into a towel, throw my arms around her. I'll have you know, I got up at 5am to make these. The gesture, the present, make me feel like I'm bare-footing cartwheels in a meadow. For breakfast, éclairs instead of toast.

*

A knock at the classroom door. It's a prefect. Itosha is wanted by Miss Thwaites, she says to Miss Moore. I glance at Lois. I've never been summoned by our daunting principal before.

I must ask you to open this package, which is addressed to you, says Miss Thwaites, formal and clipped as always. Her chin is lifted. She adjusts her specs. A large box, looming like a building over a street, overshadowing even her stately desk. My mind is doing acrobatics. Inside, another box. Inside that, straw and – a smaller box. Lift the box out and yes, another one inside that. This is strange…I say, smiling bashfully. It certainly is, is her response. Her hands are folded in her lap, and she's looking up at me quizzically. Seven boxes later, I reach in for a matchbox containing a note: April Fool! And a registered slip. A real present is waiting for me at the post-office. She cracks a smile.

Back in the classroom, laughter.

After French, Miss Moore calls me back. This is the book I mentioned in class yesterday. *The Fountainhead.* I think you'd like it. Happy birthday.
So it's to keep?
She nods.
I put my hands to my face. Why do blushes arrive so swiftly and take so long to evaporate?
Thank you Miss Moore.

At lunchtime, Jade twirls a button on my cardigan. Come on, let's fetch your present. Don't open it until we get to your house, says Lois, waving fingers dyed green from her art-class batik.

Embedding a friendship

12, Pemray Drive, 1ˢᵗ April, 2.30pm. Lois, Jade and I crouch over my new photo album, already filled. Lois in the Drakensburg, floppy hat, cheeky grin, skin the colour of a gold beach. Jade and I, dining in front of pyramids of calamari. Lois, flung up like a puppet on a kids' trampoline, just before her ankle-breaking catastrophe. The three of us yackety-yacking on the lawn at Lois's, tea things being trundled over by her gorgeous, barefoot, Afro-headed brother. Kelly the terrier, wrapped in her own mad fur.

Bourke's Luck, canyon plummeting behind me. Look at your expression, laughs Lois. You were so fearful of getting the mad staggers and toppling right over! There we are, lying on our three bellies on the hot concrete by a turquoise pool, shoulders rosy with sun. Josh too.

Wheeling up the steps of Nazareth church, Coke can in my hand. I remember hiding that can behind the holy water font. Who took the photo? It must have been Inez, my half-French Catholic friend, whom I see after mass on Sundays, because Lois is an atheist, or maybe a pantheist, and Jade is a Protestant of some sort.

The low wall at school, a line of girls, outstretched legs browning in the sun, munching iced buns from the tuck shop. Another, angled up to the first floor corridor, a crowd of us heaping over the railing, Miss Moore in the picture too, tiny beside Eve, the tallest girl in our class. The whole school in the quad, a jamboree of civvies day colour.

And I sink into this blurry, ineffable happiness.

The rosé-coloured glasses

12, Pemray Drive. All afternoon, we flip in and out of the pool. Girls, calls my Dad from the bar on the patio. Come here and have a celebratory glass of something. Itosha, you're eighteen. your pledge is over. I'm amazed, says Jade, that you lasted this long. You have iron willpower, miss!

Robert and Eleanor hoot with mirth at my spluttering. Every colour of wine, gin, vodka, martini. They all taste revolting to me.

Later, when Lois, Jade and I are getting ready for Pete's party, Mum appears with a silver tray bearing Irish coffees. *Et voilà.* A drink I can relate to.

By the time I encounter Fynn, I feel too swizzy to be shy. He's in the kitchen, attired in a dark green shirt, the brim of his Stetson tipped to cover – amusement? Music from the next room starts to move my body. Do you dance? I ask him. As soon as we sway in to the darkened room, the music switches to *How Deep is Your Love,* and we flow into each other's bodies. Mmm, I say croakily. What aftershave are you wearing? Paco Rabanne, he smiles. You're rather lightsome on your feet. Perchance, I reply, it's your own skills that increase mine. Jade flourishes a glass of champagne in front of each of us. A toast – happy birthday, Tosh. Here's to the pleasures of alcohol! She lifts the tassel of my cheesecloth top and swings it. We clink glasses and sip. I feel awash with a free sensation. *So this is why.*

Can I escort you back to your abode? My stomach is a wheeling disturbance of butterflies. But I have to decline. Lois and Jade are staying at my place tonight.

*

On Monday, my thoughts keep bursting into small explosions, and my body shakes in a mini-earthquake. My floppy school hat lifts from my head as I cycle past the boys' school, so I have to chase it along the pavement, ruffled as a choppy green sea, though he's nowhere in sight. Fear I will have to atone one day for this havoc I'm allowing to open up in my heart.

Marriage and mischief

12, Pemray Drive. Robert and Dad are on the patio, brandishing swords, roses between their teeth, when I arrive back from Lois's. Mum is bringing out a fresh ice bucket. Her closest friend, Helen, English, top heavy and hoarse-voiced from the cigarettes, and Ronan, her Irish, ex-rugby player husband, appear. Mum and Dad knew Helen years ago, in Galway, when she was married to another man. When Helen met Ronan, it was instant love, and she ran away with him. Ronan adopted her three children. I see Helen stand on tiptoe towards Dad's ear and whisper something. He nods and wanders over to the piano. Begins playing *Story of a Glass Mountain.*

Then Hedy arrives, swinging her hair, a cape of scarlet, over her shoulder, as though expecting a pop of paparazzi flashbulbs. Her personality is a fan of peacock feathers. Face a heart, chin a point, eyes a-glint, green as muscat grapes, aware of effect. A cigarette with a filter tip in her left hand. Cat-kohl eyes. Drink? I ask. Voddies for the bodies, she laughs, brandishing a bottle of vodka, a burst of peppery joy which ends in a snort, predictable as a full stop after a sentence. We pack up laughing every time. She doesn't seem to realise, or doesn't mind. When the adults begin boring her, she challenges us to a game of poker, sitting cross-legged on the floor, like us. I love watching her shuffle the pack, slick as a croupier, her long, red-painted nails clacking. Her fingers are long and brown, an emerald on the third digit of her right hand. Her wedding finger is sometimes bare, depending on her current status. She's been married twice, to the same man. Greg is a tobacco auctioneer, fit, with floppy brown hair, boyish, shorter than her. He was named in the Guinness Book of Records for being the fastest tobacco auctioneer in the world. They are both whip-smart, but she outsmarts and out-flirts him. When they are apart, she wears her wedding band on the right third digit. I see Hedy as the dazzle, the fire and air of their relationship, Greg as the earth and water. But in the slivery hours, it all gets too wolfish, too Liz-and-Richard in *Who's afraid…*and I think of the London Underground. *Mind the gap.*

My parents refuse to choose between them whenever they split, so both continue to be invited to their regular Friday sundowners. Darling, she says to Greg one night, in the hour before sun-up, let's get married again, lifting her Roman nose as she speaks. The next day, they are off to the registry with my parents in tow, as the witnesses.

She is malachite hallelujahs and marooned-on-an-island wild. How can any man keep up with her?

The bodies

12, Pemray Drive. My flamboyant father is playing *Patricia the Stripper.* Hedy steps onto the coffee table, hourglass girlish, as though she has held up Time like a cowgirl with a pistol, and made it surrender. Watching her dance is like watching a river flower around bends, upending into a waterfall. Easing her green blouse over her head, flinging it onto some man's bald pate, to unrestrained, four-noted hilarity. Piece by piece, her clothes are tossed, until she's white skin and red hair and white breasts and a red triangle, shimmying and wheeling, conducting everyone's eyes with her movements. *And with a swing of her hips…*

Marlie, Jessa and Antoinette (the Jane Blonds) are sleeping over. We're all spying from the corridor. I cover Antoinette's eyes, but she ducks. We are open-mouthed, rearranging our perceptions of Hedy, all the way to her complete nudity, some grubby man, flush-cheeked, lunging for her. Hedy bats him off with a swift retort. How dare you take liberties! she snaps, all claws and snarl, everyone else collapsing. His grotesque mutton chops and jowls sink into his collar. He pulls on the ends of his moustache, like Gertie beaking her wings in unsettled weather. *I am giving you the pleasure of looking at my body, but that does not mean you can touch!* If the adults are laughing, it is okay, isn't it? I scrutinise my parents' faces. They are drunk, gulping her in. It seems to be some kind of adult game. Even Greg, her husband (again) is grinning.

We troop back down to my room for a better view as the adults are navigated by Dad out to the floodlit garden. They peel off clothes, as easily as banana skins, and tumble into the pool naked. Oh God, I curl into my palms. Ach, man, at least they're fun, Tosh, not stuffy, like most adults, says Marlie, turning from the window, swinging her long hair.
Maybe I'm a prude. I should listen to my mum. Change the direction of my thoughts.

Event

*And below
tiny things
are growing,
one looming
into the smudged form
of a tottering figure
swinging
his little girl
on his shoulders,
the wind tugging
through the last seams
of cloud and memory
before
a landing
that,
at this speed,
must surely feel like
an earthquake...but
then you hear
your mother's voice:
Change
the direction
of your thoughts!*

First date

First a coffee at the Italian bakery in Avondale. I look at the menu, stroke the check cloth, anything to avoid meeting his steady gaze. Finally flick my eyes to his clavicle, and ask if he's read *The Fountainhead*. I don't read fiction, he says. What's the appeal? And I go all jittertalk. When I'm reading a story...it's as though time has collapsed and...there's some kind of symbiosis, I tell him. I can...literally feel the ideas of the book entering my brain. He laughs. Sounds almost sexual. His fingers are stroking his glass. What's *The Fountainhead* about? Hard to encapsulate, I say, my fingers echoing his. My body is a hive of energies. The book is like... a giant physical space, and there's this protagonist who's an architect with massive ambition. I'm feeling light-headed, floaty...and unnerving tenacity, brilliance, individuality. It's a book that makes a virtue of aspiration. Even arrogance.

Fynn's face is partly obscured by shadow and my body wants to run into his skin, but I can't sense... His eyes are watching my syllables. His manner, so Howard Roark. Self-possession, aloofness. He lifts his chin to a waiter and scribbles on the air. After he's paid the bill (with a tip) we head upstairs to the Kine to see 'Equus'. Once the lights dim, he entwines our fingers. Throughout the film, my hand is a caught bird inside his palm, and I'm in a state of enchantment that conflicts with the disturbances set off in my blood by the images on screen. When the lights go back on at the end and cigarette smoke trumpets across our heads, I twitch my nose. He releases my hand and instantly I feel ruffly, bereft, naked. No kiss when he drops me off. Maybe, sober, I'm not the same.

Impulse

It's a balmy night, stars flooding the sky. A party. Dan, who lives up the hill from our house, beckons me over to the brazier, a bunch of guys sitting around it, on logs. I recognise most of them as Oriel boys. Itosha come here a sec? Wary, I approach. Dan palms my shoulders down until I'm landed in Fynn's lap and then wraps my hand round a drink. Mortified, so in-the-stocks public, I slug the drink back without tasting it. Cringe at their ribaldry. The music swerves into *How Deep is Your Love*. Hey, that's our song, I say. Up I leap and yank Fynn along behind me to the open-air dance floor. Within seconds he's kissing me dizzy.

Trigger-alert

12, Pemray Drive. 6 August. A dull bang, like a sack of coal dropping to the ground, the house shaking slightly. And suddenly the air, like a stone, goes in and out of me. Earthquake? The news on the radio some time later announcing that it was an explosion in Woolworths in the city centre. With all the security, how was it possible to get a bomb into the department store? We listen to the names on the news, with trepidation. Eleven people killed, 76 wounded.

Rigid in bed, waiting for more bombs. And there are more, but because of the stepped-up high-security checks in all the department stores, they are planted mostly in litter bins and cars, with minor impact. My father quizzes us strenuously about our movements. A friend is caught out during the curfew and nearly shot. Bags are searched more forensically in Barbour's and Foschini's and Greaterman's. Every shadow at the back door is someone with a gun.

African violets

Saturday afternoon, May. My parents are out and everyone's off. Fynn lifts me up onto the low red brick wall in front of our kitchen, the top of it bedded with violets. A stream of their fragrance comes to meet me. His hands raise my navy tee-shirt right up, without taking it completely off. I'm wearing nothing underneath. Scent of soil and violets, warmth of the red-brick seeping through my jeans. My quivering body, which never imagined the effect of a warm mouth on a nipple. Fynn told me the other day that our electromagnetic frequencies, which are influenced by our moods, colour all our perceptions.

Buzz of a bee or wasp, a distant door banging, hum of heat in the air, the softness and fragrance of his freshly washed hair, his cool hands roaming up my hot back…my mind leaping to that moment in the field when I was twelve, wanting to freeze-frame the moment, not grow up at all. Oh, but who knew it would be like this! Fynn, my body and feelings, the universe and loops of time, all at once. So. *This* is it.

Track

Dad's gone AWOL, with a roll of cash in his pocket. On the second night, Mum begs me to track him down. You have the best chance of getting him home. Try The Howff first, then The Red Fox, and failing that, The Flagstaff, Captain's Cabin, The Blue Room.

I kerb crawl around the city, eyes peeled for his Merc. Finally locate it outside Le Coq d'Or. One arm draped around a beautiful black woman, his own curly black hair looking unruly, he is holding forth to a collection of strangers. An unsought thought jerks like a fish in my mind. Itosha! exclaims my mercurial, drunken father rapturously, as though he hasn't seen me in years. Come and meet... I walk straight towards him. Dad…Yes, yes, he flusters, we'll go as soon as I've finished this drink. While a Coke is being planted in front of me, he swiftly downs his and nods clandestinely to the barman again, who pours a second double brandy. Dad! Ah now, Tosh, don't be a killjoy. Let me finish my story. The chung chung of dim music like a carpenter sawing through wood. So, as I was saying, in 1957, I was in Budapest, visiting my girlfriend's family. This was before I met your mother, of course. His right eye is half-hooded as he trains his attention on me. Her teenage brother had got mixed up in the Hungarian revolution. The parents asked me, as I was an officer cadet in the Irish army, to rescue him. I managed to locate him just before street fighting erupted, before the tank came ploughing down the road. It didn't stop. He pauses to take a sip. I got to him somehow, and dropped down next to him. He was still alive, but moments later, died in my arms. There was no one else who seemed to know him. No one else to return his body to the family.

The words, the pauses, his voice moulded by brandy and embellishment. A goat chewing relentlessly on the same cud. I've heard this story a hundred times before.

Dad's gaze travels across the room and lands on a piano in the far corner. I wrote him a piece of music, he says. Would you like to hear it? Please, please! chorus his acolytes because, after all, he's picking up the tab. So he strides over, sits at the piano, gestures to the barman to kill the canned noise, and begins to play his Hungarian composition. Everyone gathers around. He promises me that after this one, we'll go home. The usual bargaining chip. As he plays, his eyes fill for the figment brother's tragic death, and though I know they are crocodile tears, I feel a confused flicker of love and my affinities waver. His smile of pained charm, as though he knows he's condemned to find no home anywhere, but this.

Gift

Fynn notices the warts, perched on top of my knuckles, a third one on my right palm at the base of my second finger. Hmmm, he says. I can do something about those. We're in his *rondavel*. He opens the bathroom cabinet. A trace of toothpaste scent, boyness, pungent kick of Zambuk. Selects a bottle, an ear bud, and opens my palm. This might sting a little. He dabs caustic soda on each wart so tenderly, I want to cry. From then on, every time I go to his place after school, this is the first thing he does. They seem to shrink until, one day, perhaps three weeks later, he takes my hand. They've gone.

A bowl of flames

The other girls are in heels, short dresses, lips crimsoned, a near-comic uniformity of perfect Farah Fawcett-flicked waves. As alike as mosaic pieces in a swimming pool. They leave most of the talking to their boyfriends, and one of Ivor's quips pops into my head: *silence sustains lipstick*. Ever since he told me that lipstick contains fish scales, I've never been able to consider trying it. I look down at my multi-coloured maxi and summer sandals. Dan keeps topping up everyone's crystal glasses. His parents are out. Even with white wine, I'm finding it difficult to harmonise, as though I've been handed a different instrument to play in this orchestra, and it clashes with all the others. I glance in alarm at Fynn, who slips me a wink.

So glad you broke up with that dick, Sonja. He was such a loud-mouth. Honestly, you're better off with someone like me.

The cook presents a baked Alaska on a silver serving platter.
Oh! exclaims Sonja, clapping her hands.
You've outdone yourself, Master, says Dan. This looks splendid.
The cook bows and withdraws.
Master? mouths Sonja.
That's his name, says Dan loudly, to laughter. His parents sure had a sense of humour. And speaking of humour – Dan looks at me – honestly, Tosh I don't know whether to laugh or cry when I look at you. So harem-scarem. Why can't you get a style like Sonja's?
I'm afraid I drew the short straw when it comes to hair, I say airily, though I can feel my cheeks simmer.

Dan takes a strand of my wispy tendrils between his fingers rather sadly and says I need to sort out my crazy split ends. He's suddenly inspired. Here, I'll do it for you. Whips out a lighter. Holds the flame to a strand. A sizzle emits from it, then a burning rush.

I have to trust that it was a well-intentioned gesture, one that extended to tipping my smouldering head into the flushing toilet bowl in the cloakroom, releasing me afterwards with giggles and snorts, so that I have to hold back the tumble for later.

I stare straight ahead, head wrapped in a towel, making no eye contact. My un-nameable feelings have to be sublimated. At least this trick of rearranging my emotional bearings is one thing I'm good at.

Intimations and omens

When he was taking his girlfriend back to her place in Ruwa, Ivor says, he saw wrecks of bullet-pitted farmhouses, craters left by blown-up landmines. The war has stepped up. And the newly independent neighbouring country, Mozambique, has closed our supply route from the ocean. We have to rely totally on South Africa now.

I tap my rollerball on the dining room table, mulling over Miss Kelly's history lesson. A failed uprising in Fort Salisbury, 1896. Then in the 1960s, rebels killed by Rhodesian forces in the Chinoyi Caves.

Dad says African history is not just something in the past. It's a rolling wave of long-coming revenge. Drums beating slowly on the sacred rocks of Domboshawa, like the heart of a hibernating crocodile, then building, building, luring new waves of youths. Dad says thousands more have left the country for guerrilla warfare training in military camps along the Mozambican and Zambian borders, and also in Russia, China, Cuba. They are being inspired by what's happening in the rest of the continent. Sudan, Ghana, Nigeria, Kenya, Tanzania, Zambia, Mozambique and most of the other countries up north have already gained their independence.

Though we study history, we don't seem to be learning from it, though it's shouting all down the continent. Impacting on all our little stories. Mine.

Hair

My sister sits on the verandah, pouring her hair into her lap, talking from behind its curtain as she brushes it into rabbit-fur softness.

My own hair still shows charred remnants. Split smoke.

From time to time, I can still smell the shock of singed hair, similar to the stench of a burnt-down building. Sometimes, I'm loping down the street on a hot day, in a *dwaal*, when the fiery nibs hit me again, tripping me off kilter, so I feel as if I'm walking not on the ground, but on the sun itself.

*

Does it indicate a possible brain tumour if you have olfactory hallucinations? I ask my mum. I keep smelling smouldering hair. Mum looks at me, a thin plume rising from the pink and white china teacup in her hand. Woefully, I lift my hand to the spilled brown sugar sensation of my split ends. I'm sure you don't have a tumour, love, she laughs. But it is rather a mess. I think I'll make an appointment with Robert for you. He'll fix it.

Hedy walks in the front door. She must have heard our conversation. Darling, she says to me. I think you'd look glorious with an Afro.

A comet's pulsing rose

June. Glance down at my ratty second-hand uniform, jersey wrapped around my waist, push back a strand of wayward hair. I have just flown down the long hill on my bicycle. My cheeks are flushed, my throat parched. His approaching silhouette is a long graceful line drawn with a paintbrush. A strike of lightning into my body. Even his minimalist gestures are pure and clean, slicing the air in a stroke. In his free hand, a hip flask. He offers me a sip and something takes flight inside when I discover it's water. As though he has given me a magic potion, this genie who reads my palm, divines the stars, heals warts. A car's loud bark, interrupting this weightless realm, this freeze-framed nano-second of my life.

Self-command

Booming
in your mind,
Doug's voice:
'Skydiving involves
the control
of speed
during the descent.'
You're here,
a comet
on the rim
of the sky,
as the earth spins
and hurtles.
You look up
for proof
that your parachute
is still open,
the wind
shouting
inside it.
Before and after
have been
sheared away.
There is only
this.
Now grip,
tug, jiggle,
wield
those toggles
like a weapon.

La vie en rose

July. My dad is playing and several people are communing around the piano. Fynn appears behind my shoulder and brushes my nape with his lips. Ivor is speaking in an undertone close to Dad's ear, a hand on his shoulder, Dad nodding and smiling. He launches into Ivor's favourite: *Three Blind Mice,* in various styles: starting with single high notes, veering into jazz and baroque, hillbilly, dramatic, blues, classical, then back to single high notes at the end. The French doors are flung open and at the end of the patio, Molly and Zoë are teaching the Jane Blonds, Marlie, Jessa and Antoinette, a dance that Molly has choreographed herself. I don't know, murmurs Fynn in my ear, who I love more, you or your family. And my heart is dancing like the can-can girls at the Moulin Rouge.

It's that particular time of the evening when laughter is silver and light, and it is almost possible to forget that we are a country at war. Dad stops playing and comes out to the patio. The crickets have subsided, but now we can hear the clamour of the frog colonies. *Gooach. Gooach. Gooach.* An owl whoops. The dark canopies of the trees open their wings, erupting bats which skim across the patio; a leathery glove brushing next to my ear. Robert is wearing Bermuda shorts and an open shirt, even though it's winter. I ruffle his thick bed of chest hair. How's my favourite black Prod? Mum begins to tell a joke about hirsute men, but before she gets to the end, she starts laughing, silently, as always. We know we're never going to hear the punch-line. She lifts her hand to her mouth. She ducks her head. Her body shakes. Her eyes well up. Oh dear, she says, behindhand. We are all roaring.

A shadow in the corner

Hedy and Greg have a son, Gary. He is black-haired, dark-skinned, a thunder cloud hovering in a corner of the room. At sixteen, he is still shorter than her. I wonder if he resents that.

While the adults are drinking and carrying on, Gary hangs out with us, on the few occasions he comes along. Morning breath revolts him, he told me once. He brushes his own teeth first thing in the morning, and again after breakfast, and every time food or drink passes his lips. He washes his hands four or five times a day. He fights off misery and bad dreams with sudden outbursts of violence, utters rude fragments overheard from his beautiful mother, whom he says is *as crazy as a long-tailed cat in a shop full of rocking chairs.* Her mouth, he says, won't stop, goes like a fever; then her fervent guilty nonsense, forlorn as a cellist with a never-ending melody. Their life is part fantasy, part role-playing, surging in and out of rooms, her luscious red hair, avid eyes, a desperate intent that is never entirely explicit. I listen to his stylization, barbed, hooded, extreme, withholding, bristling with puzzles. Theirs must be a weirdly schematic house of games.

He once whispered to me that he hates his mother, always lit up, dominating his father's attention, while he's left in the dark. He sometimes fantasises about killing her.

I have Ivor. Molly has Zoë. It must be terrible to be alone.

Light enters the skin

June. Fynn puts me up against a white pebble-dash wall half in shade to photograph me with my new shoulder-length Afro. I make him pose for me too. A certain expression in his eye shoots something through me and I have to rush in for a kiss.

He teaches me about apertures, light shrinking. In the intimate infra-red glow of the photography club darkroom, I watch as he develops undulations of granite hillocks, sodden leaves glinting in the lustre of afternoon light. My eye is drawn to the sun reaching down over a ladder between buildings. A bird lifting off.

I photograph his shadow climbing the stairs, a broken line flickering. His silhouette breaking the skyline with camera bag and pipe. Great trees overhead, a long light-spiked avenue beneath. I spot a boy, wait for the crease of a smile. A pair of women gossiping from two cars. A cigarette tossed and footed. Guys lifting their heads to the ceiling and blowing rings; a twilit verandah, flirt of lighters.

In his *rondavel*, I stand on tiptoe to lean my chin on Fynn's shoulder. Our eyes meet in his mirror over the basin. In my hand, a totem. I flash back to Iria's instructions. Pressed into the invisible part of him, my invisible breasts. A sting to my nostrils, as in the darkroom.

Love lessons

12, Pemray Drive. Friday. Hedy and I meet in the corridor as I'm leaving the bathroom. She and Greg have been arguing as usual, their voices drifting through my window from the patio. Why do you keep going back to Greg, I ask her, when you are always fighting? Darling, she says, cupping my cheek, it's rare to find a man for whom you feel *passion* as well as a mental connection. That combination supersedes everything else. I will always love Greg, and he will always love me, whether we're married or not.

In my bedroom, I repeat her gesture in front of the mirror. She is fun, full of surprises, generous. But then, always spiked by the vodka, there's that lava flow of her dangerous energy. And I think about what Gary said.

Several hours later, Hedy's hostile mood had become elevated, like a door whipping open, caught by a bruising wind, then slamming shut. Cruel words. Greg keeps a strangled silence.

It's a Pyrrhic victory for Hedy.

Next day she calls Dad to say they've split up again.

Thorns and spikes

August. As Dad drives out of the city, past roadside stalls, women and children selling tomatoes, or bread, or biltong hanging from sticks, I mention Benjamin's suicide in the Botanical Gardens. And Sebastian's, in the garage at home. A hot wind shoots through the window, across the bass of the car radio, snatching my words. Dad, in his usual attire of beige trousers, white shirt, socks and leather lace-ups, curls his lip. He doesn't do maudlin. Slows down at the robots and calls over a boy of about twelve selling The Herald. Slips him some coins. Thanks *baas.* He claps his cupped hands. Grey school shorts and green singlet flapping in the wind, no shoes. The boy is looking in my direction, but his eyes seem lost inside some other place.

Dad turns up the volume on the radio. *Three members of the Red Cross have been ambushed and murdered...*

He pulls up at the base of a mighty *kopje.* Huge ridges of granite, rounded and weathered, balanced delicately on needle points. Two children offer us yellow sugar fruit in a green enamel basin. What's this place called? I ask them, gesturing. Ngomo Kurira says the taller girl, gingham school dress, hopping up and down as I choose several fruit and give her some coins. Knock-kneed, skinny legs, same as me. Langton has miraculously appeared from behind a heart-booming, threatening rock. How did he know we were here?

Dad and Langton attach a tow rope to his broken-down pick-up while I study the terrain. Rock walls, ninety-degrees sheer, up from a narrow valley floor, cut deep by rainwater. The radio continues to intone: *Two black men were killed by a landmine; two black women by an explosive device.* Dense scrub, sprouting from minute patches of soil. *Five people were shot before being burnt to death in a hut.* Slabs, mottled yellow with lichen. *Two white women were shot by a terrorist gang in the Montclair Hotel.* Rain sweeps across the distant view. Thunder claps its cupped hands. The ancestral spirits are not on our side. Fear grips my insides and squeezes a hysteria out of me. *Let's go, let's go, let's go!*

Secret Places

August. Of course your stories are similar, says Mrs Smith, because you are all girls, of similar ages, living similar lives, experiencing similar emotions, going to the same school and learning the same subjects. What distinguishes your writing is *how* you process those experiences. Our minds and sensibilities are revealed through our use of language, she says. Now, let me see what you can do. Your assignment for the end of year competition is to draft an essay titled *Secret Places*.

*

I write about my apple tree in Ireland where I planted myself in a crook to read, pressing my book against a perfectly positioned branch, the warm heel of my palm flattening each page. I write about moving house and losing my tree. About moving house over and over, until eventually I learned that all I have to do to go to a secret place, is close my eyes. In this secret garden that comes with me everywhere and belongs to me only, I can breathe freely. Walk along my own private paths, even when my life is upended again and again.

I find myself writing about the fact that some people have never had a tree, or a room or even a bed to themselves. They have lived every minute of their lives in the presence of others. But no matter where anyone is in the world, whatever their circumstance, they can go to this secret place, the most intimate thing we have, more intimate even than our bodies.

*

I burst in the door, shrieking with amazed joy, waving a silver trophy at everyone around the bar. Dad pops open a bottle of champagne.

Another bite of the dust

A percussion through the house, like the wind outside. Ivor has been expelled again, along with a friend. Apparently the two of them climbed over the fence and hitch-hiked to Bulawayo at night. Came back to the school with booze, headlong into trouble.

*

My father is sitting at the breakfast table. His mood is thoughtful, quiet. So, before anyone else appears, I take a chance. Dad, I say. Ivor's like you. He's more likely to be a giver of orders than a taker of them. At least that prank showed initiative, imagination and courage. Don't give up on him.

Dad lifts his head. It was more than a prank, Itosha. He could have been killed. The school's in a hot area. A stern note in his voice. I sit down, lift a box of Willards Cornflakes and pour. Well, I'm glad he's home and safe now. Aren't you? My reward is a grunt.

*

Ivor has been enrolled at Speciss, a local 'A' Level college. So relieved he's away from that brutal place. That's the bright light opening up in the clouds. And Ivor's friend from Plumtree, the one who was also expelled, is at Speciss too, so he's happy, loving his new freedom, and especially the lack of regular beatings.

*

I know I know, that's three expulsions now. But I think I can manage to stick it out at Speciss, Ivor grins to me, once all the tensions have died down.

Only, as it turns out, he won't be sticking it out after all.

A walk on the dark side

Hedy phones my parents at four in the morning. After shadow-boxing with her demons, she says, she took some pills.

My father swiftly climbs into his clothes and drives over, takes her to hospital to be pumped. I wonder why she didn't call Greg. Or maybe she did and he refused to go over, seeing her act as a form of manipulation.

Wind-spirit

The wind outside, buffeting the house, my bedroom walls, psyche. This unquiet. And a full moon too. Can't see it, but the sky is eerie, preternaturally bright, reminding me of that night in Zambia, out by the pool, Black and I talking. And I wonder if he's alive, looking at the moon wherever he is. If he ever thinks of me. Feel shame about the colonial elitism of our lives. The way white men have made themselves the Lords of the Dance in Africa. I was more innocent then, and felt close to him, in a way I wouldn't be able to now, because of our starkly different positions. As a child, I'd never thought of him as our cook, but as a friend.

Black. What a name. Who gave it to him? Why didn't we ask if he had another name, a birth name?

My world feels like one of parallel realities. When I'm in Ireland, I belong to a formerly oppressed people. When I'm here, the mere colour of my skin grants me all sorts of privilege, based on the oppression of others.

The wind picks up momentum, jerks me to a more alert consciousness, like a teacher slapping a cane down onto the desk. My slightly open window rattles furiously. Wide wide awake, jolted-upright awake. The wrongness stares me in the face, clear as my own pale face in the mirror opposite. Feel as though some kind of message has passed, via the wind, from Black to me.

Losses

September. I peer around the door of the scullery. The hot hiss of iron on tomorrow's uniforms. Through the open window, the salt-sachet women singing in harmony, yellow and blue notes ringing across the paved driveway.

Moses, I say. Where is your family?

He puts the iron on its stand, stutters a quick, embarrassed laugh. Ah, my wife, she die many, many years ago. During the birth of our number four child. My children are in Malawi. They are grown now.

The news on the radio in the living room leaks in. *Yesterday a Viscount was shot down just west of Karoi…*

Why did you come here? I came here for work, he says, maybe fifteen years ago. No jobs in Malawi. And your fourth child? I'm leaning against the counter. Did he – or she – survive?

Belly-landed in a field…hit a ditch, somersaulted…thirty eight killed on impact…

Yes, he says, the tea-towel hanging limply from his hands. Only realise now that he looks older than I had assumed – almost a *madara*. Kindly eyes, some missing teeth. Sinewy arms. Skin light brown, close-cropped hair, small dome of a shaved head. Fine bone structure. He must have been handsome when young. Yes. Ujana. She is married now. My mother, she took her to raise, because I have to work. Do you ever go back to Malawi to see your family? He looks down at the floor and shakes his head. Maybe, one, two times, but it's difficult now.

In the next room, Dad turns up the radio.…*ten massacred at the site…ZIPRA Joshua Nkomo has claimed responsibility for shooting down the plane but denied murdering the survivors…*

Are you happy here? Moses smiles shyly. I have work and that is a good thing. I can send money home. Your mother is a kind madam.

I'm sorry, Moses. I look at him. About your wife.

He looks at the ground. Thank you.

I withdraw into the kitchen, scoop some porridge into a bowl, cover it with milk, brown sugar, smother of cream. Through the open doorway of the scullery, Moses, staring down at the ironed clothes. I head in to the living room, blowing on my first spoonful. Try to imagine having to leave your family so you can get money to feed them.

Mum pivots to face me, familiar and strange, as though it's another woman's face I'm looking at.

Desire and folly

Fingers pressed to my mouth. You sure? Yes. My grandmother left it to me. I want you to have it. Try it on. I slide the plain gold band on to the third finger of my right hand. A perfect fit. I stand on the sofa, bend down to kiss Fynn's nose. All the music in the room is streaming towards us. From the open door, the charging sky, pedestals of trees whirl in. The air, citrus.

This – thing – is a balancing act. A moment can shift it.

Fynn…
as his hand swims down my body, slides under my skirt…and it could be this moment...
My hand is a stop sign.
Fynn, I repeat, I have to wait until I'm married.
He becomes still.
It's a Catholic thing.
I gaze at the ground. Will he want his ring back?
Actually, it's a promise. To my Dad, when I was twelve.
How would he know? says Fynn, looking up at me.
I think of my father's capturing eyes every time I walk in the front door.
He just would, I say.

Fynn's whole face is a study in intensity. Will you marry me?

When did the clouds rush in, multiplying as though the sky were contagious? Saddled up, they hurl like runaway horses across the sky. Rain begins, hitting the thatch above us.

The imperative of gravity

You tip
sideways,
your head
a shield
against
the steep
screaming
wall
of wind,
against
the gigantic looming
of granite kopjes,
and tree-clusters,
breath
skinny
and you
a prong
in this amplified
stairwell, this
rush…

Not in the ditch

September. Molly and I jangle bangles on our forearms. Glances east and west of us at the airport. Bags are searched. Our white-gold bangles look like tat. In London, we go to Jermyn Street, as instructed. The man is expecting us and has a cheque ready. We deposit it into Dad's account.

You can keep one bangle each, Dad told us. If you ever land in the ditch, you can sell it.
In London with Mum, he has landed in the ditch himself. A herniated disc. Thus our emergency trip. He needs that forex for a spine operation.

*

On our return flight back home, as we approach for the landing, my body feels tense, anticipating another heat-seeking missile.

The cabin is blacked out. We begin the descent. Scrunch eyes and grip hands. This flimsy metal holding us in a precarious space between life and death. The plane has to land on a runway that will be unlit until the last second. Although we don't mention it, I know Molly's thinking about the Viscount too.

After being hit, that Viscount crash-landed in a field, then hit a *donga* and the plane burst into flames. Fourteen survived out of fifty two passengers. But not for long. Five went to look for water. Three ran and hid in the bush when they saw armed men approaching. The rest – including two children and a baby – were massacred.

Johan, the mercenary, was part of the rescue team. The worst for him was folding a blanket around an air hostess's battered, naked body. Some things, he said, weren't mentioned in the reports.

She was only three years older than me.

As the plane tips sideways, I try to block out the image of the survivors, even a mother and her newborn, shot and bayoneted after staggering from the flaming plane. Molly and I grip each other in the dark silence.

The runway lighting up as the wheels touch down. A spontaneous outburst of applause.
Dad is safe, and we are too.

Code

Outside the open window of my bedroom, very loud crickets. Rain must be imminent.

Why do you keep a diary? Fynn asks, picking it up. To process my thoughts, I suppose. We're sitting on my bed. Can't imagine not ending each day by writing in it. Call it a life raft. Keeps me afloat. I wriggle off my school shoes and ankle socks. Sometimes I write in code in case anyone pries, hint hint! I take it from him and drop it to the floor. Will you remember your code when re-reading your diaries at eighty? he winks, strolling his fingers along my outstretched leg, under the pleated teal skirt of my Form Six uniform. I giggle at the tickles, and the notion of ever being eighty.

The crickets are the loudest I've ever heard. *Kre-kre.* Suddenly, I cop on. It's Molly and Zoë, spying on us, chirping, wanting to be caught. Scram, I shout, and pull the curtains. Honestly, kids, I grin. Through the wall, I hear music. We forget about talking for a while.

Promise

Have a drink with me, Dad says. I shuffle onto a bar stool and take a chance.
Dad.
Wait until he looks up.
I don't think I'll be able to keep my promise to you, you know, about staying a virgin until I'm married. Fynn will be called up after school and…
Instantly, Dad is as alert as a soldier listening for a landmine click.
What are you saying to me? Have you slept with him?
No, no, I haven't. Not yet. But Dad, this isn't Ireland. Things are different here. There's not the same stigma. Sex…
Stop. Right. There.
His tone is a brewing storm.
Dad, I'm just telling you, because I want to be honest with you. I'm eighteen now, so you can't stop me (this just occurring to me as I'm speaking).
I can kick you out of the house; cut you off. You won't be able to…
Threats fall like rain-turned-into-steely hail. I wait for a while.
Dad, you know I've earned a bursary to go to Rhodes. And a scholarship. And a loan. I don't need your money. I can get a job for extra expenses.
Dad's expression is new. A plea. Can you at least promise to wait until you graduate?

Three more years.

I don't want to be a disappointment in my father's eyes. Seen by him as a harlot, with shame signposted on my back. Even worse, to be disowned.

Mum and Dad were virgins on their wedding night. Or so he's always said.

Once in bed, my diary open, I scrawl, the movement of my pen across paper barely able to keep up with my agitated thoughts.

Pause to think about the promise I've just made. How can his power over me be stronger than love, than my body's own impulses? Or is my promise triggered by something else?

A wife's choice

When you marry, darling, my mother says, always make sure your husband is your number one priority. Your children will leave home, and if you've poured all your attention into them, you'll have nothing left to share with your husband when they're gone.

I *will* pour all my love and attention into my children, I think. *If* I marry.

*

She is crying when I get back from school. I have never seen her cry before. Her inner life, her thoughts and emotions, I suddenly realise, have always been off-limits. I don't know my mother at all, except via surface appearances.

Mum? I say, a host of butterflies taking wing in the pit of my stomach. What happened?

Turns out marriage isn't all it's cracked up to be.

The only way to comprehend some things is via rage. I blaze out the front door, drive like an out-of-control bush fire to Helen's house. Boxlike torso, atop skinny legs, the usual cigarette. Tosh, how lovely…Don't you DARE touch me, I say as she reaches. Yank my hand away. You CUNT! You whore! You CUNT, I say again, the first time a swear word has ever left my mouth. In front of her two younger kids. Hope you're happy that you've destroyed our family. She pools her hands around her, gaping. But Tosha, you don't know the whole... I spin off, like a top, before tears start. A thousand what ifs snaking through my mind.

Brokenly

My bed, a refuge for a powerless mother. But not for long. Dad blattering in, like a wind that could tear the stripes off a zebra, dragging her out of the bed, down the long tunnel of the corridor, her wail, and I'm screaming for Ivor, and at last my brother appears, naked. There have been verbal altercations before, but this is a flailing of fists, crammed with a lifetime's worth of unexploded fury. Cave of a mouth open. Stop, says her voice. Have you no respect for your father?

Rain blurs the window. Thunder is a slamming door.

Backlash

Monomatapa Hotel. One of the uniformed buzz cuts approaches. Even from a distance, I can tell from the slope of his shoulders that it's Ivor. We choose a corner in Prospector's, the hotel bar. A song comes on the radio. As one, a dozen soldiers at the counter scrape back their barstools, stand up, lift their glasses and join in: *We're all Rhodesians and we'll fight through thick and thin…*Embarrassed, I peep surreptitiously at the black barman, who is cautiously clearing away glasses, as though handling dynamite.

Ivor, tall, but slight-shouldered, skinny as a heron compared to the other guys in khaki. His hard number one, like a convict readied for blood-thirsty challenges. Devastatingly distant, alien eyes. *I am the owner of my own life*, he said, when he told me he had dropped out of the 'A' level course at Speciss College, added a year to his age and enlisted.

I know it's not just this last outburst. A massive store of long-accumulated anger had finally reached the point of explosion. I wish I could tell him I love him without having to insert irony. All I can summon is, *What if…?* He stares into the middle distance. I don't care. The thunder of anger in his expression. Yellow butterflies of terror whip through my insides.

Sometimes, I consider how each day is unique, like an individual's gait, the way it follows its own light. Darkness too. This day I won't forget. I watch his glass as he angles it, slides beer in. The passage between glass and lip. I am partly responsible for his decision. If I hadn't screamed his name, he wouldn't have heard a thing from the *rondavel*.

Ivor: At the time, the idea of possibly dying never occurred to me. I just had to get away. Get out of the house.

Hands hanging at my sides

What, in God's name, happened? I'll never understand how my mother is cobbling herself back together, as though nothing is different.

Happiness, my mum tells me, is a decision.

I love him, darling, she says simply, and her eyes say more than just those words. And now she'll set about dissolving all the heart pain, like an aspirin in water, through denial. What must that do to the hidden pockets of the heart and mind and body?

I know that for me, my father has become muddied, ugly, diminished, banal. That grand romance I thought they had was just a charade for whatever audience was around to witness and envy it. I am crushed, despondent, and cynical about love.

The following Friday, there he is, the host, the husband, the hypocrite, lapping up sympathy for his recent op, though he's long recovered after their extended sojourn. My mother can propel herself back if she likes, but from now on, I'm instructing myself to see marriage as just another form of colonisation.

In the kitchen, a pint glass thuds to the floor, heavily. The way adults readjust seems as possible as standing that glass upright again. An emotional ripping apart, then a return to the usual behaviour. Feelings as illusory as the won't-happen-again.

It's marriage, Mum says. You'll understand when you're older. Through the window, I look at that woman, her so-called friend, back in our house, waving her arm like a wand, casting a spell over the pool.

When Mum leaves my room, tears shuffle me out of love for my father, the way a child shuffles into longer bones.

We are a family of masks.

Bolts of everything

Panting walk up the last part of the steep hill, pushing my bike, thunder and lightning jumping me every few minutes. Finally, at last, still alive, I reach our front door. Mum and Molly, whirling to Gloria Gaynor's *I Will Survive*, top volume. Soggy and giddy at seeing my mum like this, I feel an uprush of birds in my chest. Don't come in wet! Bathroom, she points. Walk on the newspapers.

As I peel off my soaked uniform, one of Dad's stories, about when he arrived home from the Congo, comes to me. Mum wouldn't let him in to the house. She ran inside, locked the door, fetched a bowl of hot water, shaving cream, razor and handed them to him through the window. You can enter when you've removed that caterpillar from your face, she'd said. And he'd shaved, there and then, on the lawn.

I love that story. My mother's empowerment. Mum says she did it because I was screaming in fear at this stranger, tall as a giraffe, who had been away for a third of my life. And she thought it would make him more familiar to me again. Also, she winked, she hated moustaches. If you can't see a man's mouth, you don't know what kind of man he is.

Mum's stilettos, changing to a sharper, higher pitch as she approaches the bathroom.

A swallow dive involves leaping up into the air, feeling its rush flow over your body, flipping, then plunging into the pool. Everything is different under water, that denser element. Sound, volume, temperature, your body, somehow magnified. A pause. Then the propulsion up, shaking water from your ears, a moment before reality shape-shifts again. That's how it feels when she tells me.

She doesn't say where they are going, or for how long. All she says is look after your father, and study hard for your exams. Then she walks out the door, taking Molly with her. Leaving

me behind.

Hollow

My fault. I was the one who urged her to leave. Not me though, Mum. Not leave *me*.

Ice-bucket tongs, one edge sharp as a mother who's left. Pressing into my palms, spindly marks. Light trickles down through the drooping willow leaves.

Owowowow! Blood from the brambles.

Ivor has gone. Mum has gone. Molly has gone.

His inability to resist the usual vultures, vodka bottles, sliced lemons. The usual ructions hammering through the wall.

I scrape at the ground. All the unrealised expressions of love, replaced by spikes, ignorings, hurtful sayings, missings. In the dirt, I doodle patterns. A skeleton of impressions.

You have your exams, she'd said. You need to stay. And look after your father.

For those three days, I didn't forgive her.

Study. Write exams. Study. Write exams. Study. Write exams. Study. Write exams.

Soon, it's all be over, and I'll be gone too.

Bones reply to the ground

Blood spilling
from your
mouth.
Rock. Fire.
A tree you clean
missed.
All the world's
rock' roll
is drumming
into your vertebrae.
Your mind splitting
from the far screaming
pulses of agony.
But you
are alive.
And already
a creaturely vehicle
is pelting
towards your radius
of sound.

Something else

The usual sessions, strangers, drunks, glassy-eyed as chameleons. Remembering what happened to Molly, I push the wardrobe against my door. Shadows, excessive as a brutal passion for alcohol. I creak my school cardigan sleeve over my eyes. Darkness. Somewhere near dawn, the music sighs into silence. Voices flick open and shut, like a door. Sleep is a garden, erasing the deafening odours of alcohol.

In the morning, doors pass me down the corridor. Into his room for lunch money. And shock. A moustache. A red-against-white. The colouration of eyelids. Purple. Cigarette smoke and something else.

Mum's muffled words heaping up in my head. *Dún do bhéal.* Keep your mouth shut.

A grey sky crosses the rectangle of the dining room window, stodgy as the porridge I'm eating. The house is thick with paused momentum.

I have to get out of here.

Illusion and invincibility

December. Twenty-two of us are heading to Kariba to celebrate the end of exams, the end of our school life. Because of the war, we must travel in convoy, herded by armed escorts. From Mukuti, the road drops dramatically into the swelter of the Zambezi valley. We slow down for the corkscrew, like a line of divers being lowered over a boat. Mosaics of light strobe across foliage. Tufty trees wave battle-scarred, foot-lopped legs in the air, as though doing handstands. I try not to think of the fact that Kariba, on the Zambian border, has already been bombed or mortared several times.

Fynn, Lois, Jade and I have caught a lift with Josh, who takes each tense bend with caution, in case we surprise an elephant or lion, or land into an ambush. In the back, we're all barefoot, feet up on the seat backs. Phew, it's hot. I wipe my forehead with my forearm. I'd say the temperature is nudging up to forty degrees. Float an arm out the window. A hot packet of air. Insects, smacking into my hand. *Thwick.* And then suddenly there it is, cupped in the palm of the valley, the starry-eyed lake, motor boats floating across its turquoise surface like dragon flies.

Wow. Some wall, I say. Scores of Italian and local builders tumbled from that wall into the water below, or were accidentally interred in the concrete while they were building it, says Fynn. Despite the heat, a shudder briefly takes possession of my body. The locals say that was *Nyaminyami,* the river god, showing his anger, he says. Our hands meet accidentally on the sticky upholstery. An electric fuzz. You heard about the Tonga tribe having to be forcefully evacuated? I nod. And Operation Noah? I nod again. Everyone talks about the *heroic* capture and relocation of six thousand animals, says Lois, sitting forward, her T-shirt drenched at the back, like a splatter of beer on a tablecloth, but they fail to mention how many more thousands died when the valley was flooded. I flap her T-shirt for her. But you have to agree that ultimately the dam transformed millions of lives for the better, adds Josh from the driver's seat. Lois is always debating with Fynn and Josh. I drift off, watching baobabs, the road and its red dirt shoulders, signs of wildlife in the bush. Woo-hoo! yells Jade, hauling half her body out the front passenger window and waving both arms at a pair of rudely rutting baboons. No more exams! No more school! Freedom! Well, freedom for a minute, says Fynn, eyes sideways at me. We'll be getting our call-up papers next month. I stare at him. Let's not think about that now.

The road loops and loops, all the way to the tail, coiled tight as a sleeping *Nyaminyami.* Tight as all the stories buried under this epicentre, with their alternative dimensions of history.

Water bird

Kariba. Time after time, I sit on the edge of the pier, skis tilted skyward as the boat pulls away, only to topple straight in. My bikini top snaps off, and I huddle in the water, scrabble to refasten it, hold on to the rope, un-splay the skis, keep an eye out for crocs. *Take it off, take it off,* shout the guys. I am a spectacle. Eat embarrassment. Have I fallen apart because of my fallout with Fynn? He is about to go to *war.*

Soldiers on R&R at the Carribea Bay poolside bar are laughing. They must have been the ones shooting at crocodiles last night, bullets striking the water like fish eagles.

Head down, I mope past the uniforms with blue SAS emblems. The heat wraps around me, clings too tightly. I can almost taste it in the back of my throat. Or maybe it's the shame. Hear my name being called. Itosha. It's Keith, Helen's older son. He beckons me over to a quiet corner with a twitch of his head. Oh god, has he heard about my showdown with his mother? Me calling her a cunt?

When I get close, he says quietly, if you want another go, I can take you out tomorrow before anyone else is awake.

*

A sluggish fan slices the humidity, to minimal effect. Barely any respite. Day-and-night sweat lie side-by-side like notes on a xylophone. Instead of sleeping, I read a Wilbur Smith novel left in the casita – *The Sun Bird* – at great speed and with total absorption. At 5am, a tap on our casita door. I tiptoe out. The girls don't even stir.

The plaited blue and pink dawn; the sky, quick and quiet. Keith starts the engine of a rocking navy and white speedboat. On the shoreline, a buffalo grazing. Tick birds balance on the tray of his back, like *demi-tasse* cups.

The smoothest way to stand up, says Keith, is not from the pier, but from deep water. We have to motor right out, to the middle of the lake, where it's colder. No crocodiles. No bilharzia.

The lake is slowly growing a veil of pink silk. We pierce into it and then he cuts the engine for me to descend the ladder into the water. Once I've given him the thumbs up, we're off. I shudder to standing. Soon I am cross-hatching the wake, trample-to-smooth, a glow-in-the-dawn glory. There's no one to see, only Keith and a fish eagle perched in the crotch of one of the charcoal tree-corpses ghosting out of the water.

Cloud in the orange tree

Carribea Bay, Kariba. The sky throwing parties of sunshine over the lake, stars flaking the evening sky, cocktails in the Portuguese-style hotel, rustic and cool. A casino, the marina, a speedboat and skiing, several pools and thatched bars. A trampoline and lawns and a beach. Distant lion grumbles at night. Bamboo ceiling fans clocketing, like irrational feelings lurking at the bottom of every thought.

Here we are, away from the parents for the first time, and I'm still all complicated. Fynn is a bristling husk and barbed wire. He's about to walk into war, while I'm flanked by Lois and Jade, two chaperones in a girls-only casita. I love your fierce innocence, says Jade, twining one of my afro curls around her finger. It's a big part of who you are.

Jade has Titch, the guy she thinks she'll marry. And Lois has already lost her virginity to Antonio, a lovely, gentle Greek guy she's been seeing, not from our school. Had to try it out. Nothing to write home about, she said at the time.

She sits on the bed beside me and makes sure I am paying attention before she speaks. Don't let any guy – not even Fynn – force you into doing anything you don't want to do, she says. If you're not ready, you're not ready.

I meet him at the outdoor bar and tell him I'm staying in the casita with the girls. Fynn doesn't understand. Who would know? And haven't we nearly gone all the way anyway? He says he'll have to break up with me unless I change my mind. I say it's not just my dad. But the truth is, I don't understand either.

Sighs and incredibles

December, Monomatapa Hotel. Mono's, a curved upright playing card from a distance. I park Mum's pale green Austin Cambridge in Rotten Row, and a young boy emerges from somewhere to mind it. The city shuffles the faces of just-out-of-school soldiers, faint trail of salt and sweat. A vendor rolls his cart past me, skimming so close that my groin jumps. Enter the lobby, cross to the Prospectus bar. There's my brother, in his new RLI uniform. He lifts his chin. We head for our corner and a waiter materialises to take our order. I hand over goodies scrounged from the pantry. And $40, the sum total of my puny savings. Thanks Tosh. You're the best. So how was training? I say. Anyone you know from school? No, he says. They're mostly mercenaries. Mercenaries? Well, how else do you think our army can hold up against forty thousand gooks with commie training and hardware back-up? I'm about to heave a sigh, when I catch myself. He's always on about me doing that. The waiter presents our drinks and Ivor takes a swig direct from his beer bottle. Don't worry. They call the RLI *The Incredibles*. And I was a crack shot during training. Dad was too, I say. Ivor gets his black-eyed look. Don't mention him. In fact, I don't want to hear anything about what's going on at home.

So, I can't tell him.

I stroke his number one haircut. He jerks away. Hey, off! A faraway ambulance wails. At the bar counter, guys in camouflage are lining up shots. I deflect, trying to keep the safety catch on. Was it tough? Not as hard as I expected, he shrugs. Lack of sleep's the worst thing – they had us up at 2am for a run, up again at 5am. He laughs. Funny how I've always had 'an issue with authority' as Mr Holme at Oriel put it, but I'm handling the military orders, no problem. That's because you're a rebel just by being in the army, at sixteen. He grins. Seventeen now. I risk it. But keep your cool, hey? No flinging your rifle to the ground, like your tennis racquet! It might go off. Ivor slugs back his drink. *Ja.* Speaking of which, a guy called Sparks was right in this bar with his fiancée after watching *The Deer Hunter,* he says. And one of his mates challenged him to a game of Russian roulette. Sparky said sure. The guy slots in a bullet, spins, aims the gun at his own head and fires. Click. Everyone in the bar cheers. He hands over the pistol. Sparks tosses back a triple, snogs his girlfriend, spins the chamber, flicks it shut, presses it to his skull. *Boom.* Right in front of her.

I put my hand to my mouth as he says it. Even in war, I suppose, death isn't something you see coming, even when it's aiming right at you. Even when you're doing the aiming.

Counter-story

12, Pemray Drive, December. There are many ways to slant a story. Mum's version goes underground, replaced by the jellyfish sting of Dad's quips. She had checked in as Ryan, he says to the Friday gathering. And the receptionist had dimpled when Callie said she was a farmer's wife from Rusape, he says. Oh, you'll qualify for the farmer's discount then. Everyone laughing.

She'd taken Molly shopping for a new wardrobe, out to meals.

He's calling it a *spree.*

The detective found her and Dad persuaded her to come home.

Was it surrender or forgiveness?

Now his counter-stories: Dad talks about the time he was asked for *his* name, spotted a magazine on the hotel coffee table and said 'Harper'. Cue hilarity. No one asks why *he* needed an alias.

Dad is like a honeymoon husband again. My parents dance together on the patio, as thousands of stars feather down around them and Dad is romantic, contrite, demonstrative. Winning her back.

White-and-noise coverings

New Year's Eve. Andrew Fleming Hospital, Salisbury. Ivor is swathed like a mummy, only eyes and a mouth-hole visible. So, how's the form? I try to disguise my fear. The fire folding into his skin. Into his face, arms, chest. *What are the white bandages covering?* Words warble out, almost incoherently. Mum not with you? She'll be along later. We're staggering visits, so you don't get sick of us. I don't tell him about the army chaplain introducing himself, saying…*I'm calling about your son…there was a gas explosion.* Mum collapsing to the ground, Molly and I rushing to her, Dad seizing the handset, crisp as crackling. What did you just say to my wife?

Behind me, a straggle of soldiers enter the room. Howzit, Sergeant, Ivor says, raising a bandaged arm. What are you doing in a place like this? The sergeant grins. What are we all doing in a place like this? A Scots accent. You're looking well. I think white's my colour, quips Ivor. Need a straw? We brought one, just in case. How are the nurses? asks one of the guys. Brilliant. They crack me up. And I get the VIP treatment. Ice-cream, strawberries. I'm going to marry a nurse when all this is over. Ivor tries to sit up and I rush to settle pillows behind him. Is the war over yet? A few uniforms huddle around the bed, some sitting. Don't worry, we'll keep it going till you get back out there. Just took R&R to celebrate New Year with you.

One of the guys tactlessly flips open a lighter. Ivor's head jerks. Oops. Sorry mate.

But you are alive.

Someone pops off a beer cap. The nurses turned a blind eye to the crate as they came in, but the noise is becoming elevated now. Pipe down in there. A querulous face peers around the door. Ah, Matron, come on. A slight gesture of the head. Have a drink with us. She waves a no thank you and closes the door. Another chorus of whispery guffaws and the room's in colour again. It's great to be here, says Ivor. It's great to be anywhere.

Fleeting, not entirely specific

Lake McIlwaine. January. I'm out the back, thrusting my arm into a huge zinc tub filled with blocks of ice, cool drinks and beers, when Keith appears. I wanted to thank you again. For Kariba, I mean. But also for inviting me to your 21st. I'm standing with a dripping Coke bottle in my hand, and a long wet arm.

He's borrowed my parents' boathouse for the party. Mum and Dad are here too. He stands so close, I can detect aftershave, booze on his breath. He briefly kisses me on the mouth. Grins and moves back inside, without saying a word.

My gaze floats through the open door, to the legs of the blond, sophisticated girls, sweat between their breasts, down their spines, arms, upper lips. Touch my own. I know he's seeing someone from my class at school. She's here.

He was just being friendly, I tell myself sternly. Catch yourself on.

Keith turns around in the doorway when I call out to say please tell my parents I'm getting a lift back, and waves, an image I'll keep replaying in my mind later, until his hand no longer raises itself, and I begin to doubt whether he had even said goodbye.

Cri de coeur

February. An aerogram. Long, dashing bursts of words, asking me to thank Mum and Dad for the use of their boathouse. Offering to take me skiing again when he gets back next week. Only, by the time the letter arrives, he's dead.

Can't put a name to what I'm feeling. It's too raw. Too sharp, planing down my spine.

Once, Ivor told me he dreamt that he was dead. Death was a cell, padlocked, blacker than black.

Keith was a regular in the SAS. He managed to survive the war for three whole years. He was a week away from completing his contract.

At the funeral, Molly takes one look at his mother's ravaged face and sobs come blurting. Helen's grief is arms wrapped around shoulders like a scarf, mouth's 'O' pressed into flesh. Helen, my nemesis, collapses into my arms, which I open to her, seeing myself as the very flower of grace and forgiveness, and there's also an ache; he'd want this.

Later, I sit with his younger brother, Harry. I wish it had been me who had died, he says miserably, crouched over, on a hard wooden seat, head bowed. He was the hero in our family. I squeeze his hand.

It was Johan, the mercenary, in C squadron with Keith, whom I overheard murmuring about the army's own faulty landmine exploding as they were setting it. Five SAS soldiers blown up. I knew one of the other soldiers too, a former Oriel boy. His girlfriend was in my class.

Sand in the coffins to weight them. Their bodies became smithereens, molecules merging with Mozambican tree clusters and pale, curly grasses, wind and levitating dust. That is their real grave, in a foreign country, with only crickets to attend them.

At least some of their elements and emanations are still in the atmosphere, not locked up in a coffin in the blacker than black underground.

Eyes like a blackout

12th February. It's better to live your own life than to live vicariously through characters in a story, Fynn says. Shorn head, that particular English intonation of his, sharper. He's home on R&R after his first contact, and already harder, a stranger. I flinch as though my appendicitis has come back. I'm about to leave for university in South Africa. A quote he self-murmurs: *everything becomes erstwhile, like time.* Heat of intimacy crossed with alienation. War has blurred or broken something. Fynn is locked up tight inside a black box. Can't intuit what's hidden in the spaces between his words.

Tenderness of knives

Another letter. *And oh by the way, Butterfly Barbara. She's an angel, tiny, brunette, with a dimple, tattoo wings, arms always open for an embrace. You couldn't call her a whore. She welcomes in all of us soldiers, gratis.*

Fynn wants me to know this. Revenge for my reticence?

My mind splitting from a far, internal screaming. A shutter flicks down, remains stuck.

Under closed eyes

A chainsaw buzz
of pain.
The seagull girl
and Antonio
(whom you know
through Lois),
pull your jumpsuit taut,
a makeshift stretcher
to protect
your shattered spine,
lift you into a VW,
yellow as the butterflies
of lichen.
I'm Kate, she says.
You travelled 15k's
beyond the drop zone!
You close your eyes.
When she lays
her hands on you,
heat charges
through your body.

Hedy's sorrow

While I am at Rhodes University, I hear that Greg is dead. Not the war, but a stroke. Everyone is devastated – he was only in his forties. Hedy has fallen apart. She is spending the days in her pyjamas, drinking almost continuously. Perhaps she could cope with their separations while he was alive because she could dream of a reunion, but now he is dead, it means that hope has died too.

Alone, her days and nights must make her feel so desolate. The colour of her life turning to ash.

*

According to Hedy, my father says, her rows with Gary are growing blacker and blacker. He's moved out. Joined the police force.

*

Hedy's 3am drunken calls to my parents are on the increase. Dad says that our family is Hedy's only refuge. How can he refuse support?

I think of that old spark of hers, which could have lit up a bonfire. What will become of her?

I am also afraid of the power of love. Is this what it can do to you?

*

One night, my father gets a call. He and Mum go over to Hedy's house together.

Oh Hedy. *Voddies for the bodies,* I hear her whisper in my ear. And then she snorts.

*

The verdict is suicide.

The day making history

18th April. When I return for my ten-day vac, Mum and Dad pick me up from the airport. Out of curiosity, we take a detour into the city.

Everything is blurred into a euphoric chaos. A flow down Jameson Avenue, past the statue of Cecil Rhodes, spilling into Fourth Street and Second Street. Women and children, ululating, transistor radios tuned to rhythmic beats. Across the street, a dog sniffs a signpost, claims it. Men hugging, running, raising their fists to the sky in jubilation, joy glinting their eyes. One guy shimmies up a telegraph pole to whoop and wave. Others scramble up trees in Cecil Rhodes Park and lie like lizards along branches, or perch on the walls of surrounding buildings to observe the celebrations from a height. There are no other whites anywhere in sight. Fear blows down my throat. But, in our Mercedes, we are ignored. This is a city of other stories now.

Dad drives us to our new house, which he's just bought. A double storey, walled boundary, impressive gates. It doesn't have anything like the personality, warmth and ambience of 12, Pemray Drive.

The Rawson family turns up to watch the news with us. The war is over, and today, the country has officially become the independent Republic of Zimbabwe.

Electricity and something else

Dad playing, the bar prop-ups watching him as though they are sunflowers facing the sun. Some things in our life are as predictable as the hands of a grandfather clock, flicking past the inevitable integers. Only everything else has changed.

Although the political wind has swivelled in a different direction, the new president's inaugural speech earlier today, all about forgiving and forgetting the sins of the war, of history, brought a tentative relief. *Whether you're black or white, join me in a new pledge to forget our grim past, join hands in a new amity and together as Zimbabweans, trample upon racialism...* There are many whites leaving the country, too resistant to change, too fearful of Mugabe and a black government, but after his speech, Mum and Dad and their friends are cautiously optimistic.

These little-town-blues....

Mum is standing in the doorway with mushroom vol-au-vents, paté and cucumber on melba toast. Robert, who notices the small things, offers assistance. Everyone is singing...*it's up to you New York, New York!* And Molly is dancing and Jack is looking between her and me, and I wonder if he sees us – two sisters – as the performer and the watcher.

I lift the empty ice bucket and go in to the kitchen to top it up, and Jack says he'll grab some cold beers and follows me.

What now? I say, meaning everything, independence, change, what'll happen to whites, to the war vets on both sides...but next thing – good grief – in the unlit secrecy of the kitchen, Jack and I are kissing.

Molly:
You were always urging me to get up and perform!

The leg of beer and the caper

I notice Dad's jaundiced fingers as he topples in a triple. (The tot measure, a present from Robert, conveniently has a hole in the bottom.) He pauses to singe another cigarette. You know, he says to the six now *ex*-SAS soldiers sitting at the bar, I was supplying salt packs to the army. Had a chat with the General and he, or at least, the Brits, have given me the contract to feed the 35 000 terrs due to arrive into designated Assembly Points. I'd like you guys to come in on it. It's a big contract.

The sound of Dad's voice sits on the air, the words sit on the cushion of silence that receives them.

Always one for restlessness and stirring, it's Jack who speaks first. Sure, we'll feed the gooks who slaughtered our mates. Dad takes hold of his shoulders. If you want to get past the war, focus on the money. After the Second World War, he reminds them, the Brits helped to rebuild Germany. Jack looks at the other guys. They shrug. What else are we going to do? says Bruce.

An hour later, there are about thirty charts on the walls, ideas spinning like shirts in a washing machine. Smoke billows towards the ceiling. It rises, like the sheer adrenalin of having survived. Dad calls order; outlines the situation. Jack snaps his fingers, one-two-three. Lifts a marker like a match to a keg. Marks the map on the wall with black crosses. Those aren't the assembly points, says Dad. No, those are the locations where our mates were killed.

Jack, I need to know you are on-sides with this, warns Dad. There will be no spicing of the meat. War is war, and now it's over.

Johan the mercenary and one-leg Bruce, Mark, Ralf, and Callum laugh Jack out of where he's headed. Ivor's healed, and he's left for Arizona, to do a pilot's course. I'm glad he's not here for this. They pour snake bites – cider-and-larger cocktails. Bruce's prosthetic limb is filled and goes clunking around the bar, like a peace pipe. I try to imagine the unending loss of his real leg, the knee he must have slapped when he was uproariously laughing, as the others are doing right now. Jack's lost limb, I think, is on the inside.

So, decisions are made, clocks wound, roads symbolically swept. And the *caper,* as Dad calls it, begins.

Assembling

6 Norman Close. July. Dad and his team have three days to source hundreds of tons of food per day for an indefinite period, and get supplies delivered to remote, still-dangerous destinations. The combatants, as they are now referred to on the radio, are already crossing borders – from the Chimanimani mountains, Chimoio, Livingstone – and gathering at the designated centres. Dad sets about leasing a plane, finding depots and lorries, taking control of logistics, analysing risks.

The night sky is leaning in through the French doors, showering the proceedings with extra-atmospheric stars (Ivor would say that's because they *are* extra-atmospheric), hours fitting into the night, one after another, like onion layers, the dogs lifting their heads whenever snacks arrive on a tray for the disbelievers, the optimists, the determined. The tearing up of old maps, marking of new ones, the lists and the bedlams, hiring the drivers and those who'll ride shotgun.

And I spend my vacs typing endless documents, rapidly improving my typing skills, and Mum and Moses start getting used to having up to twenty people for most meals. Robert is in charge of administration. Other friends are recruited to organise the supply of meat, fruit, veg, dry goods. Dad's cousin, up from Pietermaritzburg, will do the accounts. And the bar fridge and pantry shelves have to be stocked daily and Molly and I act as runners, and night sessions last well into the wee hours, Dad, loquacious amongst the motley ash trays and savage clutter, calming his team out of their revenge-talk, and they empty themselves of heavy thoughts, replacing them with a predatory interest in profit.

Nerves, in a tight-drawn wire

Dinner at Jack's place. He makes asparagus, drizzled with melted butter and lemon, for a laughing reminder of our Christmas starter at Rita and Bert's farm in Raffingora, where we first met. But I'm watchful of his moods, erratic and volatile, like Ivor's. Being with him requires a kind of mental surgery, same as with my dad. So many aspects of his behaviour trouble me.

All the unwanted truths of my motive in being with Jack I push down-down-down, like a stone deep into mud.

Trucks and trouble

6, Norman Close. The new temperament of the freshly independent country is still hidden under a downpour of change.

Dad acquires a suite of offices in Msasa Industrial Estate. I'm secretly convinced my dad took on this contract – which the British Monitoring Forces couldn't manage – because he's glad that the blacks have won their country back.

Even though the war is officially over, it could be months before the combatants are absorbed into the new Zimbabwean army. As they still have their weapons, keeping them in the Assembly Points, happy and fed, is critical.

Food, says my father, is essential during a war. And immediately afterwards.

A lorry driver – not one of Dad's – speeds fearfully through the dark spaces of former ambush territory and accidentally runs over a guerrilla. The trigger-alert combatants, assuming it was deliberate, murder him.

The delicate new peace is tainted. Conspiracies erupt. Danger pay has to be doubled for my father's shaken drivers.

An agony of sleepless nights

July. Fynn has finished his call-up, and says he's enrolled at my university for next year. I tell him I'm seeing Jack now, having assumed it was all over with us. Butterfly Barbara and all that. He begs me to give him another chance. It's difficult to love him, but it's more difficult not to. Why would you want to be with me anyway? I ask, then kick myself. Ugh, fishing. That old look, briefly. Because I want to be infected by your bottomless optimism.

Optimism?

Every day my heart and mind howl and change and howl again.

Apples and trees

Molly is out of the bath, dripping in a towel. Leave it in for me, I call. Still herself, but different too. Before I left for Rhodes, she was like a tree whose leaves have suddenly burst into chlorophyll. Now back for my ten-day vac, I find she's withdrawn, angular, intense. Entering that whirling teen-space, I guess. At her age, I was helplessly under the enchantment of Barra in Limerick; all that yearning. Wonder who she's yearning after, but sense she won't tell me. She's gone very private, a dark horse, like Mum.

The scent of apple shampoo wafts around me. Light baffles through the bathroom humidity. Turbaned and barefoot, I head back to my room. In the hallway, Molly is slipping on her sandals. She and Mum and Dad have just got back from Ireland. Jack was summoned to join them, with papers for Dad. They took a trip up to Donegal. Wonder what my family thought of him.

I close my bedroom door and open the window. A vagrancy of green growth rushes in with the cool draught. Fling myself on to the bed, too hot to put anything on. After a bit I haul out my writing paper from the bedside locker and begin a letter to Freya.

In an instant of storm

Here, in this rainy darkness, I can hear and smell the dark foliage seeping through the open window. I can't sleep. I'm thinking about Jack, and the things he's done. The wind lifts, enters through the window, breathes open a page of my journal, like a portal. *Love is an act of chance. And besides, who's to blame for a lack of humanity, only humanity?*

Robert's voice comes to me. The meaning of life, he says, is simply to be alive. To stay alive. I think about Keith, dying just weeks before the end of the war.

Lightning blinks. Details of shapes – curved, angled, sharp – seem to be wanting to speak to me. And then I see the flare of a figure bathed in the grey and tusk-yellow light, moving slowly across the garden. Thunder plays a ripple of notes, which hurl into my body. I sit up on my bed, cross-legged, hyper-alert. The smoke of his voice curls towards me again, offering me a dawn ski. After a time, he returns to his place among the atoms.

Weeks
of sponge-baths
and bed-pans
and Kate
who turns
up every day
of your forty three
of confinement.
Talks
about Aristotle
and memory
as the scribe
of the soul.
Sometimes,
mirrors.
A time
for thinking,
she says.
When you rewind,
you may
feel
vertigo.
But you also
risk
finding
your own self.

A tale of the taking of liberties

6 Norman Close. October. A loud, hot day. I'm upstairs in my room, reading Dickens. *It was the best of times. It was the worst of times.* The window faces onto the dead grass – a game of croquet being played, with hands on more than mallets. This latest crop of strangers look like mating slugs. Ugh! Downstairs, the voices raucous. Music full volume. *I put a spell on you.*

No part of this new garden giving us the preciousness of a tree's shade on these scorching days. Thankfully, we have a pool.

There hasn't been a drop in months. The sun has become an arsonist. But I'd rather kill the afternoon indoors than be out there, in front of those sly grunts.

Finally, it gets too hot and I have to go out for a swim. The lawn is dry, yellow, crackling. A naked body by the pool; he lifts his head and plops it back on to the grass. The heat runs, bubbles, streams, blooms, prickles, hangs. The dogs pant. The guy's head, a leather football whose seams have blown. He gawks at me in my bikini and sarong. I drop the wrap and dive in.

Eighteen hours since the party began, and the house is still vibrating. *It was the drunkest of times, it was the hangover of times.* He tumbles into the water behind me, a splash.

It always falls to me to escort my father's lavishly inebriated visitors to the door, wait until their cars wobble down the brick-paved driveway, as if the driver is having an epileptic seizure, then shut the gate. These randoms breezing through our lives. Shirtless, pot-bellied drunks, hunched, pigeon-chested drunks, old wrinkled drunks. This one's hot beery breath shooting into my face. A lovely figure…the boys must be all over you…Pulsing his thick lips. He wipes his face. The blurred heat. Both hands on my face. Forces my lips open. Down, down, he rams his tongue, a colossal blindworm. I wrench free, blaze back to the house and straight upstairs. Into the bathroom to wash out my mouth. *Out. Out. Out!*

No point in mentioning it to my parents. Oh he's just blotto, my Mum would say if I told her what had happened. As if that means I should laugh it off.

Out in the dead garden, several more vultures, waiting for prey.

Inferno, a day of reckoning

6 Norman Close. An explosion of chalk-white light presses against my thin curtains. I pull back the drape, and notice flutterings in the air, like grey moths. And then I see Simeon. *Aai-yaai-yaai! Aai-yaai-yaai!* He comes running to bang on our kitchen door. Black smoke is galloping into the air, and ashes the size of silver dollars have begun landing on the verandah. The sauna at the bottom of our garden is on fire! I yell for Mum and Dad, run downstairs and out the door. Simeon is staring at the blaze with a wide open mouth, a whiff of *dagga* emanating from him. Mum tears across the prickly, yellow, drought-stricken lawn in her satin gown and bare feet, going, *no, no, no, no…* Dad erupting with curses as he follows her. There's no water from the hosepipe. In our night-gowns, Molly and I help Simeon fill buckets of water from the pool but our efforts are as effective as trying to speed on a flat tyre. The building burns to the ground.

All their forex, they tell us, painstakingly acquired on the black market, was hidden in the sauna dressing room. All that security slipping away from them like leaves curling and crackling in the gush of a consuming fire. We stand helplessly, watching the orange flames and black smoke swirl into the wind. Cinder of cash notes, cinder of a drunken session – or something more ominous.

Betrayal

Dinner with Jack at the Acropolis restaurant in Avondale. Our waiter sets down two Irish coffees. The moon, or maybe a lamppost, gazing in the window.

I got a letter from a cousin, who had assumed you were Molly's boyfriend, I laugh, when you were in Donegal together with Mum and Dad earlier in the year. A bit daft of her, to imagine you'd be involved with a fourteen-year-old!

The way he is avoiding looking at me, squirming, saying nothing, now I'm not so sure.

I get up and walk to the loo. Scream into my jersey. A forest of feelings springing up in my body. Jack knows that Molly's always hero-worshipped him, ever since he said *call me when you're eighteen*. At the time, I laughed, thinking it a joke. Now a chill crawls over me.

The wall is scrawled with graffiti: *Action, not words.* A Mosi-o-Tunya of flushing, the thunder and confusion of water drowning out my hurt and fury. Taste of salt crossing the feta and olive still on my palate. Throat aching, I smash water over my face.

How far did he go? Here I am, still a virgin. *I've* been saying no for years! How is it that my father is obsessively vigilant about my behaviour, and so careless of what is happening to his youngest?

Ah, hypocrisy! Haven't I been vacillating between Fynn and Jack?

But *my sister*. An unrecognisable feeling licks at my insides.

Before walking out of the restaurant, I pause at the table. Hell with you. Lift my undrunk Irish coffee – now cool – and throw it into his stupefied face.

Midnight confrontation

I wait till all the lights have gone out, then tiptoe down to Molly's room. She's awake. Standing a metre from her bed, I ask her straight out.

She is a fish wriggling from the hook of my questions, but at least I find out she's still a virgin. She sits up in the bed, and I notice her new breasts, guava-sized, under the flimsy nightie. I thought you'd broken up. I'm sorry. I wish I could take it back.

My arms cross over my own breasts. I let the silence sit between us until she squirms.

Imagine if it had gone further...if...

The Scarlet Letter would have been pinned on her! My mind flips to my red-headed Limerick friend, Belinda, and her much-older boyfriend.

Where were Mum and Dad? I ask. They told him to look after me while they went off and did their own thing, she says. Begins sniffling. I sit on the bed. Hey. He took advantage. But he's seven years older than you! Way too old, you understand? Regardless of my history with him. So while I'm back at Rhodes, don't let him near you again, ok?

I don't think he was interested in me anyway, she sniffles. I think he was just trying to get back at you because you two had that fight after the woman and her baby fell in the ditch. I thought you'd ended things with him then.

Back in my room, I mull. All the times he'd given her little presents, flirted, petted, complimented her dancing. Made her feel visible. No wonder she was smitten. Easy bait.

I press my mouth into the pillow. Fields of unclear emotions stand around my bed all night.

Breezing through new

Seated at a pavement table with Lois at *Le Paris* café on First Street, watching flies sunbathing on the cobbles, I am conscious of how few whites are around. It's been eight months since independence, and already this is a different country. Rhodesia is no longer a geographical space, but a state of mind once created here. Now, a clamour of new shapes and sounds and colours and energies are caught in patches of light around us. A new state of mind. Lois has returned from Stirling university in Scotland, with a new look, shorter hair, jeans and green cotton shirt. I've returned from Rhodes to pick up my airline ticket for Ireland, where I'm going for the vacs.

Miss Moore strides past, as though in the direction of time itself. A walking ball of sunshine, in her own separate atmosphere. Lois and I call her excitedly. There seems to be something different about her, colour heightened, eyes sparkling high. She's wearing a floral summer dress, pink low-heeled sandals. Her toes are painted a pearly white. I glance down at my purple Indian silk dress with a white wraparound scarf, my white gold bangle dangling from the knot. What are you having? Brown cows, we tell her. Coke topped with ice-cream. She nods to the waiter to bring her one too. The sun is throwing knives, but a dusty, limey breeze offers relief. So, says Miss Moore. What is your news?

Lois has only recently come out to me after a long, fumbling preamble. Open-mouthed, I'd counted five heartbeats before hugging her. *When…? How…? Why didn't you…?* Now she says it straight out to Miss Moore, who nods sagely, her glance covering Lois with light. I'm amazed. How did Miss Moore intuit something so significant when I hadn't? Actually, she says, I thought you were both gay. She looks enquiringly at me. No, I have a boyfriend, I tell her. Well, I had! It's over now. What about you? Do you have anyone? Her response is laughter. I'm engaged, she says. As she speaks, I think of Chardonnay glinting dew in the sunshine. We both stand out of our seats to congratulate and hug her. He's from London too. I'm emigrating back home tonight, so I'm really glad to see you both before I go.

After so much presence, it's hard to imagine her absence. We slump back into our seats in a confusion of happiness that she has found someone, and also dismay. His gain will be a huge loss for all the girls here, whose doors she won't be opening into illumination now. Miss Moore tells us that all the white teachers have been removed from the school, and huge numbers of black girls have enrolled. Almost all of the white girls have left too. A new chapter, she says. For everyone.

9.

Cups of first times

Dublin. What did she say? asks Auntie Iris, sitting on my single bed, pouring tea. My first breakfast-in-bed, the morning after my first visit to a clairvoyant. Always something new in Dublin. Silver teapot, china cups and saucers, toast and marmalade. Music of the pouring ceremony rising and falling with her hands. My favourite aunt.

Faint traffic outside the window. A chill skittering across my bare shoulders. As the honoured guest, I got the bed. Nadia – three weeks younger than me, tall like her mum, autumn-coloured, cork-screw hair – is banking pillows behind her on the bottom bunk across the room. I sip the hot sweet tea, as though I'm a tree siphoning the juice of its swollen fruit.

My life will be Dublin, says Nadia, and a job I'll love, and I'll buy my own house. That's my independent girl, smiles Auntie Iris, and I remember Nadia telling me her mum has always dreamed of a home of her own. What about you, Itosha?

Oh, many lives, in various places. We laugh. And I'll always have the use of my limbs. I flash on the clairvoyant's presence, motherly, ordinary-looking, except for her slow-moving, grey gaze. When I asked why she mentioned that, she said 'because it will be your biggest anxiety'.

And my children will have eyes as blue as the sea in a Greek postcard. Blue as your own, says Auntie Iris. What else did she say? When I wondered if I'd ever live in Ireland again, she said I'd always be coming and going, like clouds.

Auntie Iris lifts my palm as if to offer a prediction of her own. No more eczema! she says. I peer closely, surprised. Oh! Hadn't noticed, I say. She laughs. Must have happened while you were thinking about other things.

Her touch suddenly reminds me of the way the clairvoyant took my hand as we were leaving. And I'd felt something from underneath coaxing up in her. Every act, she said – in the kindest, softest voice – *has a consequence*. I had forgotten that bit.

Another bend

Dublin. The swirls in the Van Gogh print on the hall wall above the phone table describe exactly how my stomach is whirling. I finger the coil between handset and phone, speechless.

Mum has just told me that death threats – from whites – have precipitated their hasty departure from the country. They have moved to Durban in South Africa. Speed and secrecy were essential, so they couldn't tell anyone. Not even me.

Poor Molly, having to evaporate from her life without warning or explanation, I think. And Zoë? I ask. She'll be following shortly. Your Dad has persuaded her mother to let her board with Molly in her new convent, and she'll stay with us at the weekends and during holidays. So at least Molly will have her.

Mum also tells me that Johan, the mercenary, went with them. He's from South Africa anyway, and he'll live with them and act as a bodyguard. Will they need one, even in South Africa?

So much is changing anyway, Mum reminds me. All your friends have left for university in South Africa or abroad. Ivor's gone to the States, and after that, he'll be travelling the world. And Fynn is coming to your university, isn't he?

I feel a suffusion of warmth and relief that Fynn survived the war. That I'll be seeing him again.

And darling, your new ticket gives you five days in Paris, says Mum. I know you've always wanted to go there.

Before the crashing new reality kicks in, I glance up at the waving sunflowers. A chorus of elements intermingling. As soon as I've put down the phone to Mum, I call Freya.

Two days later, Freya arrives on the bus from Letterkenny, guitar over her shoulder, and we take off, into the blue sky and bewitching adventure.

City of Lights and light fingers

Paris. Books on shelf after shelf, bright paths of thought. We emerge from Shakespeare & Co. with one each. I chose *By Grand Central Station I sat Down and Wept*. Freya went for *The Motorcycle Diaries*. We laugh as we imagine our choices as some sort of analogy.

We buy a crêpe from a street seller. A mole on her left cheek, single hair springing out of it. In the Jardin du Luxembourg, the sun is animating even the sounds of birds and footsteps. We walk past drifts of freshly cut grass, overlaid by the sharp sweetness of my *crêpe au sucre et au citron*. I'm wrist-deep in sugar and lick my warm skin. The yellow sky, green leaves rearranging it.

A woman at a pavement table in front of us bites the tail of her croissant. Her companion leans in, snaps his teeth over the other tail. A few minutes later, we are presented with *café au lait* and our own warm croissants. Finally, says Freya, here we are. Imagine how wildly romantic our lives would be if we could live here? This is the kind of city, I say, that changes you. Freya sighs. We could write and wear berets and become deeply mysterious and alluring.

In the plaza outside the Centre Pompidou, a busker. Bodies, including our own, gravitate to his fantastic charisma, and oh, that voice. A festival of notes and light and energy, as though these are the laws of happiness. *Just the two of us.*

Drifting through the crowd is a girl carrying his Stetson, into which people are dropping coins. Another one stands nearby, black dollop of hair, her shirt French-tucked into blue jeans. Drilling her eyes into mine. Next thing, she thrusts a note into my hand and walks off. I assume it's a flier for some art exhibition, but as I can't see a litter bin, tuck it into my jeans pocket.

After groping our way through the throng, we discover we're minus our wallets. Buddha says a crisis is a disguised opportunity, I say, giddy with the idea of sleeping in a doorway. Already conceiving of my own *Down and Out in Paris*. But how are we going to eat, without cash? Or sleep? Or get to the airport? says Freya. I don't know, I say. Busk?

Fountains and footsteps

Paris. We walk along the banks of the Seine until we reach the Place de la Concorde, where a fountain is as talkative as a pair of stranded teenagers.
You stuck? someone says in English.
He's about five foot ten – not too threatening – olive skinned, short dark hair, trim beard, laugh-crinkles. My name is Salem. Heard you mention something about losing your wallets?
We tell him our names. Where are you from?
Freya says Ireland.
And you? he looks at me. Your accent sounds different.
Hesitate, as I always do.
Actually, I'm Irish too – we're cousins – but I was raised in, uh, a few places. Er…what about you?
I am from Iran. You need somewhere to sleep? You're welcome to stay at my place. Come. It's round the corner from the Sorbonne. I'm a student there.

Behind him, the luminous fountain is a fall of glittering rain. This pure stranger in jeans and a bomber jacket. But I like his energy which lifts off, like a bird. And two against one is reasonable odds.

Freya and I glance at each other, nod, then rush after him, ducking under pin-striped awnings, deferring to pedestrians at each pavement side-step.

The balancing

You are whirly
with drugs
and the prospect
of life
in a wheelchair,
when a telegram arrives.
'Congrats,' it says.
'I didn't think
you had it in you.'
It's signed
Bernadette
(Miss Moore).
You empty yourself
of heavy thoughts
as you remember
something
she once said in class:
People forget
that Icarus
didn't just fall.
He also flew.

All you need for a travelling lamp is the sun

Paris: Two armchairs, a small breakfast table, cushion-constructed bed on the floor. Frying pan on the wall, which I'd noted yesterday. Handy as a weapon if necessary.

I sit up on my makeshift bed. Last night was a stir-fried dinner, easy conversation. And now the sun is a torch, shafting light through the window over the sink.

Door opens. Salem drawls good morning. A hasty coffee, then he heads off to his lectures, leaving money on the table for us to buy food for tonight. Such trust! On the back of the door, a calendar, print of Monet's white water lilies. While Freya rustles up toast, I deal with the crowded sink, blinking through a window that overlooks a building as tall as my joy.

Over the next four days, we are flammable chameleons, eating subsidised meals at the Sorbonne, courtesy of Salem, exploring the city. Busking under the Arc de Triomphe until we are moved on.

I'm determined to come back to Paris as soon as my degree is over. Here is where I'll find independence, my very own self. Freya thinks the same. Only she doesn't have to finish a degree first.

Serendipity, I say. Isn't it interesting how random meetings with strangers can influence outcomes? I know, says Freya. He's lovely. And he's invited me to stay.

Wind

Stay afloat, I urge the plane. It shrugs. *This aircraft is flying at 30 000 feet,* my inflight magazine tells me. Freya is beginning her life in Paris. And my family are starting over again in Durban.

I look through the porthole at the gigantic plated wing, thinking about what Mum said. No time for goodbyes. Another country, another house gone, like a cardboard box into the wind.

Mum said they couldn't bring anything but a suitcase of clothes.

My diaries.

When I asked where they were, she admitted she'd had them *burnt.* A daddy-longlegs tremor on my skin.

Even now, I feel a whirling inside, as though I'm Alice flailing into an abyss. Those diaries – from the first one Ivor bought me when I turned eleven, to the diary of my eighteenth year – were my secret place. Although I've had a week to process the news, I don't know how I'm going to manage my feelings when I actually see her.

Clean slate, she'll say breezily. It's good to travel light.

I open my new diary, bought in a *papeterie* in rue de Lancry, and take out my pen. *A cloud-forest in the eastern horizon, bruise-coloured, prophetic.*

I'll graduate in a year, and then I'll move to Paris.

Hunting for lip balm in my jeans pocket, I feel paper. Pull out a crumpled handwritten note. Briefly confused, till I remember the girl at the Pompidou Centre.

This has to be a sign.

As I glance out the window, a notion breezes through me. Do a skydive! All I'd need is twenty seconds of insane courage.

I read the note again. *'If you tie yourself to anything, tie yourself to the wind.'*

Acknowledgements

Acknowledgements are due to the editors of New Contrast, Pedestal, The Haibun Journal, The Irish Times and The Stinging Fly, who published versions of extracts from this book.

For their moral, material or literary support, I'd like to thank my brother, Ian McGlinchey, and my sister, Paula McGlinchey, and also Sara Baume, Jenni deBie, Denise Blake, Dean Browne, Lisa Burkitt, Paul Casey, Patrick Cotter, Cónal Creedon, Robert Dagge, Terry Doyle, John Fitzgerald, Mia Gallagher, Derek Matyszak, Thomas McCarthy, Susan McKeown, Bernadette McCarthy, John Mee, Tom Moore, Lesley Moir, Vanessa O'Loughlin, Ysabelle Perkins, Paul Perry, Kathy Prescott-Decie-Schneeberger, Louise Roscoe, Yvonne Saunders, Jane Skovgaard, Nick Smith, Brian Turner, Aine Wade, William Wall and Grace Wells.

I'd particularly like to thank Paul McMahon for his close, insightful editing and lovely endorsement. To Jessie Lendennie and Siobhán Hutson of Salmon Poetry, who published my first two collections and thus 'launched' me as a poet, thank you for taking me on. It's wonderful to work with you both. To Lorenzo Mari, Elisabetta Fiorucci and Gianfranco Fabbri of L'Arcolaio, I'm so grateful for your translations and publications of both my earlier collections. To Anatoly Kudryavitsky of SurVision, thank you for giving me a place to go surrealist. To Grainne Fox, my agent (I never thought I'd be saying those words) you are the best! Thank you for the questions, the encouragement and close attention to my work. I'm thrilled to be working with you. Immense, heartfelt gratitude to Cork County Council for ongoing support, and to the Arts Council of Ireland for awarding me a literature bursary, which gave me the opportunity to travel to Zimbabwe and, as it turned out, to be with my beloved, irrepressible father for the last months of his life. To Micaela and Cian Hamilton, my children, whose support and encouragement I couldn't do without. Most of all, to Michael Ray, your input and your presence in my life mean everything to me. And finally, massive thanks to my scrupulous, generous editor and publisher, Aaron Kent of Broken Sleep Books, for making a leap of faith with *Tied to the Wind*.

Glossary of Bemba/Shona/Afrikaans words and slang terms

ABF:	Code for *Absolutely Bloody Final*. Guests were not allowed to leave the house until they had declared an ABF. (i.e. the next drink would be their last.)
Amai:	Mother, a term of respect in Bemba and Shona cultures.
Bakkie:	Afrikaans word for a pick-up truck.
Boomslang:	A deadly snake, green in colouring, with black markings.
Bru:	Slang for 'brother'.
Bwana:	Shona for 'boss'.
Chongololo:	A centipede with a dark brown, almost black carapace.
Chop-chop:	Slang, meaning 'quickly', or 'immediately'.
Dwaal:	South African slang: a dreamy, dazed or absent-minded state.
Dagga:	Marijuana
Dún do bhéal:	Irish, meaning, 'say nothing' (or more literally: 'shut your mouth').
Donga:	A narrow, steep-sided gully or small ravine, usually dry except in the rainy season.
Forex:	Foreign currency. Often kept in cash notes (acquired expensively on the black market, due to sanctions).
Gat:	Gun, usually an AK47.
Graze:	Slang, meaning 'food'.
Juju:	The supernatural/magic power of a charm; karmic, for good or bad.
Khaya:	Traditional African home, usually a circular, thatched, brick or mud and wood hut.
Kopje:	Afrikaans, meaning rocky outcrop.
Kwacha:	Name of the notes in the Zambian currency.
Lobola:	Bride price, paid by the groom to the bride's father, usually in the form of cattle.
Madara:	Shona. Respectful term for an old man.
Mealies:	Corn on the cob.
Monkey's wedding:	Sunlight and rain at the same time – a sun-shower.
Munt:	A Shona word, used to refer to a man, usually a black person. Used in a pejorative way by whites during colonial times.
Mwana:	Shona for 'child'.
Naartjie:	Afrikaans for a mandarin.
Ngwee:	Name of the coins in the Zambian currency.
Nshima:	Bemba. Maize meal, or mealie meal as it is called, eaten as a porridge and also as the staple with the day's main meal in Zambia.
Robots:	Slang for 'traffic lights'.
Rondavel:	A circular dwelling or room, with a conical thatched roof.
Sadza:	Shona. The name for mealie meal in Zimbabwe.
Skafie:	Afrikaans for 'segment' (usually of a piece of citrus fruit).
Stick:	A group of paratroopers deployed from a single aircraft
Stoep:	Afrikaans. A step (or set of steps) outside a house, where you can sit.
Taking the gap:	Originally a rugby term, the phrase was used to describe those who left the country to avoid call-up. Generally derided as a 'chicken run'.
Tokoloshe:	A malevolent goblin, about knee-high, in African folklore, similar to the bogey man.
Tsikomo:	Bemba, meaning 'Thank you'.
Vlei:	Afrikaans: open grass.

LAY OUT YOUR UNREST

Lightning Source UK Ltd.
Milton Keynes UK
UKHW031824131021
392144UK00005B/123